The Handbook for
# LATCHKEY CHILDREN AND THEIR PARENTS

# The Handbook for
# LATCHKEY CHILDREN AND THEIR PARENTS

by

## Lynette and Thomas Long

ARBOR HOUSE
New York

*To Seth and Sarah,*
*our children*

*And to the hundreds*
*of children and adults*
*who have so willingly*
*shared their lives with us*

# CONTENTS

# PREFACE

From 1978 to 1980 I was principal of a Catholic elementary school in Washington, D.C. All students in the school were required to wear uniforms—the girls wore plaid jumpers and white blouses; the boys wore blue dress pants, pale blue dress shirts and blue ties. No makeup or jewelry was allowed. As principal, it was ultimately my responsibility to enforce the dress code. One problem I had concerned children wearing necklaces, ribbons, chains, even pieces of string around their necks with keys attached. From my viewpoint, these objects could be considered jewelry and violated the dress code. I was constantly reminding students who wore their keys displayed to place them inside their shirts or blouses. The keys were so common and I was so busy that I never thought to question why the children were wearing them.

As I gained experience as a principal and a deeper understanding of the problems of the children in my school, I came to realize why the children wore the keys. More importantly, I became aware of the impact working mothers and single parents were having on their children, and the impact of children on their parents who worked. Because most of my time was spent with the children, a number of problems they experienced began to emerge: children often said that it was difficult to get a note signed because they had missed seeing their parents in the morning. As a principal, I found it hard to reach parents during the day, even by telephone, to discuss school-related problems. I also found it difficult to keep children after school for remedial help or as a punishment, since their parents often waited anxiously at work for a phone call that said the children had arrived home safely.

At the end of my first year as principal, my husband, a counselor and research professor, who also had become aware of what we came to think of as latchkey children through his work on a child-abuse team, suggested that we investigate the phenomenon. He and several of his graduate students volunteered to develop a pilot instrument and interview the children at my school, provided I could get their parents' permission. We were interested in what children did before and after school, what their care arrangements were and how children felt about their out-of-school life. By this time we had identified many children who were spending their afternoons alone, and we were wondering how self-care was affecting them. Tom's search of current professional literature turned up little on the topic.

We began our interviews during the fall of 1979. My husband and I and five doctoral students in counseling from The Catholic University of America did the interviewing. We interviewed every latchkey student in my elementary school from first through sixth grade, as well as a random sampling of children who had always had adult supervision. Each interview consisted of eighty-four structured and open-ended questions; plenty of time was allowed for the children to elaborate on their answers. Each interview lasted from thirty-five minutes to more than one hour. Questions were asked about what they had for snacks, how much television they watched, what instructions they had been given and what chores they had to do, how they were to respond to an emergency, how they felt about themselves and their parents and a myriad of other questions.

The children were generally candid as the interviewers gained each child's confidence. Some answered the interviewer's questions cautiously; most were happy, even eager to talk about their experiences.

Many children told us much more about their out-of-school life than was asked.

We pooled the data from this first study in an attempt to see if there were significant differences between the groups of children who routinely spent time at home alone, those who spent time with siblings but without continuous adult supervision, and those who had always had the benefit of adult care. We looked for themes as well as the results of numerical tabulations. The results were fascinating.

We were amazed at the number of students in self-care who shared with us feelings of fear that went beyond what we normally expected from children of that age, and the complaints about feeling lonely and bored. We were shocked when the academically best student in the third grade explained how she spent most afternoons alone hidden in a closet in her house. We were also more than a little appalled when some children told us they had begun taking care of themselves at age five.

Of course, not every student told us dramatic stories; the majority seemed to be handling themselves and their particular situation well. But of the third of the school who fit our definition of being a latchkey child, about twenty-five percent seemed to be having trouble coping with self-care. The results led us on a search for more information that has lasted since these initial interviews took place.

Following the first study, we modified our initial instrument, largely by eliminating items that seemed to produce little useful information or no between-group differences; we added items in areas that seemed productive. Then we obtained permission to begin interviewing children in other schools to add to our original data. We contacted schools and interviewed children in urban, suburban and rural areas. We spoke to students in some of the poorest as well as the wealthiest communities in the United States.

Although the percentages of latchkey children changed from community to community, the problems did not. Siblings still fought and argued with one another. Children were still afraid of noises and robbers. They still had to cope with boredom and loneliness, even though suburban children often had more material things, such as electronic security systems and video games to help reduce their emotional upset.

While we continued to collect additional interview data, we also began to interview former latchkey children, those twenty- to seventy-year-olds who had spent many of their childhood years taking care of themselves before or after school while their parents worked. Most of those from whom we obtained data were between the ages of twenty and forty. Each of these adults was asked not only to describe their experiences as a latchkey child, but also to reflect on the impact these experiences had on them as adults and on their relationship with their parents. For some, looking back on the experience was a positive one; for others, it was unpleasant. Many told us that until they heard of our work they did not realize that they had been latchkey children.

Finally, in an effort to understand fully the latchkey phenomenon, we began interviewing the parents of latchkey children. We wanted to know why they chose to leave their children alone before and/or after school and how they felt about it. We interviewed both mothers and fathers, single parents and married couples in order to gain insight into latchkeyism and parents' perceptions of the impact it was having on the family as a whole. We found that most parents felt concerned about leaving their children unattended; in particular, many mothers felt guilty. Yet most told us that they felt their children were mature enough to care for themselves during the periods they were on their own. Parents tended to minimize the amount of time their children were on their own, and most parents seemed to understand only partially what was going on with their children while unsupervised.

There is still a great deal of work to be done as we try to understand what can be done to help latchkey children: what our communities can do to help; how family relationships can be improved; and what part business and industry and the government play in the way we are rearing our children.

Despite the groundwork still to be examined, we believe we have learned enough during the past three years from our own work, from serious review of available literature and especially now, from our more than five hundred extended interviews on the subject of latchkey children, to be able to share something of importance for working parents.

*The Handbook for Latchkey Children and their Parents* is a summary of our findings. It is the first book written that describes the latchkey phenomenon, its negative as well as positive aspects and projected consequences. It tells the story from the point of view of the children who live the latchkey experience, their parents, the school personnel who work with latchkey children and adults who were themselves latchkey children at one time. It uses case histories to describe how children in self-care spend their time, the problems they encounter, the successes they have, the feelings they experience, and the dangers to which they are exposed. The book examines not only the problems of leaving children alone after school, but also the difficulties of children who are alone in the morning and must get themselves ready for and off to school.

*The Handbook for Latchkey Children and their Parents* is especially important in that it suggests ways for parents to make the best of a sometimes less than ideal situation. We look at alternatives to the latchkey arrangement but, more importantly, discuss how to make the latchkey experience a more positive one when it is the only care available. This handbook offers precautions and procedures that may be followed to improve home safety, and outlines methods of reducing fear and stress.

Our hope in writing this book is that it will be a source of comfort as well as a genuinely helpful guide for parents. It is not intended to increase parental guilt. We are working parents, too, and experience the same difficulties of trying to balance the demands of jobs and of rearing a family. We hope in discussing our findings about latchkey children, we can together better understand the changes our world has brought about in our child-rearing patterns, and together strive to do whatever is possible to make childhood better for our children.

—Lynette Long
Thomas Long

# Chapter 1
# THE SCOPE OF THE PROBLEM

Coreen was asleep. A silent telephone receiver lay nearby. At 2:30 in the afternoon Coreen's mother had telephoned a handicapped neighbor in their apartment house to tell her that she was off to work. She said Coreen was napping and that her father was due at about 3:30. Coreen's mother did not hang up the telephone; instead she left the receiver on her daughter's bed. The neighbor did not hang up either. She laid her receiver on a table in her apartment. Coreen was about to be cared for by long distance, something that happens several days each week while her parents, who work separate shifts at the same plant, shuttle between plant and home. Coreen is six and a latchkey child.

Peter is five and attends kindergarten each day until 2:30. His seven-year-old brother leaves school at 2:40, so both boys arrive home at approximately the same time, around 3:00. Their mother, a teacher at a private school, usually gets home at 4:30. Her schedule varies depending on meetings, parent conferences and other functions she is required to attend. She always arrives home before her sons on Fridays because on Fridays the school where she teaches closes at 12:30. Peter's mother, a single parent, is usually able to be with her sons during vacation periods and on most school holidays. She has a problem attending them when either is ill. Peter and his brother are latchkey children.

Joshua is seven. He arrives at his apartment house after school at about 3:15. Joshua's mother doesn't trust him with a key to their apartment and so on the days mom is not home, Joshua waits in the vestibule of his apartment building until his mother returns. Joshua's mother works as a part-time cashier at a grocery store during the day and is attending a community college during the late afternoon and evening hours to improve her chances of obtaining a better job. While Joshua's mother doesn't attend classes every afternoon, she is regularly away from home two or three days each week when Joshua arrives. Despite the fact that Joshua isn't actually in their house, he is still a latchkey child.

Tina is a robust sixteen-year-old. Each day she collects her brothers Robert, age fourteen, and Stephen, age nine, and sister Diana, age eleven, at their respective schools and the four children walk home together. Tina is in charge. Since their father died a year ago their mother went to work as a secretary, leaving the four children to manage themselves and their house until she returns from work at 6:00. A high school junior, Tina is quite responsible as a care giver. If one of the children is ill, she generally stays home from school. She is especially good at organizing activities for her siblings during vacation periods when the children are home all day while mom works. Tina also watches her siblings some evenings so her mother can have a social life. Despite the fact that Tina seems to be taking charge as an effective substitute parent, all four children are latchkey children.

Irema is thirteen. At age twelve she dropped out of the sixth grade to take care of her three younger siblings. Irema's father had abandoned the family two years earlier. Her mother accepted a full-time job when she found she couldn't maintain her family on welfare payments. Before Irema reached her thirteenth birthday she was pregnant, due to a number of factors—partly boredom, partly sexual curiosity, partly opportunity and partly because she wanted a baby of her own. At thirteen she was a mother and her family now had five latchkey children. Irema's mother was shocked and angered when she found that she couldn't convince her daughter to have an abortion. Now she finds herself the sole support for five children.

## What Is Meant by "Latchkey Children"?

"Latchkey" is a term that defines children who are regularly left during some period of the day to supervise themselves, whether during that time they use group recreational programs, play in the street, stay home alone, join a gang; or for whom care arrangements are so loosely made that they are virtually ineffective. For the purposes of this book latchkey does not refer to children infrequently left alone for short periods of time while their parents run an errand, pick up a brother or sister from soccer practice or visit a neighbor. Latchkey here refers to children who regularly are left unattended; this includes both children left alone and those left in the care of an underage sibling. Some might disagree with this definition since, they might say, a fifteen- or sixteen-year old is certainly old enough to babysit. The reality is that most siblings left home together are relatively close in age so that it is more common for a nine-year-old to be charged with the care of a seven-year-old than to find a sixteen-year-old at home alone with a seven-year-old, unless, of course, it is someone else's sixteen-year-old.

Most latchkey children are school age, although there are children under the age of six who are routinely left alone to care for themselves for some time most days. Some of the most heart-rending stories might be written about children under age six, but the focus of this book is on the child between six and thirteen. In terms of number, children in that age group constitute forty-five percent of all children under age eighteen, or about twenty-six million children, fifty-eight percent of whom have mothers in the labor force. Twenty-one percent live with a single parent; more than thirteen percent live with a single parent who is employed. The child between six and thirteen is, furthermore, the one least served by organized day care services for a number of reasons that will be explored.

## The Low Profile of the Latchkey Child

Many parents who choose to leave their children in a self-care arrangement wonder if they are unusual. As a matter of fact, there is a kind of conspiracy that causes the latchkey phenomenon to maintain a low profile in day-to-day society. Parents who opt for this type of child care often feel guilty, even though they may also feel quite justifiably that they have no other alternative. Managers in business are sometimes aware of the effects of this guilt and concern. They have coined the term "three o'clock syndrome" because they often see more furtive glances at the clock, more work errors and more restlessness after 3:00 in employees who know that their children are now home alone. Parents who feel guilty are less likely to advertise their care arrangements, even to friends, and during a time of cheap labor, certainly not consciously to employers.

Parents who choose the latchkey arrangement also know that their children might be in greater physical danger if it were common knowledge that their children are unattended. Parents often advise their children never to tell callers that their parents are absent, but to use some device such as saying "Mom is taking a shower" to give the impression that mom is present but occupied.

Many parents also instruct their latchkey children to stay inside and not to have friends visit until mom or dad comes home. Because so many latchkey children are captive in their own homes, it is probable that for every two latchkey children of which one is aware in the neighborhood there is another latchkey child who remains invisible.

Latchkey children also learn to keep a low profile with adults. It is true that teachers may come to know a number of latchkey children in their classrooms, but unless they made a systematic inquiry, they would probably not know of all. And while children will often advertise their latchkey status to their friends either by wearing their key exposed or by discussing their situation with peers, they are far less likely to directly take up the issue with an adult.

Another factor that contributes to the low profile of latchkey children is a general ethic in American society that family problems are to be handled within the family—traditionally there is a great deal of hesitancy on the part of the public to be drawn into family concerns unless specifically invited. As a matter of fact, there is a good deal of resentment harbored by nonworking women when solicited to "kinda keep an eye out" for little Suzie or Johnny while their mother is at work. The national ethic of nonintervention in family matters and the often ill-disguised resentment toward parents who leave their children unattended also help suppress the visibility of the latchkey phenomenon in our society.

Furthermore, since children lack any sort of united voice or political clout, and responding to the needs of children is usually costly for the short run, though it may be cost-effective in the long run, even political bodies conspire to keep problems like latchkeyism out of public awareness.

Because of this understandable conspiracy of silence even latchkey parents are ill-informed as to the extent of the latchkey phenomenon. When articles about latchkey children appear in local newspapers, the public has, in the past, reacted with amazement. Public servants have been spared the challenge of finding the funding needed to provide adequate care for the school-age child. And parents are kept from organizing to demand better treatment for their children or gathering together to develop better care responses through mutual, cooperative action.

### How Did Latchkeyism Develop?

Children whose families could not provide continuous care have been a phenomenon in American society at least since the early 1800s. The Boston Infant School, the first day-care facility in America, was established in the 1820s as a response to a need for child-care services. But while the United States was largely an agrarian society the need was not as pronounced. Parents often worked where their children lived. If there were latchkey children at that time, they were few in number. Latchkeyism grew slowly as America shifted to a more urbanized society in which parents had to travel away from home to their place of work.

For several reasons, even with the growth of urbanization, the latchkey phenomenon progressed at a modest pace until World War I. Before that time women were less prominent in the work force outside of the home. There were fewer divorces and separations disturbing family unity. Families were less mobile, so extended families were available to provide child care when needed. Grandmothers, sisters and aunts often lived on the same city block.

The demands for additional workers placed on the nation during World War II caused an explosion in the number of working women and as a consequence resulted in increased numbers of latchkey children. This explosion abated only temporarily after the war ended.

In March 1940, of a total potential labor force of 45 million women, there were approximately 11.2 million either working or looking for work. By March 1944, there were 16.8 million women working in a total labor force of 51.3 million. Within a four year period working women had moved from comprising one-fourth of the nation's total labor force to comprising one-third of it.

During the Second World War the output of war materials depended on the presence of women in the work force. Many working women earned a national badge of honor for their war efforts. Practically speaking, many women welcomed the opportunity to replace the income of a wage earner who had gone off to war, or to supplement the family income in order to maintain or increase the family's standard of living. Emotionally, many women were escaping a difficult job as both mother and father in the home.

After the war there was a small decline in the number of women in the labor force, but the decline was temporary, as the following chart shows.

The rapid growth of the number of women in the nation's labor force only broadly outlines the context within which latchkey children exist. Not every working woman has a child, and some have thought that those that do are more likely to stay home. The above figures belie this assumption.

In 1974 the rate at which women with children participated in the labor force matched the rate at which all women participated (45.7 percent). But it was 1951 when the participation rate of women with children ages six to seventeen (34.8 percent) passed the participation rate of all women (34.7 percent). Despite fluctuations in the rates at which single women participate in the labor force, the rate at which married women participate has been on an unchanging course upward. In 1947, 20 percent of all married women were in the labor force. In 1980 this number passed 50 percent for the first time (50.2 percent), accounting for 24,444,000 workers. There were seventeen million women with children in the labor force in 1980 and this figure has continued to climb steadily since.

*Chart 1*    LABOR FORCE PARTICIPATION OF WOMEN AND
WOMEN WITH CHILDREN, 1950–1980

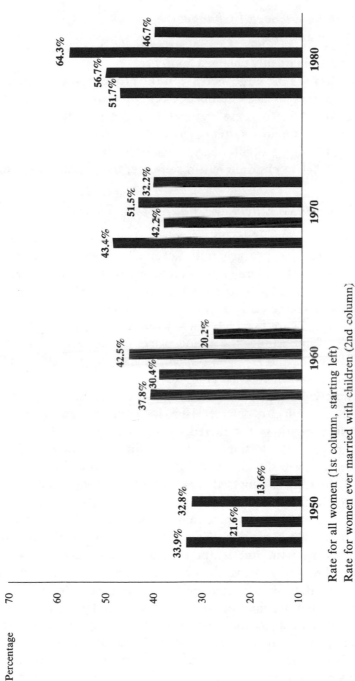

Rate for all women (1st column, starting left)
Rate for women ever married with children (2nd column)
Rate for women ever married with children age 6–17 (3rd column)
Rate for women ever married with children under age 6 (4th column)

SOURCES: U. S. Dept. of Commerce, Bureau of the Census, and U. S. Dept. of Labor, Bureau of Labor Statistics

### Significant Social Changes

Two significant changes in social structure have occurred since 1950 that have dramatically changed family rearing patterns in the United States. They are the large increase in the proportion of mothers who work, and the increased numbers of children living in single-parent households. Add to these changes two other social changes, the decline of the support system provided by the extended family and the rise in family mobility, and one sees the basis for the rapid rise in the number of children left in self-care, the "latchkey children."

### How Many Latchkey Children Are There?

The exact number of latchkey children remains elusive, since the numbers reported are generally accepted as partial and the most recently available federal study conducted by the United States Department of Commerce, dated 1976, is flawed. The fact that a current comprehensive and realistic tally of children enrolled in the various forms of child care is as yet unavailable is perhaps indicative of the low level of importance the nation places on the care of its children.

Janet Simons and Halcyon Bohen of the Children's Defense Fund, a Washington, D.C.–based child advocacy group, estimate that approximately 5.2 million American children age thirteen and under are without adult care or supervision for significant parts of each day. Other investigations conducted by various organizations and researchers present additional data regarding the number of latchkey children. In 1976 the United States Department of Commerce, Bureau of the Census reported that eighteen percent of children ages seven to thirteen cared for themselves while their mothers worked full-time. It is hard to imagine that this percentage has declined since then. In a 1982 New York City study by Georgia McMurray and Delores Kazanjian, nineteen percent of the families involved admitted that they had to leave their children unsupervised during all or part of the day, with over one-fifth of the parents beginning such practices when the children were seven years old or younger. Admittedly, this population was among the most needy in that it was the working poor, often single parents from minority groups, most of whom had lost eligibility for publicly supported child-care subsidies.

In a series of studies carried out by the authors, between thirty and thirty-four percent of elementary school children in the Washington, D.C. schools surveyed regularly engaged in some form of self-care. It is also true that among the nation's ten largest metropolitan areas, Washington's labor force has the highest proportion of working women. When the authors interviewed children in selected schools in two of the wealthiest suburban communities in the country, latch-key children accounted for between eleven and twelve percent of the children.

The authors' high percentage figures for an urban setting were corroborated by a recently released study conducted by C. D. Hughes in Phoenix, Arizona, for the Association for Supportive Child Care. Of the 144 two-income or single parent working families surveyed, thirty-one percent with children ages six through eleven indicated that their children cared for themselves on most weekdays.

Two national surveys, one conducted by Nicholas Zill of Child-trends, Inc., in Washington, D.C., found that about five percent of the 2,301 seven- to eleven year-olds he surveyed in 1976 were latch-key children. The other study conducted in 1981 by Louis Harris for General Mills, Inc., found that about nine percent of the families reported that their children cared for themselves. Both of these studies relied heavily on parental reporting.

The most recent study on school age child care (released 1983) sponsored by a federal agency was carried out under contract with the Department of Health and Human Services by Applied Management Sciences, Inc., a Silver Spring, Maryland, firm during the 1981–1982 school year. This study provides data on a random sampling of 500 households with school-age children (five to fourteen), in each of the states of Minnesota and Virginia.

Findings from this study indicate that, *overall*, next to care by one's parents, the second most frequently used arrangement for school-age children was self-care or care by a sibling under age fourteen (Minnesota 11 percent; Virginia 11 percent). But approximately one-fourth of the school-age children of *working parents* in both states cared for themselves on a regular basis (Minnesota 27 percent; Virginia 25 percent).

Two-thirds of families with full-time working parents used non-parental care on a regular basis (Minnesota 65 percent; Virginia 69 percent). Younger children tended to be in self-care or sibling care less frequently than older children. But even parents who used arrangements other than parent or self-care on a regular basis also occasionally used self-care. Parents in this study said they were more likely to try self-care gradually and incrementally increase the duration and frequency of self-care.

Depending on the percentages used, the number of latchkey children age thirteen and under can range from a low of less than 2.5 million to a high of nearly 15 million. Even conservative estimates put the figure between 5 and 10 million.

There are two important subgroups of latchkey children. One is latchkey children living in two-income families. Two children in every five live in a two-income family. The other subgroup is latchkey children living in single-parent households. One child in every five lives in a single-parent household.

The differences between these two groups are enormous. Children living in two-income families are more economically advantaged than the average family. Only about six percent live below the poverty threshhold ($8,500 for a nonfarm family of four). The median income for these dual-earner families was $27,745 in 1980. This was about a third higher than for families where only the husband worked and nearly triple the income of families maintained by women.

The group of latchkey children living in single-parent families generally suffers more economic hardships. While there is a significant and growing minority of single-parent families headed by men, single-parent families headed by women outnumber them ten to one. And the median income for female year-round full-time workers is approximately sixty percent of that of males in the same category.

In addition, only fifty-five percent of the children living in female-headed families live with mothers who are actually employed. The fathers of eighty percent of the children living in father-present, mother-absent families are employed.

While almost one in every five children in this country lives in poverty, almost one in every three families headed by a woman lives in poverty. This is more than five times the rate for married couples.

And, despite notions to the contrary, child support payments fail to help many. The most recent study done (in 1978 by the U.S. Department of Commerce Bureau of the Census) on payments made for child support and alimony showed that only about fifty-eight percent of mothers of children with no father present were given awards for child support from the absent parents. Of these women, only forty-nine percent received the full amount to which they were entitled, while twenty-eight percent received no payment at all.

The differences between latchkey children growing up in intact families with two wage earners versus those living in a single-parent household with a single wage earner will become evident as one progresses through the book. Most notably the single parent will have less time to spend meeting the same number of demands for child care. He or she will also be less likely to have someone with whom to share family responsibilities and will have fewer economic resources with which to purchase services. There are latchkey children living in intact families with a single wage earner, but the number of such families is small, especially when compared to the two other groups.

### Latchkey Children and the Baby Boom

Another factor that is influencing the number of latchkey children today is the effect of the post World War II baby boom. This was the rapid acceleration of births that occurred after the war and peaked in 1958. People born between 1943 and 1963 represent fifty percent of all adults in the United States today and all are now in their childbearing years.

As a result of the increase in the sheer numbers of people wanting and able to have children, the birth rate began to rise again in 1977 after nineteen years of steady decline. Those children born in increasing numbers in 1977 enter school in 1983. It is very unlikely that additional child-care services will have been put into place rapidly enough to accommodate these children. The possible result will be an even greater rise in the number of latchkey children beginning in 1983. And, unless something dramatic is undertaken either to provide new child-care arrangements, or to make school and work schedules more compatible, or to reduce the rate of separations and divorces, which tend to compel women to work who normally wouldn't, there should be a burst of new latchkey children in 1985. This is because studies show that parents commonly believe that when a child reaches age eight, or about third grade, he or she is mature enough to handle self-care.

## Latchkey Children and the Law

Typically the public looks to the law to protect underage children from being left in self-care. As a matter of fact in most jurisdictions parents are responsible for providing care, support and supervision of their children as long as they are minors, usually until age eighteen or twenty-one. A strict interpretation of existing laws governing the rights of minors and their parents' obligation to support their children would prohibit leaving a minor child unattended, whether that child is seven or seventeen.

As a matter of practicality, public enforcement agencies and the courts will seldom respond if the only complaint is that a teenage child is being left unattended—unless, of course, there is a disturbance or if it is for long periods of time or there are indications of neglect or abuse. Public enforcement agencies will, however, usually respond to complaints about children under age thirteen who are unsupervised. In many jurisdictions a third or more of all complaints received by child welfare agencies are about children lacking appropriate supervision.

While invoking the law doesn't seem to be an effective way of enforcing continuous child care for children, the presence of such laws should be noted. The younger the child the more likely are social service workers and the courts to interpret the latchkey situation as one of neglect.

The existence of such laws also seems to serve as part of the reason for parents who do leave their children in self-care to prohibit them from playing outside or inviting friends over, unless an adult is present. Welfare officials have wide authority to investigate conditions at the homes of neglected or deserted children, and parents generally do not wish to have their children draw attention to the family by reason of acts that could happen outside the home.

A further note of caution about the law. While in most states, except for certain specific statutes to the contrary, a parent is generally not liable for most damages and injuries caused by a minor child, there are two exceptions that can be interpreted as affecting parents of latchkey children. A parent may be liable if he or she fails to restrain the child from continuing wrongful conduct of which the parent is aware. This may be an additional reason for not starting or terminating a latchkey arrangement: when parents are or become aware that their child has set fires before, for example, or even if they know that he or she has played with matches. Absent parents generally find it impossible to restrain unsupervised children from any behavior the child can and wants to do.

A second reason a parent may be liable is if a parent negligently entrusts a dangerous instrument to a child. To illustrate: if your child shoots someone with a gun you left accessible in your house, you might be liable. Latchkey children have full access to all the contents of their homes. And the older children become, the more likely they are to exercise their ability to explore to relieve boredom, if nothing else.

Although discussion of the laws governing unattended children isn't meant to needlessly alarm parents who are already concerned about the welfare of their children, parents should certainly be aware of all possible consequences that may develop—quite unexpectedly —from the latchkey arrangement.

In subsequent chapters we will explore in depth other areas of caution and concern to parents, how to alleviate them on the one hand, and on the other, how to make the latchkey experience as positive as possible when it is determined to be the best child-care arrangement available to you and your family.

# Chapter 2
# ALONE

Between two and three o'clock school bells across the country ring and millions of children leave their classrooms. Some of these children will go home to a waiting mother, but more than half the school-age children in America will enter alternate care arrangements. Some go to day-care centers, others spend their afternoons at a neighbor's or a friend's house, some are cared for by relatives, sitters or housekeepers and many spend their afternoons caring for themselves.

Tiffany is nine years old, a third grade student at a Catholic elementary school. Both her mother and father must leave early for work, so Tiffany spends her mornings and afternoons alone. When she gets home from school at three o'clock, she calls her mother and then takes her two dogs for a walk. After exercising the dogs, she has a snack and watches TV until her mother arrives at 4:30. During the summer, Tiffany lives with her grandmother. When school is closed for teacher's meetings, snow days or days she is ill, Tiffany stays home alone.

Many latchkey children, like Tiffany, spend their afternoons alone. Some, like Tiffany, are only children. Others have sisters and/or brothers who spend their afternoons elsewhere. Younger children are often left with babysitters, rather than entrusted to the care of older brothers or sisters. Older siblings may be engaged in after-school activities. Whatever the reason, millions of children spend some part of each day alone, caring for themselves.

School children who spend their weekday afternoons totally alone can be found even in kindergarten, but there is a marked increase in the number of latchkey children per classroom beginning at about the third grade. Many latchkey children begin staying alone at age eight, an age when many parents feel their children are old enough to care for themselves. To better understand the experience of children who stay alone, we will explore in this chapter what a typical day is like during their hours in self-care: their habits, routines, problems and fears, and the ways they find to cope with them.

The amount of time latchkey children spend alone differs from child to child and situation to situation. Most latchkey children spend from two to three hours alone each day, which is the difference between school dismissal and the end of the average work day. But it is not uncommon to find children who spend five or six hours alone daily. For most families the parents' work schedules determine the amount of time the children will spend alone. A nurse who works the 7:00 to 3:00 shift might arrive home by 3:30. Her daughter may only spend a half hour alone each day, depending on her husband's work schedule. Another nurse, the mother of an eleven-year-old boy, works the 3:00 to 11:00 shift. Since she is divorced, her son spends his evenings alone. He cooks his own dinner and gets himself to bed. The only time he sees his mother is in the morning and on weekends.

Most children who stay alone expect one parent between five and six o'clock, although for some this is the earliest they can expect a parent. "My mother usually gets home at 6:00," one fifth grade girl commented. "But sometimes her boss wants her to stay after and she gets home much later." Overtime work is a major cause for parental delay, but there are others. Accidents, traffic congestion and car problems all can cause delays. Many parents stop at the grocery store for "a few things" and end up in a checkout line behind a person who can't find a check-cashing card. Each of these extends the time an expectant child waits for mommy.

A housekey on a chain around the neck has become the national symbol of the latchkey child. When worn in such a manner the keys aren't easily dropped or lost and are readily available for access to the child's house. Losing the key is a major fear of latchkey children since they usually have been coached by anxious parents to guard it no matter what. When one seven-year-old girl was asked what she would do if she lost her key she just started crying. Finally she replied, "I wouldn't. I just wouldn't." Many latchkey children can obtain a second key from a neighbor or friend. "If I lose my key I can go next door and get another one," said eight-year-old Frank, "but my mother would still be mad at me for losing mine."

Other children can get an extra key from a building manager or a special hiding place. But for some a lost key is not easily replaced, and they will spend the afternoon at a neighbor's or with a nearby relative, if such an arrangement has been made. Others know how to get into their house without a key. "I'd pry open the basement window and get into the house that way," said ten-year-old Barbara. "My mother told me if I get locked out to break a window," boasted eleven-year-old George. But for a large percentage of latchkey children, losing a key means waiting. Waiting outside or in an apartment hallway until their mother or father returns from work. Eleven-year-old Kiesha keeps her key on a chain around her neck. During recess she gives her key to her teacher so she doesn't lose it. "If I lost my key, I'd be scared. My mother would be mad. I'd go to the lost and found in school . . . if it wasn't there I'd have to wait outside until my mother got home at six o'clock." Eight-year-old Ellis wears his key on a cord around his neck. He keeps it under his shirt so no one can see it. When asked about his key, he was hesitant at first to reveal it. "My mother told me not to show my key to anyone. She doesn't want anyone to know I'm home alone . . . when I get home I look around to make sure no one is watching, and then I try to get in the house fast . . ." Ellis worries about losing his key. "I don't go outside and play after I get home from school. I'm afraid I'd lose my key. Then my mother would be real mad and I'd have to wait in the hall."

Once home latchkey children live by different parental expectations. Some receive explicit instructions on how they are to behave, others receive little or no guidance. A seven-year-old girl who spends an hour and a half alone daily said her mother told her "nothing." Other children simply get general instructions like "behave," "be good," or "take care of yourself." An eleven-year-old boy who was asked about rules responded, "Don't cook, don't play with matches and don't let anyone in the house." A nine-year-old girl who lives with her mother replied, "My mother only told me two things to do when I get home: lock the door and don't eat candy." This is not sufficient preparation for self-care.

The majority of parents, however, give their children instructions similar to these:

1. Lock the door after you get home
2. Call (usually mother)
3. Don't let anyone in the house
4. Don't tell people you are alone
5. If someone calls tell them your mother is busy and will call them back later
6. Don't cook or use electrical appliances considered dangerous
7. Call a parent in case of an emergency

The telephone is the lifeline between parents and latchkey children. It is the vehicle by which children can communicate questions and concerns to absent parents, though many must confine themselves to the initial call made on arriving home due to circumstances at a parent's workplace. An eleven-year-old girl who is alone an hour and a half per day calls her mother several times during that period. "I talk to my mother at least five times a day. She calls me once or twice, too, just to make sure I'm o.k. . . ." What could necessitate the frequent calls? "I call to tell my mother I got home safe, to ask what I can have for a snack, or for help with my homework. I call when I can't find something, to see if I can go outside and play, to ask if we can go to the store when she gets home, to tell her someone called . . ." Clearly, this girl talked to her mother by phone as readily as she might ask her a question if she were in the next room.

The telephone is also of obvious importance in emergency situations. For many latchkey children the telephone becomes their chief social link, especially if they are not allowed outside to play.

Latchkey children who are home alone generally follow predictable patterns of behavior once a routine is established. Most walk immediately to the telephone to assure mom or dad that they are home safely, then they turn on the television. A typical comment from a nine-year-old girl was, "It makes me feel like I'm not alone." Many latchkey children watch television from the minute they walk through the door until their parent arrives. Some continue watching even after their parents are home. Latchkey children watch an average of four hours a day, but it is not unusual to find some who watch television almost continuously from three o'clock until they retire.

Television provides entertainment for those children who spend their afternoons alone. They snack and do their homework while watching afternoon programming. "Watching television makes the time go by more quickly," commented an eight-year-old boy who spends an hour and a half alone each day. "I start watching cartoons and I forget I'm alone . . . before I know it my mother is home."

Television is also used by latchkey children to reduce fears. "I turn the television up real loud so I don't hear any outside noises," was another typical comment. But for many children television also intensified fears. Frightening programming such as news of murders and break-ins tends to intensify feelings of vulnerability in children who are home alone.

Some children have parental restrictions on the amount or type of programming they can watch, but it is difficult for parents to enforce these rules. "My mother said I could watch television after I finish my homework" was a frequent comment, "but I do my homework while I watch television." Other parents try to control what their children watch, banning particular shows or particular types of programs. "My mother tells me not to watch programs that say 'parental guidance suggested,' " commented a ten-year-old girl who spends several hours alone daily. "I watch them anyway; then I get scared."

Latchkey children who stay alone usually have a snack while watching television. Almost all are prohibited from using the stove, so for most an afterschool snack consists of foods that require little or no preparation, such as fruit, cookies or prepackaged cakes, or a peanut butter and jelly sandwich.

Many latchkey children are not expected to do anything when home alone, while others are expected to do the majority of the housecleaning. Older children generally must do more work than younger children and girls are expected to do more work than boys. The most frequently assigned chores are washing dishes, cleaning rooms, making beds, emptying trash and vacuuming. "I have to make all the beds, clean my room, wash the breakfast dishes, make my own lunch and practice the piano every day," said eleven-year-old John. "I don't mind it." Eight-year-old Erica also has a lot to do: "I have time to wash the dishes, clean the closets, wash the tub and sweep the floor. I like to help, but I'd like to have time to play, too."

Many children will do their homework while watching TV once their chores are completed. When their parents come home from work they usually ask if their homework is done. Whether it was done or not, the response is usually "yes." Some parents take the time to check.

Many latchkey children interviewed said they experience difficulty completing homework assignments or doing them correctly. Watching reruns of "Happy Days" or "Laverne and Shirley" doesn't help their efforts to complete assignments correctly. Those children who don't know how to complete an assignment must either wait for assistance from a parent, seek other sources of assistance, usually by telephone, guess how to do the assignment or not do it at all. Trying to do a difficult assignment by themselves is frustrating. Many children wait for help but by the time their parents return, decide not to ask since they seem too busy or tired.

Homework assignments could be a common meeting ground for latchkey children and their parents—a place where children can say, "I need you," and parents can respond, "Let me help." Instead many parents yell at their children when assignments are incomplete, making homework assignments a source of friction.

Latchkey children who are at home alone often turn to pets for comfort. Dogs are the most common pet in America and those latchkey children who have them say they feel an added sense of security. Many describe their pet using words that indicate the security the pet provides. When Tiffany was asked to describe her dogs she said, "They're big and mean and black." Other children who had dogs described them in a similar manner using adjectives like "strong" or "tough." Generally pets help reduce the level of fear of those children who stay alone, though they can occasionally make things worse. "When my dog starts barking," Mark explained, "I get scared. I think someone's outside." Cats can also be frightening to children who are home alone. "When my cat goes crazy I get scared," said seven-year-old Nikki. Ten-year-old Karen had the same fear. "When my cat races around the house, I get real scared. My grandmother told me when a cat does that, it means the devil is in the house."

These were infrequent comments, however. In addition to the sense of security pets add, they provide companionship, helping latchkey children to feel less alone. They also give the child who is home alone something to touch and talk to. Pets add responsibility, but they do make the child feel needed.

Children interviewed who don't have pets and spend their afternoons alone generally want one. The pet the child wants usually gives an indication of how the child feels about being alone. An eight-year-old girl who said she was afraid to stay by herself wants "a dog, a mean dog." Another girl who feels less frightened but is lonely said, "I want a little dog I can hold on my lap and talk to when I watch TV."

After a full day of school during which children are expected to remain fairly sedentary, most enjoy playing outside where they can run, jump and tell the world how wonderful it is to be alive. But because of safety considerations, and the violent nature of the world, many parents must insist that their children stay inside when they're home alone. As a rule younger children are required to stay inside more often than older children; city children are required to stay inside more often than suburban children; and girls are required to stay inside more often than boys. As one might expect, many of the children required to stay inside objected to it. "I seldom get to play outside," commented an eight-year-old girl who stays alone an hour a day. "I wish I could go outside since I have a new bike and I only get to ride it on weekends. I don't get to ride it that much even then since I usually have to go places with my mother." Eleven-year-old Kiesha doesn't like staying inside either. "I have to stay in all week until my mother gets home at six o'clock. I wish I could go out . . . I'm bored."

By way of explanation many parents tell their children it's not safe to play outside. Eight-year-old Gary said, "I think it's safe to play outside, but my mother said it's not, so I don't." Eight-year-old Erica's mother has her daughter convinced that it's not safe to play outside. "Going outside is a good way to get fresh air but I don't go out. I'm scared to. There are big boys outside. My mother said they might hurt me. You know how." Some children who are allowed to go outside are afraid to. "I can play outside but I think it's dangerous," said a seven-year-old girl. "I play in the back alley but cars come there too. Once they hit a dog and another time they ran over a girl's foot."

Those children who can go outside and play, usually fourth, fifth and sixth graders, have parental restrictions. Mark's situation is typical of other latchkey children who are allowed to go outside: "I can go outside if I ask . . . but I have to stay on my block." Kiesha, a fifth grader who spends from 3:00 to 6:00 alone, has more severe limits. "If I go outside I have to stay on the front porch or in the back yard. It's no fun. The kids are out front and I can't play with them." Reggie, a sixth grader, has few restrictions: "I can go out as long as I tell my mother. I feel safe when I'm outside. I'm with my friends and we look out for each other."

Latchkey children not only have less time to play outside with their friends but they also have less opportunity to have friends over to play. When they're alone the great majority of latchkey children can't have friends over, ever. Absent parents understandably worry about accidents and fighting, and don't want the responsibility of another child when no one is there to supervise. Even if they would let their children have friends over, few parents are willing to let their children play at a friend's house if an adult is not present. Twelve-year-old Carmen said, "I can't play outside but I can go to a friend's house if my mom knows my friend's mother is there. My mom doesn't want me at anyone's house where there is no adult. If something is missing she thinks I'll get blamed."

The result of the restrictions—no playing outside and no friends inside—is that approximately one-third of America's urban latchkey children spend their afternoons totally isolated, with only the television set and friends they call on the telephone for companionship. More often it is the younger children who find themselves in this position, since their parents are afraid to let them go outside.

After school is not the only time latchkey children spend alone. Illness, holidays and vacations all leave latchkey children without adult supervision for extended periods of time. On these occasions the child is not left alone for two or three hours, but eight, ten or twelve hours, depending on the time it takes a parent to commute to work. It is these times, because of their long duration, that can be especially isolating for the child who is alone.

All school-age children become ill, and through no fault of their own, often pose an extra burden for working parents. Parents who work must decide whether to send a sick child to school or let him or her stay home. If the child is not very sick, the choice is often made to send the child to school. But during childhood illnesses progress rapidly, and a child feeling slightly under the weather in the morning is usually much worse by noon. It's also difficult to tell whether a child who doesn't feel well at breakfast could be trying to avoid school. Working parents who are unconvinced of the seriousness of their child's illness usually send them to school.

Many parents questioned said they would let their children stay home if someone was there to take care of them if they made a complaint at the breakfast table of a stomachache or cold. Instead, student after student repeats the same story to the school nurse. "I told my mother my stomach hurt this morning. She told me to come to school anyway and see how I felt after I got here." Although the words change the theme is the same. "My mother told me to come to school because she has an important meeting. I'm supposed to call her at work if I get worse and she'll come pick me up."

Children who are obviously very sick must be kept at home. Most parents will take a day off if they think their child needs personal care, but many leave their children home to care for themselves with a television as a companion and the telephone as a nurse. "If I get a cold or something, I stay home by myself," explained Jimmy. "But if I'm *really* sick, my mother or grandmother will stay home and take care of me." The times when Jimmy stays home by himself, his mother calls frequently to see how he is and tells him when to take his medicine, or what to have for lunch. Still, Jimmy says he would rather go to school than stay home alone when he's sick.

Barring illness, there are many other times when latchkey children must spend an entire day alone. The school year is studded with holidays and vacations; times during which adults are expected to work. Schools are only in session 180 days, 60 days less than the average work year. Most schools give students a two-week vacation at Christmas, as well as a week-long spring break. Schools also close on all of the national holidays, plus a few local or religious holidays.

Add to that the days schools are closed for parent-teacher conferences or teacher meetings, weekends and summer vacations and it's
evident that schools are closed more than they're open.

Most parents are off on the national holidays and are also entitled
to two weeks' vacation and ten days' sick leave. But for the majority
of days when students are off, parents must work, leaving latchkey
children to care for themselves. There are no camps or other comparable programs to care for latchkey children during the times when
they are off and their parents must work. On these days most latchkey children must care for themselves all day.

One way to prevent this would be for a few families to get together
and cooperate with one another. During spring break or on other
regularly scheduled holidays, this group of parents could rotate care
of the entire group of children. Playmates or classmates make great
vacation mates and all involved would look forward to school holidays when they would have the chance to spend the day with five
or six friends. The same plan could be used to cover snow days and
unexpected school closings. Most parents can occasionally afford to
miss a day of work during unusual circumstances, but few can afford
to miss five consecutive days of work if school is closed for a week's
holiday whatever the reason. By rotating, no one would be forced to
and the children wouldn't have to spend extensive amounts of time
alone either.

Summer is the largest block of vacation time for school-age children and is a particularly trying time for latchkey children. A few
get to spend summer with their parents if, for instance, one or both
are teachers, but for the majority other arrangements must be made.
One popular alternative is day camp. Day camp programs provide
stimulation, supervision and safety within the price range of most
families. But, like school days, day camp usually ends at three or four
o'clock. Mike, an eight-year-old boy, said that he enjoys day camp,
as did many others. "I get to do a lot of things there I can't do at
school, like play outside and make things," he said. "It's fun. Last
summer I even learned how to swim.

There are also latchkey children who spend their summer vacations at the home of relatives, usually their grandmothers. Those
who have a grandmother or aunt in the neighborhood spend the day
at the relative's house and return home in the evenings. But for most,
the relative lives out of town. For some "out of town" is close enough

for them to go home on weekends and be with their parents. Many grandparents, however, live hundreds of miles away. Some children who stay with grandparents spend as many as ten weeks there without direct contact with their parents. Vacations spent with grandparents received mixed reviews: some love it while others find it boring. "I have to go to my grandmother's house in the summer because there's nobody here to take care of me," a ten-year-old boy commented. "I don't like to go. There's nothing to do there. All my friends are here." But a nine-year-old girl found the experience enjoyable: "I spent last summer at my grandma's. I like it. We go shopping and bake cookies. My grandmother's nice."

There are also latchkey children who don't have a relative with whom they can spend the summer, and for one reason or another their parents choose not to send them to day camp. Instead these children, usually fourth, fifth and sixth graders, spend most or all of their summer alone. Diane, a sixth grade girl, hates summers. She is twelve years old, a straight A student, and she is forty pounds overweight. "I spend the whole summer home by myself. I can't go outside until my mother gets home at 4:30. I sit at the window and watch the other kids play outside. I wish I was with them. It's boring to stay home alone all day." What does Diane do? "I read a lot. Watch TV . . . and eat." Kevin, a fifth grade boy, also spends most of his summers alone. "I go to camp for one week. Other than that I'm on my own. I watch TV in the morning, then I ride my bike and play outside with my friends. It's not bad but I don't like it. I have to eat lunch by myself and if it's raining I spend the whole day inside by myself. That's no fun."

On the whole latchkey children spend more time alone and less time with their friends than their parent-watched counterparts. Yet the elementary school years are a time when children learn how to interact with others. Children see their worth as how well they are respected in their peer group. Limiting those interactions can reduce their feelings of belonging and minimize feelings of self-worth. In addition, learning how to interact with and feel accepted by others is a primary task of childhood which affects how a child will interact with others in later life.

Interviews with adults who were latchkey children illustrated the importance of childhood relationships in terms of their present behavior. Many linked their latchkey experience to present shyness. Others complained that they lacked the social skills and the ability to communicate easily with others. One man who was a latchkey child from age ten to eighteen said, "I was cut off from peers when I needed them most. As a result I had trouble making friends. I had to catch up and learn how to communicate with people in college." Another man who was alone for three hours a day, from the time he was six until he was ten, echoed the same sentiment. "Spending so much time alone made it harder for me to model social behaviors. I learned them later than others. This made the world seem a more hostile place during this time."

Certainly there are children with slowly developing communication and social skills who are not latchkey children. But for those who are, it is clear that isolation is a deterrent to the socialization process. Latchkey children who are alone deal with a unique set of problems, and ways will be explored to help break up the time they spend alone and reduce isolation, which often lies at the root of the problems they experience in self-care.

# Chapter 3
# SIBLINGS

The bell rings; school is dismissed. Seven-year-old Laurie walks home with her nine-year-old sister, Linda. Laurie and Linda must care for themselves after school until their mother arrives home at 5:30. The girls have instructions to clean the house, wash the breakfast dishes, make the beds, call mom and do their homework. They say that most of the time they just sit and watch TV. Sometimes they fight. They're not permitted to go outside, nor can they have friends in.

Laurie and Linda are latchkey children. In some ways their lives are similar to the lives of latchkey children who spend their afternoons alone, but there are significant differences that set them apart from their lone counterparts. In this chapter we will explore the typical day of latchkey children who are in the company of siblings, and the special problems that they encounter.

Siblings provide each other with companionship; someone to talk to, play with, and watch TV with. On the reverse side, there's the potential for fights and arguments. In order for this arrangement to work, Linda must accept the responsibility of her younger sister who, in turn, must listen to her older sister.

Children who are home with siblings average the same amount of time alone as children who are home by themselves, about two to three hours a day. Often siblings go to the same school and walk or take the bus home together. But sometimes the older sibling is a junior high student and arrangements become more complicated. Urban children often meet their younger siblings outside their school building and walk or take public transportation home together. Suburban children attending different schools ride school buses home and meet their siblings there since the distance between home and school is much further.

The eldest child in a family with more than one child will usually start staying home after school at age eight, while younger siblings are still attending day care. This child stays home alone until the younger siblings in the family start school full-time and all children are on the same schedule. Kindergarteners are infrequently latchkey children since most such programs are only for half a day, making it impossible for older siblings who are in school until two or three o'clock to pick them up. Working parents usually send these preschool children to day-care centers or a neighbor's home after school. The popularity and rapid rise in the number of full day kindergarten programs could, however, mean an equally rapid rise in the number of four- and five-year-olds who spend their afternoons in the care of older siblings, once they're put on the same schedule.

Older siblings are not necessarily that much older than the children they watch. It is not uncommon for a nine-year-old to be in charge of a five-year-old. But some children are in charge of much younger siblings, as ten-year-old Monique indicated. "After school I watch my brother and sister. My brother is seven. I meet him outside after school and we take the bus home together. We get home around 3:30. At four o'clock the day care center drops off my little sister. I watch them both until my mother gets home at 6:30."

If there are only two children, then the oldest is placed in charge. In families with several children, parents select girls more often than boys to be the caretaker of younger siblings. "There are four kids in my family," Joan explained. "My brother Mike is thirteen. He's the oldest. I'm eleven. Then I have a sister Karen, nine, and a brother Don, six. I have to watch Karen and Don after school. Mike doesn't have to do anything even though he's the oldest. My mother says she can't trust him." The fact that most mothers trust their daughters more than their sons was also experienced by Tom, a latchkey child. "Me and my sister are only ten months apart, but my mother put her in charge of me. She carries the key and tells me what to do. I don't like it one bit."

In families where two or more children spend their afternoons alone, the house key is given to the oldest child unless the youngest child gets home first. It's unusual for parents to give more than one child a key.

Directions, like keys, are also given to the oldest sibling who is responsible for calling the parent when everyone is safe at home, helping younger siblings with homework, settling disputes and handling emergencies. Depending on the relative ages of the siblings, older children might also be in charge of making snacks, monitoring chores and supervising outside play. Younger siblings who depend on the care of their older brothers and sisters and are usually not taught how to handle emergencies, must depend on others for help.

Children who stay with siblings tend to live more varied lives than their isolated counterparts, who follow a fairly regular routine after school. They will have a snack, watch TV, do their homework and their chores, but in no special order. The number of children at home, their relative ages and positions in the family all affect how their time is spent after school. They're usually not allowed to have friends over but they're less likely to be instructed to stay indoors than children who stay alone. Those children who can't have friends over or play outside still have the companionship of their siblings and needn't deal with the isolation that only children experience.

When illness strikes, older children are treated like latchkey children who stay alone. Depending on how sick they are, sometimes they stay alone and sometimes a parent (usually their mother) stays with them. Sometimes younger children are left to care for themselves when sick, but usually their mother or an older sibling stays home to care for them.

Summer also poses a problem for latchkey children who stay home with siblings. The arrangements for these children are the same as for their isolated counterparts. Approximately one-third of them go to camp, one-third go to a relative's home and one-third stay home with siblings. Staying home with a sibling has its benefits. In most cases, it's much preferred to staying home alone. Children who stay with brothers and sisters tend not to experience the levels of fear or isolation that children alone often complain about. If the time the children are expected to stay alone is short and if the children get along well, the arrangement can be a very pleasant one. Two siblings usually get along better than three. And children who get along when their parents are home will probably get along when left alone.

Sam is eight years old and in the third grade. He lives with his mother and his sister Donna, who is nine. Sam's parents are divorced. His mother is a nursing student and doesn't get home from school until 3:30 or 4:00. Sam and Donna live across the street from the school so they are home by three o'clock. They've been staying alone for the past year. Before that the two children stayed with a neighbor across the street. They still go to her for help in an emergency.

After school Sam and Donna "fool around." "We run in the hall and flip on the bed," explained Sam. "Then we do our homework. It has to be done before mom gets home. After she gets home we can go outside and play with our friends."

Sam feels safe at home because he has the companionship of his sister and his dog, Kelly. "I love Kelly. He's a big German shepherd. He lives in the back yard. He's fun. He protects the family." Sam likes to play with Kelly, but he can't let him in the house, nor can he go outside to play with him until his mother gets home.

Sam is also very attached to Donna. He refers to her as "my Donna" and misses her when she's away. He doesn't feel comfortable staying alone and goes to Donna when he has a problem. "I worry about the darkness and creepy noises. When I'm scared I go by Donna and hide by her . . . Sometimes I have bad dreams . . . If I go to my mother she says, 'Go back to bed. I'll have no more babies.' So I crawl under Donna's bed and hide. I feel safe there."

Donna is sweet and easygoing and doesn't mind watching Sam. In fact, she enjoys his company. And even though Donna is only a year older than Sam, she tends to "mother" him. She walks him home, makes him a snack after school and provides him with companionship. Even though Sam is sometimes frightened when they're home alone, he feels better knowing Donna is there.

All children who are cared for by older brothers and sisters are not as lucky as Sam. Most are left alone for much longer periods of time, and most are not as close to their older sibling as Sam is to Donna. Many complain that their older siblings are distant at best. Fighting is a frequent problem, especially among siblings who are close in age and where lines of authority are unclear. Despite instructions to the contrary, many older children leave their younger siblings alone so they can be with their friends. Others don't let their younger brothers and sisters out of their sight for one minute to the point of being overbearing.

Of all the problems siblings experience when left alone, fighting is the one most frequently mentioned by both parents and children. Parents who leave more than one child at home unattended say they worry about it constantly. One mother of a ten- and a twelve-year-old boy expressed her fears this way: "Driving home from work, I wonder what shape the house will be in, and if both of my sons will be in one piece. Every day it's the same thing. As soon as I walk in the door both of them tell me how their brother started the fight, how they tried to avoid fighting and how the other one should be punished. The house is always a mess from their fighting. They throw things at each other and knock things over. No matter what I do, I can't get them to stop. I've tried punishing them. I even tried to bribe them by promising to take them to a movie on Saturday if they don't fight all week. But nothing seems to work."

Disputes between siblings are a commonly accepted phenomenon. Some degree of sibling rivalry is present in all families with two or more children, and is most prevalent during the elementary school years between children who are fairly close in age. Parents ordinarily see sibling rivalry expressed by endless teasing, arguing, blaming and belittling. It usually becomes most intense when parental attention is at a premium and must be competed for by the children in the family. Parents who have three or more children and only two hours a day to spend with them quickly notice their children competing for their attention. Any change in working patterns which cause a sudden drop in adult attention will intensify the feelings of rivalry already present.

Children competing for attention generally fight even when their parents are home. Parents generally check sibling disputes before they become too intense with a simple phrase, "Cut it out, you two," or "Linda, stop teasing him." When left alone, however, children must settle disagreements themselves. Minor disputes can quickly get out of hand and often will end in a fight when an adult isn't present to impose a solution or prematurely end the argument. Many siblings report that they fight daily between themselves.

Children alone will fight over everything and anything, from whose turn it is to walk the dog or do the dishes to what TV show to watch. One parent explained that she could never predict what her children would fight over. Once she controlled one problem they found something else to fight over. "Last week they fought over who was supposed to sit in which chair. At times it seems as though they're looking for something to fight over; that they intentionally annoy each other." Many parents expressed having the same problem.

Most latchkey children need to express their frustrations and fighting is one way in which they accomplish that. They arrive home from school tired and in need of nurturing, a need that can't be immediately satisfied. The child must also try to cope with conflicting emotions: frustration from a hard day at school, some degree of resentment from either having to watch or be watched by a sibling and anger at parents for not being there to see them after school. No one is there to dissipate these emotions by providing reassurance, making a snack, listening to that critical event at school, and as a consequence these disappointments and frustrations are frequently expressed as anger. Because of their proximity and relative safety, siblings are frequently the target of this anger.

George and Tina are latchkey children. Their mother, a high school teacher, returned to work this year, since she felt her children were old enough to stay without her for an hour after school. George is eleven and Tina is eight. George is supposed to be in charge but, according to their mother, Tina is the more responsible of the two and does most of the work. Everyone in the family agrees that one of the major problems in leaving George and Tina alone is fighting. According to Tina they fight almost every day. "He's always teasing me. I scream at him and tell him to stop but he doesn't listen. He starts calling me names, and sometimes I get so mad I hit him. He hits me back. We just keep hitting each other until I run upstairs and lock myself in my mother's bedroom. I call her from there and tell her what George did to me. Sometimes George takes the phone off the hook so I can't call. Then he comes upstairs and tells me I'd better not call or else he'll really beat me up tomorrow . . . When my mother comes home I tell her everything that happened. She yells at my brother and tells him to stop teasing me, but it doesn't do any good. He acts the same way the next day."

Calling on the telephone for parental intervention is not uncommon. Children depend on parents to intervene when they are home, so they also expect them to intervene when they're at work. Most working parents are upset by the frequent phone calls they receive from fighting children. Not only does it interrupt their performance at work, it raises their stress level since they can neither intervene nor monitor their children effectively. Most are at a loss as to how to handle phone calls from children who are home alone. Calling a parent at work to say "George hit me. Tell him to stop" is one way children use to get parental attention. Whether the parent responds to these cries for help and demands for action neutrally ("I'll take care of it when I get home"), angrily ("Both of you are going to get it, I don't want any more fighting"), or positively ("Put George on the phone. Let me talk to him") doesn't matter. The child's objective of receiving parental attention was met. Even negative attention is better than no attention. The cycle of fighting and calling, which is the reason for fighting, is reinforced. Calling for intervention in a fight is also a way of saying, "We need you. We can't stay by ourselves." Indirectly, the child that seeks intervention is telling his parent that he doesn't like staying home with his siblings without adult supervision.

Parents who want to discourage frequent phone calls over minor disputes should develop another system of handling complaints. One system that one parent found effective was to listen to all complaints and problems as soon as she got home from work. This way she could hear both sides of the story after the emotional energy had dissipated and she could give her children her complete attention. In effect, this woman has a short family meeting with her children every night in which she helps them deal with the conflicts they had that day. She doesn't punish them, but instead gets them to discuss their differences and make commitments to change.

Other parents try to reduce the phone calls they receive by eliminating conflict. They try to decide as much as possible in advance so that there is less to argue over. Clear rules and policies can do a great deal to reduce fighting, although some children will continue to argue no matter what. One parent got so frustrated with the fighting among her three children that she assigned each of them a room of the house where they were to wait for her. "They weren't allowed to interact at all," she said. "If anything went wrong, I just punished the person that wasn't where he was supposed to be." This parent felt compelled to go to extremes to keep her children separated. If children fight so intensely that they can't be trusted to be together in the same room, then they shouldn't be left alone—one or all should stay with a babysitter.

In some families the fighting becomes so intense that accidents or injuries occur. Scratching, biting, hitting and kicking are common methods of fighting used by children that result in cuts and bruises. In some instances methods of settling squabbles are even more intense. One girl reported going to her bedroom and getting a bullwhip and chasing her younger sister around the house whenever a fight began. Another girl reported that her younger brother went into the kitchen, got a butcher knife and threatened her with it in the midst of a fight. Reports of sibling fights that result in death are not unheard of. These are the infrequent, though still alarming, instances when children run to the bedroom and get their father's gun or knife and use it in the heat of anger. Injuries requiring medical care or that result in death may also accidentally result during arguments. One girl who was fighting with her sister fell through the storm window and had to have numerous stitches in her arm. A young boy suffered a broken arm when his brother pushed him during a fight and he fell on concrete. Fights that result in serious injury can, of course, occur when parents are home, but it is less likely since children who are seriously threatened will quickly run to an adult for help. When no adults are present, the children must contain their own anger, which many don't yet know how to do.

Children who spend their afternoons with siblings much older than themselves are less likely to fight, but the experience still may not be a positive one.

Mark is eight years old and lives with his mother and sixteen-year-old sister. His parents were recently divorced. His father and fourteen-year-old brother live nearby, but he seldom sees them. Mark walks to his cousin's house after school where he meets his sister. She drives him home. Although his sister is sixteen and a sophomore in high school, Mark and his sister are latchkey children. When they get home Mark does his homework and watches TV while his sister takes a nap. "I'd like to go outside and play or have friends in," Mark comments, "but my sister won't let me. All she wants to do is sleep." As a result Mark never goes outside in the afternoons; instead he spends the time "making rockets" or playing by himself.

Mark's mother doesn't get home from work until seven or eight o'clock in the evening, so his sister fixes dinner and the two of them eat together. Mark sees very little of his mother except on the weekends, when they go shopping together.

Mark says that he watches four to five hours of television a day. He has no limit or restriction on the amount of TV he watches. Sometimes he finds the television programs frightening. When he's scared he says he just "sits quietly." When questioned further, he said he has recurring nightmares about a witch.

Mark's grandmother lives nearby. She cares for him when he's sick and when school isn't in session. Although Mark is never alone, he is seldom with his parents, and doesn't seem to have a close, loving relationship with anyone. When he has a problem he goes to his sister for help. They aren't as close as Sam and Donna, but she is there for him to talk to.

Unfortunately, Mark's mother doesn't realize how lonely he is. She's a grocery store cashier and spends a lot of time worrying about financial concerns. She assumes Mark is satisfied with the current arrangements because he's home with his older sister and because he's a happy child who doesn't complain. As should be the case with other parents, Mark's mother should take the time to question Mark to find out how he really feels about the arrangement. In this instance, with a couple of close relatives nearby, she might be able to schedule one day a week for him to spend with his grandparents and one day with his father and older brother. This would not only give Mark the variety he needs, but would give his sister relief from the responsibility of watching him.

Other children also complained that their siblings are present physically, but not psychologically. "My sister's always on the telephone," remarked eight-year-old Karen, "she never plays with me after school." Judy's brother doesn't spend any time with her after school either: "Chris brings his girl friend here every day after school. He knows he's not supposed to let anyone in the house. All they do is sit and talk and hold hands and leave the room."

Although these children feel lonely even when they're home, many younger siblings complain that their older sisters and brothers actually leave them alone. "My brother goes outside to play with his friends," said six-year-old Tracy. "He tells me if I tell my mom he'll hit me. He knows he's supposed to stay with me." It's not uncommon for older siblings to leave their younger sisters and brothers alone to go outside and play, go to a friend's house, participate in an after-school activity or go to a neighborhood hangout for a couple of hours. In most cases, the children's parents don't know that this is happening. Certainly it's not unreasonable for older children to want to be with their friends, but an arrangement should be worked out to meet the needs of both children, such as enlisting the aid of a babysitter for one or two days a week to give the older child a needed break from the responsibility.

Not all older children take advantage of their arrangements as Tracy's brother does—most take their role as caretaker seriously and don't leave their younger sisters and brothers unattended. Instead they see their role as a surrogate parent, helping younger siblings with snacks, changing clothes and providing comfort when needed. Still, this type of interaction between siblings isn't always positive. Some get carried away with their role as substitute parent and try to control their younger siblings excessively and discipline them when they behave inappropriately.

Older children who care for younger siblings must make sure they behave correctly when adults aren't home, and normally have parental guidelines to help them. One common rule is that older children aren't supposed to discipline their younger siblings directly. "I was told not to correct my sister but to let my mom correct her when she got home," explained a boy who is responsible for watching his sister, who is three years younger than himself. "If there's a problem, I'm supposed to take care of it," said one eleven-year-old girl who watches her two younger sisters after school. "I tell my mother what happened later. But if the situation is serious, I call her at work."

The directions given by parents and what actually happens are, however, usually very different. Older siblings often carry their responsibility too far. "When daddy's not home, I'm the man of the house" and "I'm the boss and you have to do what I say" are frequently heard from children left in charge of younger siblings. Older children left in charge often act like a "little mother" or a "little father," disciplining younger siblings the way they think their parents would. Younger children reported being yelled at, hit and punished by older siblings. "If I misbehave, my oldest sister says she's going to tell my mom. If I still don't listen, she sends me to my room."

An additional problem is that the older child is in the position of arbitrarily deciding what constitutes a punishable offense. Some children feel that their younger siblings are bad because they touch something that isn't theirs or eat something forbidden. "My sister knows she's not supposed to eat candy before dinner," explained a ten-year-old boy. "When she does, I call my mother right away." Other older siblings expect immediate compliance with demands and when they aren't met they get mad. "I tell my brother to take out the trash," explained an eleven-year-old girl. "But he keeps watching TV so I turn the TV off and send him to his room. He's afraid upstairs alone, but he should listen to me." Another girl punished her three-year-old sister because she wanted to play with her toys. "I told her to sit on the couch and watch TV. She wanted to play with her toys but I was tired of cleaning them up. So every time she got off the couch I spanked her. She cried, but she has to learn."

Younger siblings also tend to think that their older siblings behave incorrectly. A common complaint is that older siblings control the three t's: television, telephone and treats. "My sister's always on the telephone. I never get to use it," or "I want to watch cartoons after school, but my brother won't let me. He always wants to watch his programs," are constant cries of unfair treatment. Another complaint is that older children make younger children do more than their share of the household chores. "I always have to do the dishes. My sister's supposed to do them, but she hates to put her hands in the dirty water so she makes me do them." A woman, the youngest of three girls who grew up in Long Island, New York, found being the youngest very difficult. "My oldest sister was very dominant and bossy. I found it hard to take orders from her and that put a great deal of strain on our relationship. She was often verbally punitive . . . our relationship was terrible. We fought constantly." Another woman who started staying alone with her fifteen-year-old brother when she was eight also complained that he was too bossy. She said he yelled at her and hit her if she did anything wrong. "I would rather have been left alone or stayed with neighbors," she commented. They also fought frequently. Twenty-five years later, they still don't get along.

Girls who stay home with older brothers often complain that the experience is less than pleasant. Felicia started staying alone with her brothers, Jose and Juan, when her parents got a divorce. Felicia was ten, her brothers were thirteen and five. Although they were only home alone for an hour a day, Felicia hated it. "Being the only girl I was the odd one out and my brothers teased me constantly. They took my shoes and hid them, made fun of me or tickled me." But Felicia had problems with her brothers even when her mother was home. "They were always mean. It's just when we were alone that things got worse since no one was there to stop them."

Mary also had trouble with her brothers. She started staying alone with her older brother, John, and her younger brother, Norman, when she was eight. The three of them spent two hours after school alone every day. They were allowed to go outside and play but they weren't allowed to have friends inside the house. Mary stayed with them until she was eighteen and started college.

Mary complains about the problem of being watched by an older sibling, especially a brother. "My older brother tended to be bossy. We fought constantly since he was always telling me what to do." Mary's brother, John, was three years older than she was. Her problems with him got worse when he became a teenager. "He became interested in sex. It got to the point where I was afraid to be in the house alone with him, so I would spend my afternoons playing outside. Once he cornered me and started to touch me . . . I threatened to tell my father and he stopped."

Mary never discussed the problems she had with her brother with her parents. "Talking to my parents wouldn't do any good. Even if they yelled at my brother nothing would have changed. When we were alone, no one was there to stop him from bothering me. If I would have told my father on John, he might have beat me up. It only would have made things worse, not better."

Advances from older brothers to younger sisters are not uncommon. In fact, there is a great deal of sexual abuse at the hands of older siblings, even though it is less frequently reported than father-daughter incest. Most girls don't tell their parents about their interactions with their brothers because most advances are accompanied by threats or bribes, and girls generally feel that an older brother has the ability to carry out such promises. Even a girl who isn't afraid of her brother still wants to maintain the approval of her parents, and telling them that she's been coerced into some sort of sexual activity with her brother is frightening. Many girls are afraid to tell their parents because they worry that they will be blamed. Even when such behavior by an older brother does come to the attention of parents, they seldom seek professional help in order to prevent intervention from an outside agency. Some parents feel that seeking help might somehow jeopardize their son's future. At most, parents will punish the older child and leave him alone with his younger sister as little as possible. But for working parents finding alternate child-care arrangements for their daughter is often difficult and costly. Some parents who become aware of such a problem don't understand the seriousness of it—traditional family roles aren't upset as they are with father-daughter incest, and many parents view sibling incest as two children simply "exploring their sexuality" or "playing doctor," rather than a responsible sibling taking advantage of a younger child. In many cases sibling incest doesn't really involve both children— it is often a preadolescent or adolescent male using his younger brothers and sisters for his own gratification.

Sexual exploitation by an older sibling is an even more frightening experience for a latchkey child, since she knows that she's under her brother's care frequently and that he can take advantage of her whenever he wants. Even if intercourse is not attempted, the younger child no longer trusts the older one, who has violated his role as brother and caretaker. Instead of a sense of family unity, there is now tension whenever the children are alone, and their relationship is permanently affected in a negative manner.

Gina was a latchkey child as long as she can remember. "Both my parents always worked. My mother was a secretary and my father had his own business. My mother didn't get home from work until after 6:00. Sometimes it was as late as 7:00. It seemed like my father was never there. I know he was but he was always out working so that we could have all the things he didn't have when he was a kid."

Before Gina started school she spent her days at home with a babysitter. "When I was little I didn't go to nursery school. It wasn't like it is now where everybody goes to nursery school. I stayed home and a sitter watched me while my mother worked. I didn't mind it. We had a lot of fun together." But when Gina's brother, a high school student, came home from school at 3:30, the sitter left. "He was in charge of me and my sister Mary every afternoon. He also watched us in the evenings and on the weekends when my parents went out. Mike was a lot older than the both of us. He's twelve years older than me, and nine years older than Mary."

"One afternoon when I was four, Mike lured me up to his room. 'Come here, I got something I want to show you,' he said." From this point on Gina was forced to have sexual relations with her brother, including intercourse. "This went on for three years, until I started second grade. Mike was afraid I'd tell my teacher at school. I was bigger and coming in contact with more people. His threats didn't frighten me as much anymore and he knew it. I found out later that he'd done the same thing to my sister until she was seven. He was afraid she'd talk, so he turned to me. I was four and a lot easier to control."

Gina never told anyone what was going on, in spite of her threats to do so. "Looking back it's hard to believe I didn't say anything to anyone, but you have to remember how a four-year-old thinks. Mike told me he'd kill me if I told anyone. He said he'd beat me or make me do something worse. I believed him. My sister and I were helpless against him. No one was there to protect us . . . plus I thought that if I told my mother she would yell at me and say it was my fault. Mike was always her favorite. I thought she'd believe anything he told her."

Although the case of Gina and Mike illustrates the most frequent form of sibling sexual abuse, homosexual experiences are also frequent. Older brothers will initiate sexual activity with younger brothers, and it is not uncommon for sisters to participate in sexual exploration with each other.

Sibling sexual abuse manifests itself the same way as does any form of sexual abuse. The signs that parents should look for are not unique because the abuser is an older sibling rather than a stranger. Physical signs, including genital trauma, genital soreness or genital infections are the easiest for the parent to observe. But parents should be extremely cautious before confronting an older child and investigate the situation carefully since genital trauma could also be self-inflicted. Parents who suspect abuse should also be alert to suspicious stains on their child's underwear or bedsheets; behavioral indicators might also provide a clue as to the nature of the relationship between siblings. Children that seem unusually close, always touching each other and doing things together, might be more involved than it first appears. Or if a child is involved against his/her will, signs of stress might also be apparent. The child who all of a sudden protests when asked to stay alone with an older brother or sister should be questioned. Sexually abused children often protest violently—usually fabricating reasons why they don't want to be left behind—when parents announce that they are going out and leaving the child in care of an abusing sibling. The child who is abused might also suddenly show aggressive behavior toward the abusing sibling in the presence of parents or, on the other hand, act frightened when that sibling enters the room. A precocious interest in sexual issues by the victim might also provide the alert parent with clues as to possible problems. Somatic complaints such as frequent headaches or stomachaches, which are also signs of stress, might be indicators of abuse. Abused children also often exhibit the other common signs of stress: a sudden drop in school performance, sleeping difficulties and eating problems.

Unfortunately, there is no indisputable sign that indicates sexual abuse. Physical trauma may be self-inflicted and behavioral indicators may be a reflection of other stresses. However, parents who have strong reason to suspect abuse should talk to their children before reaching conclusions. If abuse is confirmed professional assistance should be obtained immediately.

## Problems of Older Siblings

Usually siblings who are unwilling partners in a babysitting arrangement won't be happy. Younger children are dissatisfied being watched by their older brothers and sisters, while older siblings aren't pleased with the arrangements either. Even though they're in control and don't fear verbal, physical or sexual abuse, they still don't enjoy staying with their sisters or brothers. Many complain that the responsibility is too great, and it reduces the amount of time they have to be with friends. Some children complained that they didn't like being responsible for their younger brothers and sisters because their mother punished them if something went wrong. "I have to watch my seven-year-old brother," complained ten-year-old Michelle, "and that's not always easy. He runs ahead of me when we walk home. He won't hold my hand when we cross the street . . . If anything ever happened to him, my mother would kill me." Twelve-year-old Cindy doesn't like watching her two younger brothers either. "They fight and play rough all the time. If they break something I get in trouble, since I'm in charge."

Others complain about the restrictions watching younger siblings puts on their lives. Older siblings are usually required by parents to come straight home after school, making it difficult for them to participate with any regularity in school clubs or after-school sporting events. "I hate watching my sister," was the complaint of one girl, a sentiment echoed by many.

Some children resent the responsibility of watching their younger brothers and sisters without the authority to go with it. They find it frustrating to try to control them when they can't punish them. "My sister doesn't listen to me. She knows I can't do anything except call my mother," one girl complained. "And by the time she gets home she's too tired or too busy to do anything about it." Because of the restrictions imposed on older children, the frustration and resentment they feel is often seen by younger siblings as anger and disapproval. Expecting older children to watch younger children joyfully, when internally many feel angry at them, is an unreasonable expectation. It's important to remember that older siblings are still children, too, and need understanding in the things that frustrate them.

The problems of caring for younger siblings are magnified if older siblings are expected to watch several children, to watch children who are physically or mentally disabled, or to watch step-sisters and -brothers rather than natural siblings. Karen, the oldest of five children, is twelve years old and in the fifth grade. Her parents are divorced. She lives with her mother and four younger siblings in a row house in Baltimore. When no adult is home, Karen is in charge. "I don't do too well in school . . . this is my second time in the fifth grade. I guess it's because I'm absent so much. My mother works at a factory. When she doesn't work, she doesn't get paid, so if any of the kids are sick, I have to stay home and take care of them." Karen also stays home from school to watch her five-year-old brother if their babysitter isn't available to pick him up after kindergarten.

Karen has a lot of responsibility. Being the oldest child, her mother also depends on her to do a lot of the work around the house, including cooking dinner, helping with homework and putting the children to bed when her mother works late. Although Karen seems to be coping with the responsibility of watching her brothers and sisters, it is a great personal sacrifice. Talking to Karen, you sense that she is proud to be contributing to the family, that she enjoys playing mother. But Karen has given up her childhood to be the caretaker of her younger sister and brothers. She is no longer another child in the family, but her mother's partner in running the family. Her schoolwork has suffered because she is absent so frequently, and because she has little time to do her homework or study in light of all her other responsibilities. By keeping her daughter home from school to watch her younger brothers and sister, Karen's mother is communicating to her daughter that school is not important, that Karen's first responsibility is to the home. Karen doesn't mind being kept out of school now since she isn't doing well, but chances are she'll resent it in later life.

Karen's situation could be improved if her mother didn't depend on her to watch her younger brother when the babysitter is unavailable. Instead, an alternative arrangement could be worked out with a back-up babysitter or by enrolling her son in a day-care center, where the care would be more reliable. Additionally, she has far too many responsibilities for a child of her age. If her responsibilities remain at the same level, it's likely that she'll miss more and more school until she eventually drops out.

Edith is thirteen. She gets up at six o'clock and makes breakfast for her six-year-old brother, Reggie, helps him get dressed and walks with him to school. At three o'clock they return home together, change their clothes and watch TV. Half an hour later their younger sister, Tayna, who is developmentally disabled, comes home by a special bus. She is three years old, but she can neither walk nor talk and still wears diapers. Once home, Edith must undress her, change her diaper and feed her. After she's fed, Edith carries Tayna into her bedroom and puts her in her crib with her rattle. Sometimes she puts her in her stroller and lets her watch TV. "She likes the noise and colors, but I know she doesn't understand it," Edith commented. Edith's father gets home at 5:30, at which time Edith usually goes outside to play.

Watching both Reggie and Tayna for two hours a day is a great responsibility for Edith. Luckily, Reggie is well behaved and normally spends all of his time watching television, leaving Edith free to care for Tayna. Watching Tayna severely restricts Edith's life—she doesn't have time to watch TV, do her homework, talk to her friends on the telephone or play outside until her parents come home. When her parents get home, much of their time is also spent caring for Tayna, so Edith and Reggie don't have as much time to do things with their parents as they would like. A disabled child places a strain on any family and families with latchkey children are no exception.

Edith so far is willing to sacrifice virtually all of her time after school to care for her sister, and while taking care of her sister can teach Edith an important lesson in responsibility, it still shouldn't be at the expense of robbing her of having any time for herself or of having time with her brother.

Parents may decide, after considering all the alternatives and weighing the advantages and disadvantages, that leaving their children unsupervised in the afternoon is in their children's best interest. Still, leaving children alone on a regular basis is not the same as leaving them alone once in a while to go to a movie or to eat out. Even children that get along well must be properly prepared for the experience.

Preparing siblings for self-care is more complicated than preparing a single child to stay alone. Each child must be able to care for him- or herself, if necessary. This means that parents must teach each child, not just the oldest, how to handle household emergencies, use the telephone effectively, prepare snacks and do whatever else is necessary to remain successfully alone after school. Preparing all children will not only remove some of the responsibility from the oldest child, it will teach the younger children in the family to be responsible for their own actions.

## Handling Conflicts between Siblings

The easiest way to reduce conflicts when they occur is to reduce the necessary interaction between children. Siblings who are close in age should be expected to act independently of each other. Not only do younger siblings resent being bossed by siblings who are only a year or two older than they are, older siblings have difficulty controlling their slightly younger brothers or sisters as well. When siblings close in age are left alone, no one should be "in charge." To begin with, each child should have his or her own key. A key is a symbol of power and if it's given to only one child it could become a source of conflict. Struggles can be kept to a minimum by limiting other areas of possible conflict also. What television programs will be watched and where each child will sit while watching; what they will have for a snack and where they will eat it; what chores each child will be responsible for and the amount of freedom each child will have to go outside can all be decided in advance. The number of advance decisions necessary will vary from family to family, depending on how the children are getting along. Children that get along well might be able to stay alone with less structure, with parents adding rules as the number of conflicts increases. Children who have numerous conflicts will need their day more tightly structured. But whether children get along well or poorly, it is important that parents develop a systematic method for handling conflicts. This can be done by establishing a formal grievance procedure or setting up regular family meetings. Whatever the method, each child must feel he or she will have an opportunity to be heard.

In families where there is a substantial difference in age between siblings, the oldest sibling is generally in charge. But giving an older sibling unlimited authority often leads to difficulties. Parents must train older children to be loving and helpful as well as understanding. Older siblings are generally very capable of enforcing house rules, and are quick to remind their younger counterparts to take their feet off the couch, hold their food over their plates while eating, or zip up their coats before going outside. They provide the authority of an adult figure, but too often will punish their younger siblings unnecessarily and give them little understanding. Parents who leave older siblings in charge of younger siblings shouldn't also give them the authority to punish them. Instead, older siblings should report problems to parents when they come home from work.

Another way to assure fair treatment of younger children is for parents to limit the number of decisions older children can make. Again, deciding in advance what the younger children should have for a snack, if and when they can go out to play, what they should wear after school, what shows they can watch on TV and when they should do their homework, will reduce conflicts when parents are at work.

A matter of equal importance to establishing rules and making advance decisions or limiting authority is teaching older children how to relate to their younger siblings effectively. Parents need to explain to older siblings the importance of providing quality care to their younger sisters and brothers. If they are too young to understand that their younger siblings miss their parents, can become frightened and lonely and need both supervision and love, then they're too young to be placed in charge of younger siblings on a regular basis. Children eight or nine years old are still too egocentric to understand the perspective of a younger child.

Once the oldest sibling clearly understands that his or her responsibility to the younger children is not only to be a caretaker or rule enforcer, but also to provide nurturance, the parent can begin preparing him or her for this new responsibility. Of course, training should include household safety, telephone and emergency procedures and other skills necessary for self-care. In addition, parents will find it helpful in the long run if they work closely with older siblings to teach them how to help younger siblings with homework, how to resolve conflicts and listen to problems. The parent can accomplish this both by modeling appropriate behavior and by supervising the older child when helping the younger one, pointing out how and when to provide assistance. But even with extensive advance preparation, parents who leave siblings alone need to monitor the situation very carefully and make adjustments in policies and procedures as problems arise.

## Stepsiblings

Stepsiblings, more and more common in today's society of frequent divorce, don't have the relationship natural siblings do to help them work out the problems that frequently arise when children are alone. Natural siblings may not always like each other, but they share a common bond and are accustomed to each other's idiosyncrasies. Stepsiblings experience all of the same problems that natural siblings do but, because of the lack of relationship and hidden competition between them, the problems tend to be magnified.

Quarrels are frequent among stepsiblings. When two families

merge there are often hurt feelings, misunderstandings and jealousies. A child who had two natural parents after a divorce often feels as though he or she has only one. When this parent remarries someone with children, the child now has to share his or her "only" parent with his or her new sisters and/or brothers. Jealousies are sure to arise when a child is asked to share his or her prize possessions with strangers. Any attention the parent gives to the stepchildren is sure to become a source of contention. When stepchildren are alone there is a risk that these jealousies will come out in fighting between the children.

Another common source of jealousy for a stepchild is in his or her parent's relationship with the new stepparent. "That's not my daddy, why are you kissing him?" is a frequent statement made by young children. The children of remarriage are torn between loyalties to their absent natural parent and their developing relationship with their stepparent. It's not uncommon for this jealousy of the new parent to be transferred to the children of the stepparent. These new family members become "them," and afternoons at home alone can escalate into an "us-them" situation.

Perhaps the major adjustment stepsiblings must make is a change in family position. The oldest child who was accustomed to being in charge of a younger sibling might now find him- or herself second in command and taking orders from a new brother or sister. This sort of change may give rise to power struggles and conflicts during afternoons alone. "You're not my sister! I don't have to do what you say!" are frequent statements from a child who is being watched by a stepsibling. Other changes in family structure also produce conflicts. The only daughter in one family might now have the competition of another sister. And certainly the youngest child in one of the two families will no longer be the baby and receive the constant attention of the others. Working out new family relationships is a major task during the first two years of remarriage. Children who spend time alone after school will spend a lot of time on this task in both a positive and negative manner.

Another major adjustment which affects latchkey children concerns squabbles over territorial rights. Usually when two adults with children remarry they move into the home of one of the two families, since few couples today can afford to buy a new house. This means that one set of children basically maintains their household while the other set of children becomes "guests." Rooms, toys, the television and the telephone all must be shared. During afternoons when there is no adult supervision, the "host children" will be quick to remind their "guests": "This isn't your house," or, "This is our TV so we can watch whatever we want." Normal conflicts that latchkey children experience over the television, telephone or snacks are more intense and emotionally charged when they occur between stepsiblings. Parents can resolve these conflicts in the same manner as they would with natural siblings, by predetermining rules regarding television, snacks and other conflicts as they arise, but during the initial adjustment period a good deal of patience and understanding will be required from all parties.

# Chapter 4
# FEARS AND DANGERS

Interviews with latchkey children provide insight into what these children fear while alone as well as how they cope with these fears. The most frequently mentioned fears are about break-ins, physical assault, fires and sibling conflicts that might result in injury or property damage.

At the slightest outside noise many project the worst: a break-in or an attack. Eleven-year-old Christopher is a child who has experienced continuous fears during his four years as a latchkey child. Christopher lives with a mother, a stepfather and a twenty-one-year-old sister. All of the adults work full-time jobs. Morning is a process of four people getting up and preparing to leave the house. Mom, a secretary, and dad, an architect, drop Christopher off at school on the way to their respective jobs. When school is dismissed at 2:30, Christopher walks home alone. He lets himself into the house, changes his clothes, rests, calls his mother (usually several times) and watches TV, mainly cartoons. "I don't like being home alone," Christopher says, a common complaint from latchkey children without siblings for company.

Christopher began staying alone in the first grade. He said that he was "real scared" when he heard noises then. His strategy was to go outside or to a friend's house when he was afraid. He confided that noises still scare him, and he generally handles them in the same way. Although he's not allowed to let people into the house or answer the door, "If I think someone is in the house, I call my mother or go outside," he said.

Christopher is one latchkey child who is allowed to go out of his house, although his freedom is restricted to a four-block perimeter. Like many latchkey children, if something dangerous should happen Christopher is supposed to go to a neighbor's home. "But," he said, "there are no grown-ups at home in my neighborhood, only other kids."

In more than four years of being a latchkey child nothing "really dangerous" has happened to Christopher. His fears seem to be generated by noises or by what he sees on television. His mother told him to avoid "sex movies or movies with lots of killing." But sometimes he begins watching a scary movie and is too afraid to turn it off. "I can't watch scary movies," he says, "because then I can't sleep. I keep picturing that something will happen to me, grab me and kill me."

Most children are occasionally afraid. Fear is a common reaction to a threatening world, and children daily face a world that is imperfectly understood. Even children at home with an adult are fearful. "I'm afraid of the dark" or "I'm afraid to go down to the basement by myself" are statements expressed by children whose mothers are home. All children experience fear, but they are more likely to experience fear when they're away from an adult, even if it's a distance of just one or two rooms.

Because of the lack of presence of an adult, feelings of fear are more frequent and enduring for latchkey children than for children who are under continuous adult care. For the latchkey child feelings of fear are also experienced more frequently because of their own hypersensitivity to household noises, the impact of extended hours of watching television, the communication of possible danger passed on to them by concerned parents, the real dangers of the latchkey situation and the fact that children simply feel more vulnerable when alone. The fears of latchkey children are also felt for longer periods of time. The child who is frightened by an attic noise will run to mother for solace and perhaps an explanation. Fear then subsides and the child is off to play again. Latchkey children, however, don't have the benefit of having a fear immediately relieved. As a result they must grow up much faster. When the child is home alone and fears occur, there is no one they can run to—sometimes no one even to call. Christopher, for example, ran outside only if something dangerous happened, not every time he was frightened. Children must develop their own strategies for ridding themselves of fear, or must cope with their fears until mom or dad comes home.

Many latchkey children protect themselves in the face of fear, but aren't successful in removing the fear entirely. As a result, a fear once produced is endured for a much longer period of time than a similar fear produced when mom or dad is at home. About one-third of latchkey children experience fears that are recurring and against which they develop strategies for defending themselves, rather than ways for allaying the fears.

Eleven-year-old David is a child who hears things in his attic. He says that he hears these noises about once a week. When he does, he locks himself in the bathroom and stays there until his father arrives at about 5:15. In an effort to cover the attic noises, David turns up the TV very loud as soon as he arrives home each day. "My father thinks I'm deaf," he says with a shy smile. David began to stay home by himself only this year, but in seven months he has not yet mastered his fear of the "attic" noise. When asked if he ever mentioned his fear to his parents, David said, "I asked to stay alone and I have to show I can do it." David, like many latchkey children, doesn't like the alternatives to self-care he thinks are available to him and seems to prefer an occasional afternoon in the bathroom to being in the home of a babysitter.

Twice as many preteen children who are home alone experience fears that are enduring or repetitive as children do who are home with siblings or friends, even though no adult is present. The companionship of a peer provides some sense of safety, if only in numbers. Siblings also help create their own noise which can serve to drown out unexplained house noises. They also tend to keep each other's attention focused on some activity or other, and off noises. Children alone often complain of boredom and a bored child is more attentive to possible distractions, even noises in the attic.

Nevertheless, children at home alone together are still more frightened than children at home with an adult. They are frightened by noises if they hear them; they are influenced by television; and they occasionally experience the real fright of a break-in, a fire or an accident.

Parents often wonder why their children will subject themselves to television features that they know are frightening. Children have a fascination for being frightened, and scary movies are the perfect means to that end. Children are also apt to disregard the consequences of watching "Dracula" or "The Phantom of the Opera," or even some of the odd creatures shown on reruns of a series like "Star Trek." Sleep disturbances such as nightmares and insomnia are common in developing children, but they seem to be more frequently experienced by children home alone and less by those under continuous adult care.

Siblings in self-care also experience some threats not experienced by the only child who is at home alone. The major threat is that they will accidentally injure one another or that one will break something for which the other, usually the older child, will be blamed. For some children, arguments lead to pushing, shoving, wrestling or fist fights. Children are afraid of these altercations, since no referee is present.

Sibling rivalries do, at times, also interfere with the ability of siblings to comfort each other in time of external threat. The sometimes ambiguous role of the older sibling as a substitute parent frequently leads to arguments about who is in charge, interfering with the older sibling's ability to fill in the role of nurturing parent when the need arises. The result is that the presence of siblings is frequently a stop-gap measure for holding fears at bay and may indeed elevate stress that must be endured until an adult appears.

Frankie is a second grader who stays home after school with his twelve-year-old sister until their parents arrive between 5:00 and 5:30. Frankie began staying home alone with his sister as soon as he started a preschool program that lasted as long as his sister's school day did. Frankie may have been as young as three at that time.

Frankie recalls feeling mad when he first started staying home alone. While this may only be a short-term projection, he is very adamant when he says, "She [his sister] didn't like taking care of me; we'd argue." Now eight-year-old Frankie says he's really mad. "I wish I could stay home by myself so my sister didn't have to take care of me. Let her stay at her friend's house. Dad thinks I can stay home alone, but my mom doesn't think I can stay by myself."

Frankie says the only things that frighten him are scary movies. "When scary movies come on I get a blanket and the dog and watch the movie. I like them. Besides, there's nothing else good on." Frankie and his sister watch a lot of TV, in fact they watch almost constantly until bedtime.

Many latchkey children begin caring for one another when one or both are quite young. As in the case of Frankie and his sister, it often happens that neither of them is mature enough to develop a truly nurturing relationship, yet in times of stress they need each other because no one else is available. Despite the fact that Frankie would like to stay home without his sister, when asked who he usually goes to for help when he has a problem, his ready answer is, "My sister."

## How Do Children Cope with Fears?

In the face of fear it is common for latchkey children to hide in places they think are safe. They lock themselves in bathrooms, hide in showers, under beds, in closets, and, if they are small enough, in bathroom or kitchen cabinets. Sue Ellen, an adult who was a latchkey child from age five to eighteen, coped with her fears by playing in a closet. She said as a young child she built a cozy and protected play setting to which she retreated frequently when frightened.

Another method latchkey children use to deal with fears is to turn on the television as soon as they arrive home. The noise of a blaring television drowns out other frightening noises and alerts possible intruders that someone is home. It also distracts the child. Some children go from one room to another turning on lights as soon as they arrive home.

Other children cope with fear by conducting routine security checks. Philip, a fifth grader, has a baseball bat stationed in the umbrella stand near his front door. As soon as he locks himself in the house after school, he conducts a systematic check of all the doors and windows of the house, looks under all the beds and inside each closet. Philip carries his baseball bat with him during these inspections. Other children reported carrying "weapons" for protection, such as an old shoe, knife or stick.

While younger children hide, older children often use the telephone to overcome fears. Calls are made to parents when something especially frightening happens, or to get mom to act as referee when siblings argue. Calls to friends provide more routine comfort and companionship. It's not unusual for older latchkey children to spend several hours on the phone.

All of these activities may be signs of fear. If a parent returns home and finds the television or radio blaring (often without anyone paying attention) or all the houselights burning, these may be signals that the child is frightened. If a parent calls home each day and usually gets a busy signal, it may be that the child needs solace. If a returning parent often finds his or her child asleep and it's much too early for bedtime, it may be that the child has discovered sleep as an escape from fear. Fear is stressful and must be acknowledged and dealt with. It can keep a child from accomplishing what he or she wants during a day; it may slow the child's development or stifle the child's adaptation to family change.

## How Do Parents Discover if Their Children Are Afraid?

The first step is to establish and maintain open channels of communication with one's child. Most latchkey children understand that their self-care arrangements are not ones their parents prefer. These children listen to and accept the reasons given by their parents for self-care. They accept their parents' problems as real and refrain from intentionally adding to them. When an eleven-year-old girl was asked why she didn't tell her mother how frightened she was to be alone, she said, "She has it hard enough working and trying to make ends meet. She doesn't need to worry about me, too."

Parents of latchkey children must convince them that they want to know the truth. This means that parents must cope with their own guilt about leaving the child alone so that they can communicate to the child that they will be receptive to problems. Many parents discourage their children from being honest by repeatedly emphasizing the child's maturity and responsibility. Robert, age twelve, said, "Mom always tells me that I'm mature. Mature children aren't afraid."

Parents must listen, but being a good listener is difficult even under the best of circumstances. Returning from work, a tired parent's first view of a house in disarray can quickly lead to nagging, judging, lecturing or criticizing and just as quickly cut off any input by the child. When asked what she liked least about being a latchkey child, a little girl responded, "My mother's always too tired for me." A parent returning home should allow herself a few minutes to gain her composure and then listen to her children before she says or does anything else.

Sometimes, however, a child is reticent and being a good listener isn't enough. Parents may have to express their concerns first. In this way, children come to know that "this is something we can talk about." Ask questions that show interest and give your child a chance to open up.

## Inquiring about Specific Problems

If parents don't wish to be shut out of their child's problem world, then they must be willing to inquire into that world. Children seem to respond well if their parents ask whether they have a special hiding place or are curious as to whether the child enjoys playing in the closet. These benign inquiries can lead the parent into a discussion about the reasons for the hiding place, or the duration, frequency and circumstances of closet play. When asked, children will often proudly tell inquiring parents about their plans for conducting security checks. Elaborate plans for self-protection can be an indication of a highly elevated level of fear, or might show that the child has adapted well to a stressful situation. The more elaborate the plans, the more likely the child is experiencing threat.

Does the child have recurring nightmares or other sleep disturbances? By far the most common sources of insomnia are fear and agitation. Fears, conflicts and mechanisms for coping with them can often be expressed in a child's dream life. These secondary sleep disturbances are common in developing children. By far the majority are transient and, though a source of irritation and concern for parents, are in themselves inconsequential. When these disturbances are overwhelming and/or persistent, however, or combined with other signs, they may be indicators of serious fear.

Is the child depressed? Regressive whining, clinging and all kinds of manipulative acts can communicate the child's strong fears of being left alone or of feeling helpless and unloved. Chronically depressed children usually appear sad, uninterested and inhibited in age-appropriate activities. They often show a low frustration tolerance and are prone to intense, aggressive outbursts and periods of restless irritability. Depressed children will often cover up their negative feelings by aggressive, provocative behavior, by daring pursuits or by clowning. Other frequent cover-ups for painful feelings of fear, despair and sadness are: overeating and maniclike hyperactivity alternating with complaints of boredom and fatigue, a drop in school performance and difficulty in concentrating, belligerence, a tendency to bravado, occasional running away and delinquent acts. Does the child play with fire? Fire-setting is viewed as a means by which children retaliate against those aspects of the environment that they feel have rejected them, or as a means of getting attention.

Ask your children what frightens them most. Many children will tell you that they become panicked when their parents don't appear as expected. This is especially true among children being reared in a single-parent household. Parents know the sinking feeling they experience when, upon arriving home, they find their child absent and have no inkling of his or her whereabouts. Parents often protect themselves against this happening by insisting that their children stay in the house. Others set up well-defined limits for their child's outside play and insist on being informed of where the child will be at every moment.

A single parent with two sons, only one of whom is a latchkey child, told of her developing panic when, upon her return from work at four o'clock, she found a note from her ten-year-old latchkey son that said simply, "I'm riding my bicycle." When her twelve-year-old son returned from school at 4:30, she sent him out to look for his brother. Forty-five minutes later, the second son returned to report that the first child was nowhere around. She called the police. "By 6:00 I was a basket case," she said. Her son appeared at 6:30, explaining that he had ridden to their former neighborhood, an explanation the recently divorced woman could understand, but one that hardly removed the disaster scenarios she had been conjuring up for two hours.

Children often behave in the same way when parents fail to appear. The fears produced when a parent or child isn't where he or she is supposed to be are an amalgamation of the multiple dangers that surround us each day—accidents, sickness, assaults and other injuries. It's important for parents as well as children to keep each other informed of their whereabouts or if they'll be late in returning home as one way of allaying their collective fears.

## Dangers

By the very nature of their circumstances, latchkey children are always faced with risk. Dangers can generally be classed as threat of injury from accidents; the threat of fire, explosion, or other triggered or natural disasters; the threat of violence, such as burglaries, assaults or abuse; the effects of sickness; and nuisances such as obscene phone calls. While no segment of the population is free from any of these possible dangers, unattended children are particularly vulnerable. The younger the child, the greater the danger.

The most common danger they face is injury due to accidents. Accidents constitute the number one cause of death to children. From 1963 to 1973, there was a sixteen percent increase in the number of deaths from accidents among children in the five to fourteen age group, and a decrease of eighteen percent for children under the age of five. During this same period there was a great growth in the labor force participation rate of mothers and a substantial growth in care facilities for preschool children, but not for school-age children.

In 1977, of all American children ages one to fourteen, almost 10,000 were killed in accidents. This figure was three times the number of children in this group who died from cancer, the next leading cause of death. Accidents during 1977 accounted for forty-five percent of total childhood mortality. Motor vehicle accidents were responsible for more than twenty percent of childhood deaths, drownings for eight percent and fires for six percent. Other common types of fatal accidents are those resulting from poisoning, falls and use of firearms.

Of a group of forty-three adults who were interviewed because they had been latchkey children, six recalled calling the police or fire department when they were home alone. Three called about suspected dangers and three about emergencies occurring at the time. One of them called the fire department when her brother set the house on fire. The blaze was extinguished without personal injury, although damage to the house was substantial. A second woman, charged with the care of several siblings when she was only twelve, called the fire department because of a fire in progress that started outside the house and spread to the interior. She was unable to rescue an infant sister during the blaze, and by the time the firefighters got to the child, she was dead.

## FIRE

Fire is an important danger because it is visible, produces panic, leaves evidence and children attempt to extinguish fires themselves. They are sometimes unsuccessful.

Because of their fear of a fire starting, many parents of latchkey children tell their children not to use electrical appliances, such as the stove or toaster. Still, children will occasionally try their hand at cooking or prepare a piece of toast, despite their parents' sanctions. In one such case, a flapping curtain was ignited by the toaster, and "In a minute," said the child, "the kitchen was on fire." As often happens, the child extinguished the blaze.

An eleven-year-old at home with his nine-year-old brother, on the other hand, was not so fortunate. The eleven-year-old was making candles on the stove while his brother was playing with their Atari. The eleven-year-old became distracted by his brother's play and soon became involved in Atari himself. He was reminded that he had candle wax burning on the stove when he saw flames leaping from the kitchen. The boys got out of the house, which was extensively damaged.

With regard to fire, there is no such time as a "safe" time to leave children home alone or without alert, mature supervision. Actual recent cases from files of the National Fire Protection Association (NFPA) show what can happen when children too young to act wisely are left unattended or under poor supervision.

A nine-year-old girl in Detroit was left in charge of a little brother and sister while their parents worked. While the child was making breakfast, fire broke out in the kitchen.

The youngster, who had received no emergency training, opened a window "to let out the fire," then went to school. When she got there, her teacher smelled smoke on the child's clothing, learned about the fire, and ran to attempt to rescue the tots. The little boy, age two, died and his year-old sister was seriously burned.

Of all child deaths by fire, most occur when children are left alone. Fire deaths are disproportionately high among younger and older people. The young are not skillful at tasks that may put them in danger. They are curious to try what they see adults doing: toying with matches or cigarette lighters, using stoves, tending fireplaces, practicing cooking. Children aren't always able to foresee the consequences of their acts. They may be insubordinate or testing the adult world by playing with matches, even though emphatically told not to do so. Too frequently, they also haven't been trained in the rudiments of self-preservation.

Children left unattended are often helpless if a fire breaks out. Every year hundreds of children suffocate in their sleep from heat and smoke; others die in vain attempts to escape. Firefighters have a rule: never leave children without competent supervision, even briefly. The supervision of a "mature" minor is inadequate if he or she is not trained properly for such an emergency.

Most fatal fires occur in residences and a disproportionately high percentage of victims are very young. No national count has been made of how many unattended children are fire victims during a given year, but a rough estimate is that one-third of all fire victims are children. In some jurisdictions, such as Newark, New Jersey, estimates are that one in six calls responded to by the fire department involve children alone at home.

If children are going to be left unattended, they must be educated both in fire prevention and self-preservation techniques. Unfortunately many children are not taught how to react to fire, while others are given instructions that are positively dangerous. When asked what she was told to do in case a fire started in her house, one little girl said, "My mother told me to grab all the valuables and run out of the house." When asked what valuables she was to collect she only identified the TV set. Her mother's recalled instructions may immobilize this child in case of a real emergency. Some children will try to play the hero. One eleven-year-old said that in case of a fire he would put it out with a hose. A nine-year-old said he would turn on all the faucets in the house and leave.

Not all children are poorly instructed. Some parents teach their children good fire safety rules, and then practice responses to emergencies through mock fire drills and other types of emergency training. Children need such training in order to make parental admonitions and instructions operational.

Furthermore, every child needs to be taught important safety procedures. Children left alone are usually given better and more detailed instructions than children at home with siblings. When siblings are at home together, parents seem to depend on the oldest sibling to be the home fire marshal. Sometimes this child doesn't react well to emergencies; sometimes the demands of an emergency are more than the child can handle; sometimes the oldest child is not present. By teaching each child how to respond to an emergency, all children are better protected.

Generally, children at home in the care of an adult are not well instructed, since parents feel that the adult caretaker can handle all emergencies. But even parents routinely at home with their children can't count on being able to reach their children in case of an emergency. A valuable safety precaution is to practice with each child what to do in case of an emergency. The fire prevention office of the local fire department is usually equipped to conduct instructions for even small groups of children. Organize your neighborhood and request such instruction. At the same time you could request a home safety check, if your local station conducts them.

All families, not just those with latchkey children, should plan and practice home fire drills, devising an escape route from each room of the house. Secondary escape routes should also be planned in case primary routes are blocked. Practice using these routes, particularly at night. Determine a meeting place outside your home to assure that everyone is out safely. If your house has two stories, buy a commercial escape ladder to use in case the stairway is blocked by flames.

Children who live in apartments should be taught safety tips pertaining to apartment residents: if the fire is in your apartment, get everyone out of the unit and close—don't lock—the door. This allows the fire fighters access but helps to keep the fire contained to your unit. Next, sound the building alarm *and* call the fire department. If the fire is in another unit, instruct children to feel the apartment door before opening it. If the door is hot it shouldn't be opened. If the hall is clear, they should proceed to the nearest exit using the apartment stairs rather than the elevators.

Teach children how to dial the fire department and give their name and address. Children should also be taught what to do when their clothing catches on fire (stop—drop—roll), and how to leave a smoky room by crawling on their hands and knees.

Install a smoke detector, and let your children hear what it sounds like when it goes off. If it runs on a battery, the battery should be checked regularly. A home with more than one level should have a smoke detector installed on each floor.

Buy a fire extinguisher and place it in the kitchen where most fires start. Then teach all members of your family how and when to use it.

INJURIES

Non-fire-related injuries can also occur, and adult neighbors may not be available for assistance. Mom or dad often work at a distance from home and children must cope with these emergencies themselves. One former latchkey child recalling an emergency she had as a child said, "I was playing hopscotch at a friend's home. I fell and broke my leg. I rode my bike about three-quarters of a mile home and waited there until my sister arrived. By the time she did, my leg was badly swollen."

Many children don't know how to reach nearby emergency aid and will first call mom or dad. If they can be reached, parents frequently can't assess the seriousness of the emergency over the phone and in case of real need, are often too far away to be of immediate help.

One youngster was seriously cut by a jagged piece of glass while playing in his back yard. He waited for his mother to return from work before receiving medical attention. Another girl said her sister was cut falling through their storm door. Even though the mother was called immediately, the thirty-five-mile trip she had to make to get home took an hour. Some children, when injured, will go to a neighbor for help. Others will call an ambulance or the fire department; some will handle the emergency themselves by going to a hospital's emergency room or their doctor's office. The most frequent response to cuts, broken bones and other similar physical injuries, however, is to wait for mom or dad to return home, or to call them for help.

Children must be taught to recognize an emergency that requires them to call the number for the police, fire and rescue squad in their area first. Under most circumstances public emergency services will be able to reach a child before the parent will. After calling for public emergency assistance and reaching safety, the child should be instructed to then call a parent. In other kinds of emergencies they must learn to obtain assistance from an adult as quickly as possible and not try to handle the emergency themselves or wait for their parents to return home.

All children who stay alone or with siblings should know basic first aid. The following list of treatment procedures should be part of the basic training of every latchkey child:

*Animal Bites.* Children who have a pet or are allowed to play outside should know how to treat animal bites. Animal bites should be washed out thoroughly with soap and water and covered with a bandage. Animal bites should be reported immediately to the local humane society (if it's a strange dog) and to the child's doctor, the numbers for which should have been posted with other emergency numbers. If the animal that bit the child was wild (for example: a racoon, squirrel or snake), the child should be taught not to try to catch or chase the animal. If the animal was a dog or cat, the child should get the name and address of the pet's owner. If the child doesn't know who the owner is, he or she should at least be able to describe the animal. If poisonous snakes are a common threat in your area, teach the child how to treat such a snake bite.

*Burns.* Children often burn their hands and arms while cooking or playing with fire. The best way to treat burns is to prevent them. Teach children the dangers of playing with fire and how to cook safely. Children who receive minor burns regardless should be instructed to place the burn under cold running water or hold an ice cube on it until it no longer hurts. They shouldn't be taught to put butter or any other substance on a burn. If a child is seriously burned he or she should be told to call an ambulance immediately.

*Broken Bones.* Children who fall are often quick to cry, "I broke my leg, I broke my leg." Obviously, most of these cases are false alarms. But the complications from moving a broken bone are serious enough that if a child genuinely suspects a broken bone, it should be treated as such. It is often difficult even for a professional to tell if a bone is broken without X rays. A child who suspects a broken bone should not move the bone, but call his or her parents and the family doctor for advice.

*Cuts and Scrapes.* Cuts and scrapes are an everyday occurrence for many children. Parents should teach children to wash out a small cut or scrape with soap and water and place a bandage on it. If the cut is bleeding profusely, direct pressure should be placed on it until it stops bleeding. Then it should be washed and covered with a bandage or gauze, depending on the size of the cut. If a child has a cut that is gushing or spurting blood and the bleeding can't be stopped, he or she should be instructed to call the police or an ambulance immediately.

*Insect Stings.* Children playing outdoors are likely to get stung by a bee or a wasp at one time or another. Children should be taught to care for insect stings by *scraping* the stinger out with their fingernail or pulling it out with tweezers and applying ice to the injury. Children known to be allergic to bee stings or other insect bites, or who experience nausea, vomiting, tightness in the chest, nose or throat, should contact a physician immediately.

*Nosebleeds.* Since nosebleeds are bloody and messy and often occur without warning or for no apparent reason, they can be very frightening to a child home alone. In order to reduce this fear and assure proper treatment, all children should be taught what to do in case of a nosebleed. Nosebleeds should be treated sitting up, not lying down. A child with a nosebleed should be instructed to sit calmly in the kitchen so blood isn't trailed all over the house. Then the nostril of the side of the nose that's bleeding should be pressed against the center of the nose. If both sides of the nose are bleeding, the nose should be pinched between the thumb and forefinger. Pressure should be applied for about five minutes. If the nose hasn't stopped bleeding at this point, a cold compress should be pressed against the side of the nose. If this doesn't work, a physician should be called. In any case, children should be urged not to blow their noses while they are bleeding.

*Poisoning.* The best way to treat poisoning is to prevent it. Parents should place poisonous substances out of the reach of children. They should also point out the warning labels on the containers and urge their children not to touch substances with these markings. In case of emergency, the number of the poison control center nearest your home should be posted near the telephone. Keep ipecac in the house to induce vomiting, show your child where this is in your medical kit and how to use it so he or she is prepared to do so. Teach your child how to identify and read the contents of labels of bottles and jars so he can read the information to poison control if necessary.

## FIRST AID KIT

It is essential that every child home alone have a first aid kit handy to use in repairing minor injuries. Parents should assemble the kit with their children and teach them what every item in the kit is for and how it is to be used. The kit should be located in a readily accessible place in the home and maintained to be of use. Once items are used they should be replaced immediately.

*A basic first aid kit should include:*

- a box of bandages in assorted sizes to dress small cuts
- sterile gauze pads to dress larger cuts
- a roll of adhesive tape to hold gauze pads in place
- a small scissors to cut adhesive tape
- a triangular bandage to make a sling
- an elastic bandage to wrap sprains
- tweezers to remove bee stings
- calamine lotion or baking soda to treat insect bites and poison ivy
- iodine or peroxide to clean cuts
- cotton balls to use with peroxide to clean cuts
- thermometer to check for fever
- a bottle of aspirin to reduce fever
- an icepack to limit swelling
- a small bottle of ipecac to induce vomiting in case of poisoning

Take the time to review the items in the kit with your child periodically. Stress with your child the need to exercise caution and avoid accidents.

## TRAFFIC ACCIDENTS

Children who are allowed to play outside and those who walk to and from school are in danger of being involved in traffic accidents, whether they are latchkey children or not. Approximately five percent of the children interviewed, or their siblings, had been involved in a traffic accident while unattended. One woman, a former latchkey child, recalled that when she was twelve her younger brother was hit by a car. Since she could not get in touch with her parents, she had to deal with the police. Being in a traffic accident is traumatic even if the incident doesn't result in injury. The police are usually involved and for many children this is quite upsetting. Children hit by an automobile often feel that they are responsible. All too often they have done something careless or unthinking.

If a child witnesses an accident, particularly one involving a sibling, the child should be taught to immediately call (or make sure someone else calls) the police emergency number for assistance and then offer comfort to whoever was injured in the accident. If a brother or sister is involved, he or she should be kept calm and still until professional help arrives.

Many parents reduce their own anxiety and attempt to protect their children by not allowing them out of the house while they are away. Doing this does offer a little more parental peace of mind, but also serves to isolate the child, particularly if he or she is alone, and can impede the child's social development.

BREAK-INS

Children who aren't permitted to go out once they arrive home are still not free from outside assault. One of the latchkey child's greatest fears is also an all-too-frequent reality, that is of being burglarized or attacked.

Approximately seven percent of the latchkey children interviewed had experienced one or the other. Most burglaries occurred while the children were out of the house, but in two instances children returned home while the intruder was still in the house. One ten-year-old who had this experience said, "The thief ran out with some of our property still in his hands. When he left, I shut the door and locked it good." When asked whether he called the police, he said that he hadn't.

Karen, eight years old, came home after school and noticed her front door ajar. She said that when she entered the house, "A man ran out the kitchen door." The house had been ransacked. Dresser drawers were emptied on the floor; even her penny bank had been smashed. The girl called her mother.

A mother reported that her son came home and noticed a ladder leaning against an upstairs window. The quick-thinking nine-year-old went next door and called his mother. "I came home," she said, "and called the police." The police officer who took the call asked where she was calling from. "My house," she said. "Get out now," replied the officer. "We learned a lot by that experience," the woman said. "We're better informed now about how to handle a break-in. I didn't think that the intruder could still have been in my house."

Children, as well as adults, should know what to do if they are home when a break-in is attempted and what to do if they approach their house and something looks amiss. In general, don't enter the house if something appears out of the ordinary. If a window that was shut is now open, or if the door that was locked is now ajar, don't go into the house. Instruct your children to get to a neighbor's and call home to see if a family member came home unexpectedly. If not, the child should call the police immediately and wait at the neighbor's until the police arrive. If a child is home alone and someone tries to break in, the child should call the police immediately, then remain quiet so he doesn't alert the burglar that someone is home. At the first opportunity, the child should get out of the house as quickly as possible and run to a neighbor's for help. If the child can't get out of the house safely, he should lock himself in the bathroom and wait for the police to arrive.

Parents can minimize the chance of a break-in by following crime prevention techniques recommended by the local police department. Some police departments will even send officers to do a security check of your home free of charge. In general, keep doors and windows locked. Don't hide a spare key outside where someone else might find it, and don't store a ladder outside because it can be used to climb through a window. Also, in suburban or rural areas, be sure to keep hedges and bushes trimmed so that burglars don't have a ready hiding place.

Children are also vulnerable to attacks by strangers when playing outside. It's not uncommon for children to play outside when instructed by parents to stay home. It's likely that these children, if attacked or approached by a stranger, won't tell their parents because they know they weren't supposed to be outside in the first place.

All children, but especially latchkey children who walk home from school or play unsupervised, must be alerted to the danger strangers pose to them. Children must be taught *never* to talk to strangers, to get in the car with a stranger or accept gifts from strangers. Children are safer if they walk home from school with friends and stay on main streets. If a stranger approaches your child, he should be taught to run away and find safety where there are other people, such as in a store or at a neighbor's house. If grabbed, children should be instructed to kick, scream, bite or do whatever is necessary to get away and then report the incident to the police.

### SEVERE WEATHER AND OTHER NATURAL DISASTERS

Each year thousands of children find themselves home alone during severe weather emergencies. Many are frightened, and not without just cause, since hundreds of people lose their lives each year from severe weather in all its forms. The type of disaster prevalent depends on what area of the country is involved and what season. Snowstorms, blizzards, ice storms, thunderstorms, tornadoes, hailstorms, lightening, flash floods and hurricanes, in addition to natural disasters such as volcanic eruptions, earthquakes, or tsunamis are all common in various parts of the United States.

Some types of severe weather and natural disasters can be predicted hours ahead of time, allowing for emergency preparations. However, other types of severe and dangerous disaster occur quickly, with little or no warning. Due to their sudden occurrence, it is likely that a parent will *not* be home when these disasters strike. It is therefore important for parents who live in severe weather and/or natural disaster areas to prepare themselves and their children to act quickly and correctly in emergency situations. Knowing when and how to act will not only reduce the fear of weather emergencies that children in self-care experience, but will reduce the likelihood of injury if an emergency does occur.

The National Weather Service issues two types of storm alerts: watches and warnings. A watch means that weather conditions are right for severe weather, while a warning means that severe weather is imminent and emergency action should be taken immediately.

Parents who live in a severe weather and/or a natural disaster area should discuss the various events that can occur in their area with their child. These discussions should be straightforward, but should not be put in such a way as to frighten the child unduly. The discussion should include the nature of the event, the associated dangers and the protective action to be taken. In addition, a "storm re-hearsal" in which you and your child pretend a storm is coming and the child practices the proper safety actions can reinforce these discussions. Children should always be taught to save themselves and their siblings first. *Never* instruct a child to save some material possession or protect the house before he can get to safety.

When working parents are aware that severe weather is predicted, they should call home, inform and reassure their children and remind them of the proper safety measures that should be taken. Sometimes, however, parents can't get through by phone; the lines are down or the child is on the phone. It is therefore imperative that children home alone know the signs of a severe storm or other weather emergency and what to do. Older children can be taught to tune into local radio stations to get the latest weather information.

Many severe weather emergencies have predictable effects such as power failure. If the power goes out, children should know where a flashlight is and how to use it. Children should not be told to use candles during a power outage, which would only create a fire hazard. They should, however, be taught to call a parent to report the power failure and to turn off appliances to avoid a sudden power surge when electricity is restored.

Another typical consequence of a storm is water entering the house through broken windows and doors, or temporary basement flooding. Older children can be taught to clean up broken glass, wipe up water, or temporarily hang a towel or place some large object, such as a box, in the opening to cover a broken window. Children should be instructed *never* to turn on an electrical appliance that is wet, or to turn one on while standing in water or on a wet surface.

Gas leakage, which is extremely dangerous, may occur during earthquakes, hurricanes and floods. Children should notify their parents immediately if they smell gas. They should also be taught the location of the main gas valve and how to shut it off. Children should then leave the home and go to a safer place, if possible.

One way to prepare your child for these emergencies is to assemble a "severe weather kit." Your child should know where the kit is located, the purpose of each item in the kit and how to use it. The kit should always remain in the same place and items in the kit should never be used for other purposes, lest in a real emergency necessary items would not be available.

*The severe weather kit should include:*

- a portable radio
- a flashlight
- extra batteries
- food which needs no cooking or refrigeration (1–2 day supply)
- clean plastic containers for water
- a first aid kit

Thunderstorms are the most common of all weather emergencies. They occur regularly in all parts of the United States, except perhaps along the Pacific coast and in Alaska and Hawaii. Latchkey children are frequently home alone or outside playing when a thunderstorm strikes unexpectedly. In many cases thunderstorms are accompanied by high winds, thunder, lightening and hailstorms, all of which are very frightening to children. Children need to recognize the approach of a thunderstorm and to get inside before a storm strikes. If they are near home they should go there, but if they are any distance from home they should be instructed to go to a large building or a nearby friend's house, since thunderstorms often last only a few minutes. Once inside, children should stay away from windows and doors, not use the telephone except in a real emergency and turn off the television. Children who are caught outdoors should be taught to get away from all metal objects, open water, lone trees and hilltops.

Flash floods often accompany thunderstorms, tornadoes or hurricanes, all of which may bring heavy rains within a short period of time. A flash flood is sudden and violent; it can sweep everything in its path, including cars, bridges, houses, trees and mud. Walls of rushing flood waters may reach ten to twenty feet high. No area of the United States is free from the threat of flash floods. They are especially dangerous because there is little advance warning. During a flash flood, children should be taught to move to safe ground immediately. Know the elevation of your house and tell your children where to go in case of a flash flood if it isn't safe to stay in your home. Make sure your children understand not to attempt to cross flowing water when it is above their knees. Children should also be instructed to keep away from storm drains, streams, irrigation ditches, canals or other waterways.

Tornadoes are short-lived local storms that contain high speed winds usually rotating in a counterclockwise direction. Tornadoes occur in all fifty states and at all times of the year, but occur most frequently in the spring and less frequently in the winter. Tornadoes are extremely dangerous. Their strong rotating winds haul all kinds of debris—rocks, glass, dust and dirt—for many miles. They can devastate large buildings, roll cars and buses over and demolish homes. Children (or anyone, for that matter) are in danger whether outside or in a building.

When a tornado *watch* is issued, children should use the portable radio in their emergency kit and tune to a local radio station for further information. When a tornado *warning* is issued, children should be instructed to go to a previously determined safe place, generally under the stairs in the basement. If there is no basement, they should go to an interior bathroom, closet or hallway. Children should also be instructed to stay away from windows, doors and outside walls and open the windows a little if they can.

Major hurricanes are rare in certain parts of the United States, but occur frequently in coastal states from Texas to Maine. A hurricane is a great whirlwind of air, traveling at least seventy-four miles per hour, around a low pressure center called the eye. While hurricane winds do much damage, most of the deaths associated with hurricanes are caused by drowning since, as the storm approaches land, it brings with it huge waves and storm tides, called "storm surge." Hurricanes also bring torrential rains which may cause flash floods in inland areas. A hurricane warning is issued when a hurricane is expected within twenty-four hours. Hurricanes are tracked very accurately, and parents shouldn't leave their children unattended when a hurricane warning is issued.

Winter storms are a seasonal threat in the central and northern parts of the United States. Winter storms include ice storms, freezing rains, heavy snow or blizzards. Children are often dismissed from school early when a winter storm threatens and must care for themselves until their parents return from work. The major physical dangers to children resulting from exposure are frostbite, hypothermia caused by freezing temperature and injuries resulting from falls on icy surfaces. Children must understand that during any winter storm the safest thing to do is stay inside. Children home alone often play outside for long periods of time while improperly dressed and are frostbitten. Children who want to play outdoors even for short periods of time should be taught to dress warmly and wear hats, scarves and mittens, as well as jackets and boots.

APPLIANCES

Children alone will often use and abuse appliances unless instructed otherwise. The best way for parents to avoid problems is to take their children on a house tour and point out the appliances that are permitted and those that are strictly forbidden. In order to make sure your child understands what appliances cannot be used, put a bold DO NOT USE list on the refrigerator door or mark each such appliance. This list should probably include irons, a food processor and power tools, at the very least. Instruct children how to use appliances that are on the permitted list and watch them use them in the evenings or on weekends to make sure the appliances are being used correctly. Instruct your child on general appliance safety. Make sure they know how to pull the plug out of the socket by the plug, not the cord, and that they understand *never* to use a wet appliance or use an appliance while standing in water.

Leaving children home alone is never completely safe, but the risks can be minimized if children are properly prepared.

# Chapter 5
# STRESSES

Stress is a fact of life. Tension and relaxation form the natural rhythm of living. Stress builds up, is resolved, builds up and is resolved again. Things happening in the world may increase stress, reduce it, block its resolution, or alter its rhythm. Individuals vary in their capacity to withstand stresses without damage—that is, without seriously reducing their ability to function or to resist future stresses. This quality of resilience seems to vary from birth, but it also may be developed or inhibited by conditions in the environment, especially during childhood.

Latchkey children experience the ebb and flow of life's stresses. They vary in their capacity to withstand stress and in the degree of their resilience. One latchkey child might thrive on that which undermines another.

Latchkey children of today need more stamina and a greater resilience because conditions in today's world produce greater fear than they did a generation ago, a greater sense of abandonment, and heightened belief that one must take sole responsibility for one's survival. There is today a diminished sense of family and community support. And there is today a great deal of pressure on children to grow up rapidly, to arrive at a state at which adult care is not needed. The result seems to be that today's children are exposed to more experiences that tax their adaptive capacity than was the case for children a generation ago.

Latchkey children as a group are presented with challenges that may make their parents wince. Not only are they exposed to sex, violence, and drugs daily seen on TV and elsewhere, but a much higher percentage of them live with other bewildering changes occurring in the social environment—divorce, single parenthood and dual-career parents. Furthermore, latchkey children are left for periods of time to contemplate the results of any or all of these differences as they become the temporary lords or mistresses of their homes. More than being exposed to social change, latchkey children soon learn that their survival depends on their ability to adjust to change without admitting fear, confusion, pain or stress.

Children of the 1940s and 1950s were less frequently left in self-care. Today thousands of children younger than five (Current Population Reports Series P-20, #198, October, 1976) and millions of school-age children are left to supervise themselves. Most children of the 1940s and 1950s had a sense of the continued presence of mom in the home. Today more than half of all American children know that mom's attention is divided between home and work.

Today's parents are faced with a world moving too rapidly, with lightning-fast communications, rapid role changes, eruptions of personal and professional uncertainties. Many of these occurrences seem to be completely out of their control. No wonder parents seek to reduce their stress, at least at home. If child-rearing is stressful, then by hurrying children to grow up or by treating them as though they were adults, parents limit their own stress burden. In fact, they shift some of it to their children.

Many latchkey parents select self-care for their children precisely to reduce parental stress. It is not simply the cost of child care or the lack of a suitable child-care facility that leads many parents to decide in favor of a latchkey arrangement, but the stress caused by the combined pressure of cost, facility, transportation and the confining schedule that out-of-home care imposes. These parents seem willing to accept the burden of guilt a latchkey arrangement exacts in favor of release from other stresses, especially when convenient, inexpensive, adult-supervised care arrangements are not available within easy walking distance of the child's school or accessible by low cost transportation.

Parents of latchkey children do not mean their children harm in choosing to leave them in self-care, but are more likely looking for the least stressful care arrangement. As a society we have come to believe that it is good for children to mature quickly and so as a society we tend to support these parents' choices. We look for signs that children do well when presented with circumstances demanding more maturity and responsibility. We often find what we seek: some latchkey children appear to thrive.

But not all do. There are casualties as well as apparent successes. The question is if, overall, we do children more harm than good by hurrying them into adulthood by saddling them with adult responsibilities.

### Differences between Children

There are evident differences in the way children react to the latch key arrangement. By way of example, here are two acquaintances, both attending the same school:

Brian and Richard are both eleven years old. Both live with a mother, a father and one older sister. Brian has a nineteen-year-old sister; Richard's sister is seventeen. Both boys walk to school. Both live in a single-family dwelling. Neither is allowed to have friends visit while he is at home alone. Both can play outside after school. In both instances, their mothers arrive home at about 4:30.

Brian began staying home alone while in the fourth grade, when his sister took a job after she graduated from high school. He doesn't like to be alone. "Whenever I hear noises that scare me I call someone," Brian said. "I know movies aren't true, but I'm still scared of them," he said. Brian continues to have occasional bedwetting episodes and hates it when he "messes up." "When I'm bad I feel like jumping off the house or running into a wall. I don't like to disappoint people," he said.

Brian sees his neighborhood as dangerous. In case of an emergency he is supposed to go to a neighbor's house. "There usually aren't any grown-ups there either," Brian said, "only other kids." He calls his mother several times each day at work, usually when he hears the noises that scare him.

Richard began staying home alone when he was in the first grade. His sister was a junior high cheerleader who usually arrived home sometime after he did. At this age he was not allowed outside until his sister got home. Now that he's older his sister seldom comes home until after his mother arrives, but Richard says he's not afraid to stay at home alone. He spends a lot of time practicing sports after school and doesn't seem to have time to be lonely. Richard seldom has sleep disturbances.

Richard is a very well-functioning child. He has good feelings about himself, his family, and his life. Being a latchkey child has apparently not caused him problems of which he is particularly aware.

Brian, on the other hand, seems to have experienced more stress as a result of his latchkey experience. His grades, which were average or above average at the outset of his being home alone, continued to fall as the school year progressed. He expressed fear, a sense of danger and exhibited a somewhat clinging attachment to his mother.

Unfortunately, there is a tendency for parents to stereotype their children. In certain areas children are lumped together as reacting to a given set of circumstances. Parents frequently think of their children as infinitely flexible and, as such, able to adapt easily to adult schedules, needs and interests. Stresses experienced by parents induce them to put their needs ahead of those of their children. Indeed, all too often, parents are led to think of childhood as a period free of conflict, fear, struggle or stress.

Parents who are under stress—and it's difficult to maintain a home and a job and not be—tend to become self-absorbed and, consequently, have trouble seeing their children as complete personalities. Additionally, they lack the energy necessary for dealing with issues apart from those concerning themselves. As a result of parents' stress, children are often dealt with as convenient stereotypes: reliable and mature, or irresponsible and childish.

Many parents will think of their children in such a way as to reduce their stress, compressing a child's personality to fit the parents' needs. Children left in a self-care arrangement are therefore most often seen as capable, reliable, responsible and unafraid.

Whether this description is more fitting of children today than those of the 1940s and 1950s is debatable. Whether children left alone today are a unique or a more able subset of children is even more debatable.

## Greater Stress Today

That today's young people are under greater stress than those of a generation ago is reflected in the increase in stress diseases among this population. Physicians are reporting more youthful patients with ulcers, headaches, stomachaches and allergic reactions. The suicide rate among the ten- to fourteen-year-old population has increased fifty percent in a ten-year period.

Divorce has become part of the status quo—the accepted, almost inevitable conclusion of a marriage. In Marin County, California, for example, it is the odd child who lives in a household with both biological parents still in their first marriage. This is quite a contrast to those children of the 1950s who were ashamed if their parents divorced. The majority of children in the 1980s now live in a household in which one or more of the following social conditions exists: divorced, separated or single parents; dual-career parents; or a parent living with a mate outside of marriage.

Before the Second World War, children asked to take on an adult role generally understood the straits, usually financial, in which their family lived. Now it is hard for many children to really understand why they must move into a small apartment with only one parent, or why they have to be sent to a day-care center, or why they must stay home alone until their parents arrive.

## Stressors

Latchkey children today are more afraid of something "bad" happening on their way home from school or of someone breaking into their home. But everybody seems more afraid than was the population of a generation ago. The threat of violence is a permanent fixture in American society. Fear is a stress coped with by all children, but especially by latchkey children because their parents are distant or unreachable during many stress periods.

The world is a more insecure place. As people have developed more instruments to control the world, we seem to have produced even more that are out of our control. Children experience either directly or vicariously the effects of this technological revolution and of inflation, rising prices, recession and the mobility a shifting parental employment picture seems to demand. Latchkey children are especially stressed by these changes. These children are more routinely confronted with the employment insecurities of their parents, either because the child is asked to be involved with the family as an equally contributing member in terms of maintenance of the home, as is often the case of a child living with a single parent—or parents tell the child of their insecurities as a means of justifying their current care arrangement.

Many American children are constantly "on the move." The families of more than forty percent of school-age children move in any three-year period. This high degree of mobility often removes the child from the support system that an extended family or long-term neighbors can provide. And moves are often connected with family upheavals, making them all the more stressful.

There are a variety of other things that can also produce stress, though it should be remembered that stressors are not good or bad of themselves. They are simply special demands with which one must cope. A child can feel stress because of a move, a new teacher, separation from a parent, the birth of a sibling, a new bicycle, winning the Little League championship, an illness or the loss or gain of a pet. But certain stressors appear to demand more adaptive energy from children than others. There are four categories of stressors that deserve special comment in the context of latchkey children: separation, changes in life patterns, threats and changes in responsibility.

## 1. SEPARATION

Even in nuclear families in which one parent has chosen to remain at home children can experience the stress of separation when a parent must travel on business or is separated because of illness. But children today, especially latchkey children, experience separation most frequently because of divorce. Separations that occur as a result of marital discord are often forced upon children at a much earlier age than separations they would experience as a result of the death of a parent. Furthermore, absence caused by death is less detrimental than that caused by the voluntary separation of parents.

Recent years have witnessed a dramatic increase in divorce in this country. During the years 1960 to 1978, the divorce rate went from 9 per 1000 married women to 22 per 1000. In 1978, there were 4.5 million children under eighteen living with a divorced parent compared to 1.3 million in 1960.

During the period 1960 to 1978, the percentage of children under eighteen living with two parents declined from eighty-eight to seventy-eight percent. Those living with both biological parents declined from seventy-nine to sixty-eight percent. By 1980, one in five children lived with only one parent.

Whereas a generation ago the largest proportion of single parents was widowed, today the much larger percentage of single parents is divorced or separated. Since 1960, the proportion of all children living with a widowed mother or father has remained constant but the number living with a divorced or separated parent has quadrupled. If present trends continue, by 1990 one-third of all American children will live for some time with a divorced parent.

Divorce generally means that the child must adapt to a two-household existence. Not only is one parent now absent, and this absence is often acutely felt, but the child must also adjust to a new living environment or experience the departed parent in a new living arrangement.

Jane and Sally, ages eight and ten, were separated from their father when their mother left him, taking the two girls with her. The girls' father was very angry at his wife. He determined to leave her with nothing and so her first move was into an unfurnished apartment. "The girls and I slept on the floor for a month," their mother said. "I didn't have a penny. I had to get a job immediately." Jane and Sally were moved from a furnished, three-bedroom house where they had lived their whole life to an unfurnished apartment in a new neighborhood. They were asked to give up old friends, attend a new school and support their mother in her decision to leave their father. Because their mother initially had no income and had to find a job, the girls became latchkey children as soon as their parents separated.

Jane and Sally experienced the friction and family disorganization that preceded their parents' separation. They lost the impact of a father and suffered the immediate effects of their mother's greater economic insecurity. Jane, a bright youngster, began to show evidence of the effects of her father's absence and her new environment.

Her normal A and B school grades plummeted and have failed to rebound. "I want her to study and do her homework, but I don't want to force her," her mother said. "She's been through a difficult time and with working I don't have a chance to really help her."

The year after their parents' divorce was especially problem-filled for the girls. Their mother was also experiencing outrage and anger. By the end of the second post-divorce year, the girls' mother thought they were adjusting well to the separation. "Then something happened that told me there was a lot of unexpressed anxiety," their mother said. "One Saturday night, I had just finished getting the girls to bed when the doorbell rang. It was John (her former husband). He might have been drinking a little, I don't really know. It was unusual for him to drop by unannounced. At any rate what began as a calm, though distant conversation soon looked as though it was going to become a real shouting match. I asked him to step outside for fear of awakening the children. We must have been outside for quite some time arguing about one thing or another. Anyhow, when I finally went back into the house I found both my daughters huddled together in the foyer crying. I can still hear Sally's voice asking me where I had been. "We thought you'd left us," she said. I spent a lot of time comforting them and getting them back to sleep. But about 3:00 A.M. Jane woke up vomiting. I don't think it was because of anything she ate. I think it was more nerves. Anyhow, I was really struck that they thought I might go away and not come back. I've spent a lot of time reassuring them since then. And I try never to go anywhere without telling them exactly where I will be, how to get in touch with me and when I will return. I never was much for being on time. Now I'm compulsive about it with the kids."

Many single parents of latchkey children remark that their children's greatest expressed fear is that the remaining parent will fail to reappear. Mary, a parent of an eight-year-old in Oxon Hill, Maryland, commented, "My son seems to be adjusting to being home alone. He's not afraid of any of the usual things like noises or robbers, but he is very afraid I won't come home again. Maybe that's just because his father left and not because he's a latchkey child. This year has been hard on both of us."

Two-thirds of mother-child relationships deteriorate during the year after divorce. Their relationships become less cooperative, angrier, less trustworthy and often filled with disorder and tension in daily living. Boys eight and older are most poorly treated. Their mothers withdraw from them more frequently than they do from girls, and older children are given less special attention than younger children.

During the same period, the custodial parent becomes more important to the child. Mothers more often than fathers become the primary custodial parent, although the latter group is growing. Separated parents turn to older children more for emotional support and assistance with household maintenance. If these demands for emotional support are not excessive, greater communication of concerns and plans can lead to more companionship between separated parents and their children. The greater participation of young people in family decision-making and household chores may lead to accelerated self-sufficiency in children. But too much independence and responsibility can also make youngsters feel overwhelmed, incompetent and resentful.

Sometimes separation comes as the result of the death of a parent. Shortly after the Second World War, death accounted for the majority of households in which a child lived with a single parent. Today such children are in the minority. This change has brought about a sometimes unanticipated phenomenon. Now children whose parents die often find themselves the odd person out. Naturally, there are other classmates living with a single parent and of course there is no stigma attached to a father's dying by reason of a sudden heart attack, for example, but a child who loses a parent by death is often the one child in the class who has no possibility of seeing his or her parent again. This makes a difference.

Anna, an only child, is also the only one in her rural Pennsylvania school who lives with a widowed mother. Now age ten, she became a latchkey child a year ago when her father died. Because of her husband's continually poor health, Anna's mother has been the sole supporter of her family for almost eight years. Anna's father served as the primary care-giving parent; at least he was always home until his death.

Anna's mother, who commutes sixty miles one-way to work, said that her daughter has adjusted well after her father's death, except that she now feels different from her classmates. "Not having a father who might show up someday bothers her," she said. "The other kids living alone with a mother miss their father, but they at least know there's a chance of seeing him again."

## 2. CHANGES IN FAMILY LIFE PATTERNS

Every change causes stress, and changes in any life pattern of a family will demand that each member of the family adapt to it. Conditions within the family that lead parents to decide that their children can or should care for themselves are usually major changes creating a great deal of stress. This stress is acutely felt by everyone in the family, but especially by the children who begin to take care of themselves.

When children begin the process of self-care, another set of changes occurs that is stressful. The relationships between children and parents as well as between siblings are all made different because of the new care arrangements. The benefit or harm produced by these changes largely depends on the attitudes of the people involved and the physical complexity of the arrangement.

If parents focus on the contributions the latchkey child is making to the family's well-being, the child's self-concept can be enhanced. Telling one's children that you appreciate the sacrifices they are making in taking care of themselves in order for mother to work, for example, can help them feel like participants in the family rather than abandoned and unloved. Acknowledging that self-care is sometimes lonely, frightening, boring and bothersome lets your children understand that you are attuned to their world and understand some of their troubles. When parents communicate a positive attitude, the stresses caused by change can lead to growth and a new feeling of mutual appreciation between parents and children.

On the other hand, if parents focus on their own concerns, the guilt they feel in choosing to leave their children unattended or the bother the care of children causes, then children will feel diminished in their parents' eyes as well as their own. They will become a burden, a source of pain, unlovables. Stresses caused by change that are handled in a negative fashion will most likely lead to a loss of self-esteem in both parents and children and widen the gap between them.

Parental reactions take both forms and family patterns change accordingly. Children who read in their parents' attitudes love, acceptance, understanding and concern respond to the challenges of self-care in better and more growth-producing ways. Parents who show irritation, a lack of acceptance, understanding and concern, or guilt about what they have chosen to do, produce children who find the latchkey experience more difficult and these children adapt less well.

Leaving siblings at home alone together also creates a demand for change in their relationships. Parental mediation is removed and children must interact with each other directly. They must control themselves and one another without the benefit of a parent's restraint. The stresses caused by these new opportunities can draw siblings together as they join forces to overcome common challenges, or they can create rifts between them that even in later life are never healed.

Of course some of the adaptations between siblings leading to new life patterns between them will emerge out of their own personalities. But parents can help by setting the family scene for cooperation rather than conflict. Children who see cooperation between their parents will be more likely to model that cooperation when on their own. Children whose parents volunteer help will be more likely to volunteer help. Children who observe parents caressing one another, talking softly and kindly to one another and being solicitous of one another will be more likely to mirror the same kind of nonviolent behavior when alone together.

On the other hand, parents who are aggressive, who control by threats and punishments, whose interaction with others in the household lacks generosity and is filled with criticism will find that their children not only mimic this behavior but expand on it, often because children have not learned sufficient control to cope with frustrations.

Parents can help reduce the potential for developing negative interactions between siblings, and consequently the less desired changes in life patterns that may occur, by establishing strategies for friendly cooperation between siblings. Carefully laid rules that capitalize on each child's strengths and preferences should be set. Plan cooperative projects the night before that give each child something satisfying to do in order to produce a mutually satisfying product. Cooking or art projects lend themselves to this. Divide duties to be responsive to each child's strengths and preferences. Where two or more children have a preference for doing the same thing or dislike the same thing work out a rotating schedule or pull that item off the menu of duties altogether. Be certain to review duty assignments regularly at family round tables.

The attitudes children develop as a result of being in self-care will have an effect on their relationship with their parents as they grow up and in later life. Children who learn independence, who handle their fears and the complexities of self-care well and who come to trust themselves as a result of their ability to master being latchkey children will feel better about themselves and will behave better. This usually causes their parents to like them better, treat them more maturely and establishes a positive pattern of communication.

Children who cannot handle the stresses or complexities of the latchkey situation and whose lack of maturity elicits criticism from their parents will feel badly about themselves, behave less well and have less rewarding interactions with their parents. A downward spiral in family life is begun.

Because there is no clear dividing line that determines at which point one pattern or another will go into effect, it is important for parents to exercise a degree of caution, erring if they must on the side of being too understanding. In families in which there are two parents present, periodic examination of the latchkey situation between both parents is necessary. Acknowledge to each other that this is a mutual responsibility and establish a time for both of you to discuss your observations together. In single-parent families solicit the advice of a trusted friend who might discuss the matters with your child, observe how the child interacts with you, and then act as a sounding board for your observations and concerns and possibly help you in planning strategies for improvement. All parents of latchkey children should also solicit information about their children from neighbors. From time to time, neighbors will notice your children doing something they ought not to do while in self-care. At other times they will relate things that will bolster your confidence. In any case, make use of all the information available to make the best judgment possible of how your child is faring. Your family patterns depend on it as do the life patterns of your children.

3. THREATS

Children experience stress from threats, real or imagined. The presence of adults is usually a solace to children. If no helpful adult is accessible the stress caused by most threats is usually prolonged.

Nine-year-old Patrick, telling about his most frightening experience, said that it was the time some boys followed him home from school. The boys never did anything to him or said anything to him. "They just stared at me and followed me," Patrick said. "I started running as soon as I could see our apartment house. I ran up the stairs and dropped my key twice while trying to get the door open. After I locked myself inside, I called my mother. They had to page her, since she wasn't on her floor. I looked out the window to see if the boys were still there. They were. They were just standing there, staring at me. It was a long time before my mother called me back. By then the boys had gone."

There is no way to tell what the boys in the street intended to do, if anything. Something about them frightened this nine-year-old to the point where even after he locked himself in his second floor apartment he didn't feel safe. Patrick called his mother, but she wasn't immediately available. Latchkey children who feel threatened usually call their parents first. By the time Patrick's mother called him back the immediate threat had subsided, but the recollection of that event lingered on. Eighteen months after it happened, Patrick still recalled it as his most frightening experience. He is now very cautious when he passes the corner at which he first saw those boys, and he goes out of his way to have a friend with whom to walk home.

If parents like Patrick's mother understand that children at home alone will, occasionally, experience threat when the parent is not available, they can set up a fail-safe for their children. Patrick's mother, the head nurse of a unit, knew that all calls to her were received by the receptionist in her unit. Patrick could easily have been coached to tell his problem to the receptionist if his mother couldn't be reached. The receptionist, at least in this case, could have been asked to be especially sensitive to calls from this woman's child and to find out what the problem was if his mother was occupied elsewhere.

Setting up such a plan means that parents must feel secure enough to share with others the fact that they leave their children unattended. The presumed stigma often makes it difficult for parents to make such an admission, especially to working colleagues. In this nurse's unit, as a matter of fact, she was not the only one with children, and not the only one using self-care as a child-care arrangement. It would have made sense at a unit meeting to have had all those on a shift make plans as to how they could help their children in case of need, especially when one parent or another wasn't readily available.

Sometimes threats are real, as when children receive crank or obscene telephone calls. At other times they are imagined, as when a flapping curtain in winter causes a child to think there is a ghost in the house. Threats can come from outside the home, as in the case of an attempted break-in. At other times the child lives with threat, as when an older sibling mistreats a younger one. One girl said that her older brother played a game with her in which he would put her into a large trunk in their house and sit on the lid. He wouldn't let her out until she began to cry and beg. "I never told my parents he did this," she said. "But I hated that game. It wasn't a game to me."

Parents must understand that threats are stress producers, and that even when a threat is removed, the stress residual may linger on. As with many suggestions in this book, the first thing parents should do is discover what threats, if any, their children experience. When you know what the problem is you will be better equipped to deal with it. Having children share with you those things that frighten them depends to a large extent on the closeness of the relationship you have built with them.

Being aware is half the battle. If Patrick's mother knew that her son continued to be afraid that the boys might follow him again she might have helped him make even more firm plans to have a friend accompany him home. She may have arranged for his school bus to drop him off in front of his house, or at least she may have provided him with a police whistle to carry in his pocket.

Had the girl whose brother locked her in the trunk told her parents about the incidents, they could have taken steps to control their son and perhaps gotten rid of the trunk. Admittedly, threats from within are more difficult to control. Frightening or abusive behavior occurring in the house between siblings might be good reason to seek day care for one's child, depending on its severity and the parent's confidence that it can be successfully controlled.

Crank or obscene telephone calls are best handled by instructing the child to hang up immediately. At least your child's lack of response won't further encourage the caller. The resulting stress of this, however, needs some patient parental counseling. Talk with your child about the feelings he or she still has as a result of the calls. Try to build in the services of a nearby adult whom the child can reach if the unwanted calls continue. Sometimes just knowing that there is somebody nearby will reduce the threat for your child. And of course consider having your telephone number changed or your listing removed if the calls continue. Many parents of latchkey children have unlisted telephone numbers.

Occasionally threats come as the result of a severe trauma that is not easily put aside. One seven-year-old was abducted and molested by a man on her way home from school. She and her family obtained counseling to help them to deal with the incident. Then, two years later, "seemingly out of the blue," said her parents, she began to draw pictures of the man with large genitals, nooses around his neck and words on the paper that indicated her continued thoughts about and hatred for the man. Her parents wisely reinstituted counseling.

## 4. CHANGE IN RESPONSIBILITY

The simple fact of self-care increases children's responsibility for themselves. In addition they are often asked to shoulder chores and duties at home as a means for further sharing family responsibilities, or because parents believe that assigned duties are a good way to keep children active and less bored. Some parents are so concerned about boredom that they overstructure their child's time alone. One girl whose mother filled her afternoon hours with numerous activities said to her mother, "Please, Mom, give me a break. Sometimes I just like to come home and do nothing."

In a study of third grade children's planned after-school activities, Joan Bergstrom of Wheelock College found that children were involved in two to four planned after-school activities a week on the average, with two-thirds of them involved in such activities for three or more days per week. Planned activities accounted for an average of three and a third to six hours out of the twenty-seven and a half to thirty-seven and a half hours of time usually available after school, although some children in this middle-class, suburban Boston community spend as much as ten and a half hours in planned activities.

Structuring of children's out-of-school time seems to be more important for working than nonworking mothers. And working mothers with boys schedule more of their boys' time, usually with sports, than their girls'. Boys are also given much more responsibility for getting themselves to and from practices, lessons, clubs and the like, than girls.

Children at home with mothers generally depend on them to get to scheduled activities that are not within walking distance. Children at home alone are generally responsible for getting themselves to structured activities. And boys more frequently than girls are allowed to exercise this responsibility. This constitutes a marked increase in personal responsibility for unattended versus attended children and boys versus girls.

Working parents who are concerned about increasing their children's responsibility for their own mobility may need to go to unusual lengths to arrange safe transportation for their children by way of carpools, private taxis or escort services, for example. Working parents concerned about their children's social, physical and intellectual development may want to help their children structure out-of-school time in accord with their children's wishes and abilities. Being a latchkey child then increases the responsibility of both parent and child if normal social, physical and academic development is to be maintained.

Looking at the world from the child's perspective, children already carry a lot of responsibility. School itself is highly structured and demanding. The work of children in our complex society to learn enough to become productive members and to become socialized is an enormous undertaking. Childhood looks so simple from an adult point of view, but bewildering from that of the child. Even establishing good peer relationships offers an exceptional challenge. There are few clear rules and yet many a child's future depends on his or her ability to develop and maintain friendships.

When the normal responsibilities of childhood are added to, stress increases. As with other forms of stress, children can grow as a result of these changes or be overwhelmed by them. The outcome is determined partly by the child's own resources, partly by the extent of the demands and partly by the resources available in the child's environment.

Children at home alone are not only expected to maintain their normal academic and social progress, they are also often asked to do this with less help from their parents. The drop in readily available adult assistance for latchkey children is perhaps one reason for the success of the Dial-A-Teacher program sponsored by the Indianapolis, Indiana, public schools. This homework assistance hotline was designed to help students complete more difficult homework assignments. It has succeeded in accomplishing this and more. In many cases the service, which operates every Monday through Thursday from 5:00 until 8:00 P.M. when school is in session, also helps children handle other responsibilities.

The latchkey experience alters the impact specific adults have in fostering the social dimension of a child's learning and development. As children have less time available during which to interact with their parents, the responsibility for developing those mental structures that mediate between those that children develop from within (collective knowledge) and those imposed from without (academic instruction) shifts and changes. Sometimes the impact of another adult, such as a teacher, is enhanced; at other times parental behavior, now observed in a compressed time frame by the child, is enlarged.

The acquisition of mediating structures, or learned responses that children pick up from adults, occurs only if children are personally attached to the adults. Mediating structures are not *specific* responses to a particular person or thing, but a way of responding. For example, a child who observes a parent reacting with fear to a stranger will often learn not a specific response to that particular person, but a way of responding to people in general. The child will abstract, not imitate, a common pattern from the parent's behavior. Abstracting from a parent's actions is a more powerful and generalizable process than imitation.

Self-concept, trust, autonomy and problem-solving styles and strategies are all learned patterns of behavior and thinking acquired from adults who are important to the child. Such mediating structures once learned are difficult to unlearn. Because these structures are not acquired through direct experience, but indirectly through association with important adults, they aren't likely to be changed by direct experience. They are changed only as the child becomes attached to someone with a different point of view. Such is the nature of prejudice, for example.

The attachments children develop thus become very important in forming or replacing mediating structures. Children deprived of adequate interaction with their parents can shift their attachment to significant others in their environment, a teacher or day-care worker, for example, and therefore shift the impact or responsibility for developing mediating structures away from parents. At the same time children risk developing dysfunctional mediating structures or only loosely developing them when in the care of someone other than their parents. Many parents worry about such shifts in responsibility, which can cause stress for parents and confusion for children when conflicting mediating structures are present.

The presence of mediating structures is all the more reason for parents to develop and maintain a close relationship with their children. Working parents, whose time with their children is more severely limited, must go out of their way to allow their children to spend as much available time with them as possible. This doesn't have to mean that housecleaning or yardwork always gives way to play with children. It does mean that parents must find ways to involve their children in as many parental activities as possible. Often a child is more enthused at being allowed to help dad repair a broken piece of furniture than dad's attending his hockey match or taking him to a movie.

## 5. OTHER CHANGES IN RESPONSIBILITY

Emergencies change the amount of responsibility a child has to carry. Children generally rely on other people for help in an emergency, usually their parents. Children at home with parents often are not coached as to how to handle an emergency, and often fail to recognize their responsibility in such a situation. The same is not true for latchkey children, whose parents are more likely to advise their children about emergencies, impress on them their responsibility for responding and provide them with procedures for coping. Some parents put together emergency kits for their children. The kind they carry with them might include money for phone calls or transportation and a list of emergency numbers. The stationary kind, located in a specific place in the house, often contains first aid equipment, a flashlight and portable radio. The very existence of such survival kits impresses on latchkey children their responsibility for their own safety and often the safety of their siblings.

Children in the five to thirteen age range often act on assumptions they make based on limited information. Because of their level of development, children in this age range often cannot alter their reactions to take into account new or contradictory information. In addition, children in this age group sometimes have difficulty distinguishing between thought and reality.

The result is that many children up to about age thirteen follow patterned responses very well, but if forced to cope with a situation in which they have to depart from a plan or schedule, will experience problems. For example, as often happens, a latchkey child discovers one winter's day that he has lost his house key. He goes to the neighbor for a spare key. The neighbor is not at home, so the child sits on the porch of his house until his mother arrives.

Parents have to help their latchkey children cope with increased responsibility by developing structured responses for their children, but they must also help them in developing flexible problem-solving skills. Actually parents can make a game of such instruction by developing mock emergency situations and then asking their children to handle them. The more realistic the charade, the more fun the game and the better the learning for the child. Then alter certain aspects of the mock emergency, see how the children respond, and help them to think through alternatives.

Children asked to accept responsibility for care of siblings on some regular basis encounter more stress than children without siblings. Most children accept such challenges seriously and actively try to protect their brothers and sisters from harm.

Families in our society often give children responsibility for taking care of one another, yet little is known about the quality of such child care, the extent of the older child's responsibility or the limits of the child-care skills of children. Early adolescents, at least, are often assumed to be competent enough to protect the well-being of younger siblings. Many, beginning at about age eleven, are hired to babysit for children outside the family. In fact, many parents indicate a preference for babysitters between the ages of twelve and fourteen.

While data is sparse, evidence indicates that eleven- to fourteen-year-olds today are given much more responsibility for younger children than in the past, and that such child-care responsibility is undertaken by children in the elementary grades as well. A study of Oakland, California, youth showed that sixty-six percent of eleven to fourteen-year-olds care for younger siblings at some point in the week. Ten percent of these have daily child-care responsibilities.

The practice of older children caring for younger ones is widespread in nonwestern societies, and the children are prepared for the responsibility. But because mothers have traditionally been the primary caretakers in western industrialized societies, little attention has been given to child care by children. Psychologists and child-care specialists are in fact divided about the advisability of giving child-care responsibility to young adolescents, particularly children under age eleven. Little is actually known about how this age group handles child care in unsupervised situations. Some experts suggest that because young adolescents are preoccupied with how others see them, this could cause difficulty in their understanding a younger child's point of view.

Girls more frequently than boys have daily child-care responsibilities. And the expectations about the role older children should play in taking care of younger ones vary from family to family. Even cross-cultural studies show wide variations across and within cultures in care-taking styles and organization in relation to the number of siblings and the work load of parents. Because real data are lacking and the practice of using older siblings as caretakers for younger ones is common, parents should exercise caution so as not to give older siblings too much responsibility for family child care too soon.

When the decision is made for an older child to take care of a younger one, parents should be confident about the maturity of their caretaking child. Confidence can be developed by gradually allowing the child to accept child-care responsibilities while under supervision. Sibling care is not a decision that should be rushed into, despite the fact that for many families the circumstances leading to sibling care come about very quickly.

Before starting sibling care the responsible child should be well coached by his or her parents. Adult assistance should always be available, and parents should provide their caretaking children regular times during which they can calmly discuss any problems associated with sibling care.

The tasks of sibling care are made easier for caretaking children if parents have constructed a safe environment, developed a set of effective rules, set up a good communication network, taught simple child-care principles, and if they monitor their children's performance closely. Still, there are built-in problems to the arrangement which must be acknowledged. The child acting as a parent substitute is really a sibling and as such may gain little authority over other siblings. In other cases, a caretaking sibling may have managed to win real authority over younger siblings and then found it difficult to release this authority when the parents are at home.

For many families having an older child watch younger ones is a successful child-care arrangement but it must be noted that not all children are capable of such responsibility. If children are ineffective in caring for siblings or dislike providing sibling care, the arrangement will most likely produce negative effects and parents would be wise not to force the child to do it. Children should feel that they can tell their parents that such an arrangement is not working out, and parents should also be alert to signs of trouble. In such situations, other arrangements for child care should be made.

Although these are the main causes of stress to latchkey children, there can be others as well, depending on the stability of the family and the dynamics at work within it:

### Stress Caused by Communication Blocks

Many adults who were latchkey children throughout their childhoods beginning at a very early age—five or six—indicate that they learned to suppress their need for a parent because they felt their parent or parents weren't able to respond. Some said that as they grew older, there were moments when they thought they could have approached their parents, but found that they then couldn't directly express their need for nurturance. Most of these adults said that they simply couldn't express their needs or that when they tried to, the interchange ended in a quarrel. Many latchkey children find it difficult to identify exactly what they want apart from the more concrete requests for goods or services. It is highly likely that at those odd moments during which an absent parent seems accessible and the child tries to take advantage of this accessibility, the child is not able to articulate clearly what in the way of nurturance or other emotional support he or she wants, although it is evident that something is wanted, and the parent becomes frustrated.

Sam, a six-year-old, suddenly is unable to tie his own shoes or pull on his socks when his parents arrive home after work. He asks for help to get a drink of water or adjust the TV set. His parents frequently explode at these cries for attention, not realizing that they are strong but indirect requests for nurturing.

Parents need to be alert to these communication blocks, especially to their child's cries for nurturing or emotional support. Don't hesitate to continue to be affectionate with your children as they get older. There is no rule that says you must stop hugging your children at age five or seven. Plan ways to express affection for your children. Caresses, pats, hugs and kisses are the most direct and impact-filled ways in our society. They are much more effective than telling children you love them or writing them love notes, although both of these means should be used as well.

Because of their limited amount of time at home, parents of latchkey children should also work to make sure the positive communications they perhaps feel in the middle of the night reach their children when they are awake. Since working parents often feel tired and frazzled when they arrive home from work, perhaps in no mood to be affectionate, it may be better to set aside some cuddle time with children each day at a later time. Pick out an overstuffed sofa or chair and snuggle up in it with your child. Read a book together, talk about the day's events, but make certain that there is plenty of physical contact. If you have more than one child make certain that they each have some individual cuddle time, no matter how short. While there may be times when you want or need to share this special time with all your children at once, each child is an individual and should have a chance to develop a special relationship with you apart from the crowd.

Don't be afraid to make a fuss over the cuts, scrapes and bruises your children bring to you after you arrive home. These special concerns of your children are ways in which they make contact with you. Your children won't become "crybabies" because you show concern over their hurts. Fathers especially with sons must temper their fears that their boys will not grow up able to master the hardships of adulthood if "old dad" pays some extra attention to his child's hurt. As children grow older, they will have plenty of opportunity to learn that the world doesn't stop each time they get a nosebleed.

Because of the way we have, in the past, acculturated boys, fathers sometimes have to make more of an effort to show affection to their children than mothers do. Fathers who sense a distance with their children should look for ways that fit their individual personalities to bridge that gap. For some a good romp in the woods, a bicycle hike or a game of football will be just the ticket. For others reading a book together, attending a concert or going to a museum will provide the opportunity.

Children are often especially pleased when dad, or mom, takes time off from work to be with them. Of course, you may lose some pay, but who are you earning this money for anyhow? Try taking your child out for lunch or to a ball game on a day when things are slow in the office. He or she will appreciate this special contact with you more than a new video cartridge. Many children interviewed said that their best times with their parents were when they helped dad repair the car or worked a puzzle with mom or went rock climbing together. It's very likely that if *you* enjoy whatever it is you're doing your enthusiasm will be transmitted and your children will come to enjoy the activity as well.

If your child seems to want to tell you something but has trouble expressing it, don't be afraid to help him or her put the need into words. Of course it may be something you don't want to hear, but it will benefit both of you in the long run if you try to draw out what's on his or her mind. Besides, you may be pleasantly surprised to find that your child is trying to express something positive towards you.

Little Gretchen stuttered repeatedly as she tried to ask her mother a question. Her mother, who was busy doing housework, paused for a moment, a bit exasperated, stroked the back of her hand across her forehead and said, "What is it, Gretchen?" It took a few more stutters before Gretchen was able to say, "Can I help you?" Fortunately Gretchen's mother had not been so preoccupied, distracted or exasperated to stop her cleaning. The result was two more small but willing hands to help with the housework. Gretchen's mother even had the good sense to make a bit of a game of it.

Many adults who were latchkey children said they experienced their need-stress as a pull in two directions, a need for parental care and a fear that the need wouldn't be fulfilled. Some said that they felt that they could only obtain their parents' attention by acting as their parents' helpers. It's a good idea to allow children to help, but doing chores shouldn't be the only time when things are shared between parent and child.

### Changes in Family Income

It is possible that the detrimental effects of a separation or divorce on a latchkey child may be due largely to the reduced income of the custodial parent. In fact, some researchers suggest that low income has a greater effect on child-rearing practices than father absence among divorced mothers.

After a separation, the drop in income can be precipitous. In a national longitudinal study of families, when women were separated or divorced and retained custody of the child, their income-to-needs ratio fell by thirty-five percent. When fathers retain custody, the financial problem is much less severe. It is also well established that divorce is more common among families with low and unstable incomes and that the latchkey phenomenon as a percentage of the population seems to be more pronounced in the lower income, single working-parent category.

Low income is associated with stresses that make household and child care more difficult, e.g., poor quality of housing and neighbor-hoods, or the need for mother to work. If the family change that preciptates a latchkey situation is associated with lowered income such as that occasioned by a divorce, the child may experience the stress of further social isolation brought about by a move to a differ-ent neighborhood. Such moves tend to be made to areas with higher risks to personal safety, fewer recreational facilities and less adequate schools, in addition to the loss of familiar friends, neighbors and schools.

On the other hand, latchkey children in dual-income families generally live with a higher than average family income. Depending on the timing and rationale for the addition of this second salary, it may or may not provide a source of stress for the child.

Jorlee, the youngest of three daughters in a stable family, resented her mother's decision to begin working when Jorlee entered the first grade. She did not appreciate the addition of a second source of family income and instead interpreted her mother's decision to go to work as a sign that her mother loved her less than her two sisters, during whose grade school years mom had stayed at home. When mom began using her added income to purchase presents for Jorlee, the child's stress grew. Now an adult, Jorlee says, "I thought mom was buying me off. While I liked the presents, I still resented my mom's working and continued to believe that she loved my sisters better."

Often a young child doesn't have a concept of money. What the child does understand is that mom is not home, that it gets dark early in winter and it's frightening when you're alone. When a six-year-old's mother told him she had to go to work to earn money so that they could eat, he replied, "No, you don't. You can just go to the bank and write a check."

A second income may be necessary to stabilize a family's standard of living; for others it may serve to advance the family's living standard. Two-career families often hope to increase opportunities overall. Two-career couples usually hope to be able to afford a better home in a better neighborhood, send their children to better schools, take vacations more frequently or own two automobiles. These goals are understandable, but with many young couples the drive for the better things in life often becomes a whirlwind that draws them into debt and soon increases their need for two incomes. As children experience the advantages technology has to offer, and as moves to better neighborhoods put them in touch with a group of friends who can afford computer games, a trip to the seashore or a second car, the child comes to learn that he must contribute to maintaining this standard of living. For many children, their contribution consists of spending a few hours at home alone, growing up a little faster and shouldering some extra responsibilities, like cooking supper or making beds. While these children may dislike their self-care arrangements, they clearly enjoy the advantages the incomes of both their parents bring. Children in families affected by a change in income, whether for better or worse, feel the same pull of stress, but many will keep quiet about the problems of self-care in an attempt to help out the family in the face of such a change.

## The Reflected Stress of Multiple Demands

Multiple demands on single working parents or dual-career couples may prevent family life from having the regularity that helps children go to school well prepared and on time, get to bed at a regular hour each school night, or have a well-balanced and timely meal. Parents of latchkey children are often in a rush in the morning, exhausted from a day's work at night, concerned about maintaining a social life, and of having time to relax alone or together without the children. They must also find time between work, children and self to do the shopping, pay the bills and maintain their dwellings, even if their children are unusually helpful with household chores. Like everyone else striving to do well on the job, parents of latchkey children carry home with them work concerns, worry about locating the next contract, threatened reductions in the work force or inter-personal problems with co-workers or superiors. The multiple de-mands placed on parents can be reflected in their home behavior and ultimately are reflected as a source of stress for the child.

Two parents, both professionals and very involved in their individ-ual careers, said: "The mornings aren't so bad for us, even though the children (ages three and six) are in a rush to get to school. But one or both of us works late an average of three nights a week; sometimes neither of us arrives home until after 8:30. Getting the children to bed at a decent hour is always a problem, since they don't want to go to sleep without spending some time with us. Often this means bedtime comes after 10:00. While we're concerned that we see our children each day, the later they stay up, the more upset we become, so bedtime often loses a lot of the peacefulness that it ought to have. If the children get to bed late, they're cranky when they get up and getting them off to school is often less than pleasant." These children not only miss seeing their parents during much of the day, but the time they do spend with mom or dad becomes strained since so much gets compressed into such a short period of time.

### Handicaps

Some latchkey children have special problems, including physical handicaps. These can make self-care more hazardous or stress-filled. One sixteen-year-old latchkey child who is blind and has been in self-care for six years, three hours a day, said, "I can take care of myself. I feel my parents look after me very well considering that they both need to work." When asked if she had encountered any particularly frightening experience while home alone, she said, "Yes, one time especially. I kept hearing noises out front and when I pushed the intercom that linked our house with the next door neigh-bor's, no one answered. We live in a rural area and there's just our two houses close together. I began asking 'Who's there?' but no one answered. When I tried to call my mom the phone didn't work. I began screaming and screamed until I passed out. Meanwhile, our neighbor came in, noted that the intercom was on and came by to check. The noise was the wind blowing through a leaflet someone had stuck in the door handle."

In general this girl dealt with the latchkey situation very well. She said, "I don't feel being home alone has had any effect on me. I never realized anyone was concerned about it until now." Despite her ability to function well, being alone and handicapped has posed some special problems and extended some common ones. Though now sixteen, developing friends has proven a continued problem. "Because of my lack of sight I have very few friends. Since mom is not home and I live in the country, I can't easily get to many social functions or to friends' houses. I think, if anything, that's the main effect being alone has had on me—it's more difficult for me to visit friends."

Many parents of handicapped children are financially pressed. And as their children get older the pressure on both parents to work increases. Then too, parents of exceptional children frequently find it difficult to find adequate supplementary child care. Despite the fact that the blind girl's story above is shocking to some unaccustomed to blindness, it is not an isolated case. It is true that parents of exceptional children try not to leave them unattended, but they are frequently left in the care of siblings.

One mother of a retarded twelve-year-old became quite angry when she discovered that the fifteen-year-old daughter left in charge had gone to a Superbowl party, leaving her retarded sister alone. The mother, a single parent who earned a living as a real estate salesperson, tried never to leave her younger daughter alone. Her flexible hours and her daughter's schooling made this possible much of the time, but some child-care responsibility still fell on the shoulders of the fifteen-year-old. As both girls got older, the fifteen-year-old began to resent her own confinement more and more and began to engineer a few escapes to favorite activities.

Children with less evident handicaps are more frequently left alone or in the care of siblings. A child who is diabetic or epileptic may be able to function quite well under most circumstances, but with the onset of an insulin reaction or a seizure, help is needed immediately. If such children are unattended, the attack could prove fatal.

Every handicapped child presents a special case. Parents must be thoroughly acquainted with their child's capabilities before leaving a handicapped child in self-care or with siblings. The parents of the blind girl knew that their daughter was generally capable around the house and they had provided a special communication link with a neighbor. What they failed to do was to assure themselves that there would always be someone present to receive messages over the inter-com, or to develop a back-up system if the neighbor had to leave. Their informal arrangement usually worked, but there was no guar-antee. The blind girl came to trust her structured plans so much that the one time they failed in a suspected emergency the girl panicked. This is not an uncommon reaction for younger children whose planned responses fail.

The blind girl's parents could have entered into a more formal arrangement with the neighbors so that in case they weren't present to monitor the intercom they would have been responsible for mak-ing other arrangements, providing a companion for the girl or taking her with them, for example. Such formal arrangements usually de-mand the services of an exceptionally close neighbor or relative or the exchange of goods, services or money in order for them to work. In addition, the girl's parents might have provided a daily visual inspection of the house before their daughter entered. In this rural community the neighbors may have been the logical choice or, per-haps, the school-bus driver.

Parents who leave handicapped children unattended should make certain that the local police, fire or rescue squad knows about the unusual circumstances in the home so that, when they receive an emergency call at that address, they may respond quickly and with good information. Of course, latchkey parents are unlikely to so inform public emergency assistance units because of the fear that emergency personnel will think them unfit parents. Even if prior arrangements with local emergency units are impossible, handi-capped children should know how to communicate full information about themselves and their situation to adults who can help.

This need for the communication of complete and accurate infor-mation in a call for emergency assistance is one reason that unat-tended retarded children are in great danger. No matter how docile the child and how well-structured the emergency plans, it often takes a good deal of quick thinking based on a few rapidly assessed varia-bles in order for anyone to respond appropriately to an emergency. Some retarded children are simply not capable of making such re-sponses and can be harmed while trying to exercise an emergency plan not suitable to a particular emergency.

Visibly handicapped children such as the blind or those suffering from spinal cord injuries or those whose facial contours make it evident that they are different are, unfortunately, often shunned by their peers. Because the latchkey experience can add to this isolation, it is wise for parents to make special efforts in planning for out-of-school activities for their handicapped children. In many cases parents of exceptional children can obtain public assistance to allow their children to participate in such activities.

The social isolation experienced by handicapped children can also cloud the social activities of siblings who are required to provide child care, as in the case of the sister of the retarded twelve-year-old. This is, of course, not always the case—some handicapped siblings themselves make excellent care givers for their brothers and sisters.

When children have silent handicaps, as in the case of the diabetic or epileptic, both the handicapped child and his or her siblings need to be instructed as to what to do in an emergency. Moreover everyone needs to know what an emergency is like. Seizures are frightening and siblings need to know how to communicate accurate information to emergency personnel. This means they need to know exact terminology in relation to the particular handicap and not be afraid to use it.

Living with a handicapped child is stressful on all members of the family, and siblings will occasionally try to escape the stress. When parents understand that stress is building, it is time to call a family conference to talk about it, or quietly sit down with the child whose behavior seems to be signaling stress to discuss the situation. Non-handicapped siblings sometimes find it difficult to admit that stress is produced from wanting to get away from a handicapped brother or sister. But the feeling is common and should be dealt with calmly and in a straightforward manner, rather than have feelings of guilt at wanting to get away add to the child's stress.

### Television as a Stressor

Children in self-care tend to spend a good deal of time watching television. Very often they watch TV because they can't think of anything else to do. Many of these children average four to five hours a day in front of the TV, though they may not always be closely attentive to what is being aired.

Many parents consider television a companion, while some professionals see it as a mental anesthetic. There is, however, an equally strong argument that television produces stress because it provides too much information in too rapid a sequence to allow for reflection. David Elkind, a professor at Tufts University, suggested that the real stress of television is the difference between how much information is beamed at children and how much they can actually process.

When television simultaneously presents children with information that is too violent (as in cartoons) or too complex (as in the relationships developed in soap operas) or abstract (as in much news coverage) for them to process, stress can result. Further, many of the themes shown on television—sexual involvement, adultery, incest, prostitution, or violent themes like war, murder or rape—prove stressful for children who are as yet unfamiliar with their own sexuality or who do not yet possess a mature level of impulse control. Children who see adults unable to master their own impulses or who view lack of impulse control as leading to hurtful consequences, might come to fear their own angry feelings or sexual desires and therefore experience stress.

In another way, television increases stress because it interferes with active play. Play is considered a stress releaser. Tense executives are often advised to take up a sport to relieve stress. A child propped in front of a television for hours sacrifices play and therefore loses the benefit of physical activity and its properties as a stress reducer.

Television is also a model for behaviors that can produce stress in real life. Many parents notice their children exhibiting aggressive behavior after having watched hours of cartoons on a Saturday morning.

Lynn, the single parent of a six-year-old latchkey child, tries to catch up on her sleep on Saturday mornings. Her son watches cartoons from 7:00 until about 11:00 A.M. When Lynn and her son finally get together, she complains, "He seems restless and demanding when I'm just waking up. If I don't respond to him immediately, he gets angry, shouts, throws things, even hits me. It sets the whole day on edge. I don't know why he acts like this."

Many adults notice the empty feeling that often results from an extended session in front of the television. Adults frequently respond to this feeling by eating, drinking, smoking, falling asleep or getting out of the house. It must be assumed that this empty feeling is also common in children. But the ways that adults deal with it are often not appropriate or possible for latchkey children, especially getting out of the house. The result seems to be increased stress as wants or needs go unmet. Children have difficulty understanding what's going on, in particular the effect prolonged television viewing has on them. Suggestions for ways to monitor the amount of time children spend watching television can be found in Chapter Twelve.

### School Burnout and Premature Structuring

School burnout is not necessarily or exclusively a product of children in self-care. Children at all levels of educational, racial and economic backgrounds can experience chronic unrelieved stress from being in school, no matter what their care arrangements. These children lose enthusiasm for school, hate to go to school, become alternately tense or lethargic when confronted with school, and might show physiological or behavioral systems that result from their ineffective attempts at dealing with their stress-filled encounters with schooling. What makes latchkey children different is that some of them cope with this particular type of stress by avoiding school altogether. In these cases, home is a ready haven in which they know they will not be hassled because they'll be alone. By avoiding school whenever possible, these children voluntarily extend their self-care as the least painful of their alternatives. Many then resort to television watching, alcohol or drugs to relieve creeping boredom.

Dropping out of school or truancy is more common for the adolescent latchkey child, but it also occurs among elementary-school-age children. The following example is true, though uncommon. As children get further into adolescence, however, more situations like the following can develop.

Devon, a seventh grader, had had it with school. Since both his mother and father worked, he found it easy to miss school often. When he first began cutting school, he stayed home for fear that someone would notice him on the street and report him. He spent his time sleeping, eating and watching television and exploring the closets and drawers of his house. It was during these discovery trips through his house that he came upon his father's extensive collection of pornographic magazines, a hidden pistol and minor drug paraphernalia. Such explorations into the secret places of one's house are not uncommon for latchkey children.

Devon began spending a lot of time browsing through his father's magazines and it wasn't long before he was experimenting with his father's marijuana. As Devon took more days off from school, he fell further and further behind, making school even more difficult. Soon he stopped going to school altogether. He also grew bolder in his excursions away from his house. He soon managed to find a cadre of unemployed dropouts with whom he found something in common. He was able to supply them with small quantities of his father's marijuana, which kept him in generally good standing despite his age.

Devon's school did not contact his parents about their son's continued absences until the boy had virtually dropped out. This was a mistake on the part of the school, but nevertheless a reality. When his father found out about his son's truancy, he was furious. Devon and his father had an all-out confrontation that caused the boy to leave home.

The new runaway took up residence in a vacant garage for a while. While he attempted to avoid his parents, he would break back into his family's home occasionally while his parents were at work for food, clothing and drugs. Before winter set in, Devon had fallen in love with a twenty-one-year-old waitress who took a fancy to him and let him move into her apartment. She began supplying him with what drugs he wanted and accepted him as her lover. In less than a year, Devon, son of a Ph.D. and a high school teacher, was on a constant high, had contracted a venereal disease and was floating in a circle of people more than seven years older than he. His response to dragging himself to school day after day was to use his latchkey situation to avoid school altogether. Readily available drugs softened the impact of stay-at-home boredom and before he would have completed the eighth grade, muscular, attractive Devon had aged ten years.

Devon said some years later, "I became street-wise quickly. School wasn't the only thing that frustrated me; I never had a good relationship with my father. In some sense I thought my parents wanted me to grow up quickly, so striking out on my own at thirteen wasn't really all that hard. In my case it wasn't that my parents couldn't afford me. They just wanted to do their own things. I guess what I did was give them what they wanted with a vengeance."

Latchkey children, especially those left unattended in the morning, can avoid school simply by staying at home. Unless schools have a policy of telephoning parents to check about absences children can often miss many days of school before their truancy comes to the attention of their parents.

Missing school doesn't relieve stress for young children, it simply shifts stress or increases it. Falling behind in schoolwork, being truant and otherwise operating behind parental backs usually creates a great deal of stress for children. The more stress these children try to avoid, the more stress they often manage to create for themselves, as was the case with Devon.

Parents of latchkey children would do well to check on the school attendance of their children from time to time. Occasional phone requests for information, regular teacher conferences and periodic school reports combined can keep parents alert to the children's school activities before a problem has time to develop.

School personnel are usually good friends to concerned parents. Cultivate your child's teachers each year and be certain to become acquainted with the school counselor, if there is one. A good home-school relationship can be an enormous help in developing ways to relieve your child's stress both at home and at school. Despite Devon's difficulties at home, he might have been less inclined to skip school if his experience there had been better.

Children at home alone for any length of time will begin to explore any areas of the house accessible to them. If parents of latchkey children want to keep certain items away from children that will normally draw their curiosity, there is no substitute for a good lock. Guns certainly should be locked up. Devon may not have avoided marijuana had his father kept his stash locked, but he wouldn't have found it so available. Of course everyone is better off if drugs, weapons and other "adult only" items are not kept at home.

### Stress and Suicide

Increased stress during childhood is not to be taken lightly. For many children it becomes a matter of live and death. Among adolescents, suicide has become the number one cause of death. What is more startling is emerging evidence that even children under the age of five try to commit suicide. "People can't believe that kids could kill themselves, but we have treated children as young as four years old who tried to commit suicide by jumping from a window," said Dr. Bennet Leventhal, director of the University of Chicago's Child Psychiatry Clinic.

Intentional death-seeking behavior in children under five years of age remains an unappreciated phenomenon, but there are documented reports of children under three who stop eating for weeks, threaten to throw themselves in front of automobiles and bite or puncture themselves to the point of bleeding. Health professionals believe that such examples are only the tip of the iceberg of a bigger problem of preschool and school-age children who commit suicide and whose deaths are misdiagnosed as "accidental."

Because childhood has become a time of increased stress, children are becoming more vulnerable to disappointments and frustrations. When the traditional support systems are reduced or removed, stressed children become especially vulnerable.

When children come to believe that they have no significant people in their lives, their own survival often seems irrelevant to others. If the child's family has also become rootless, unable or unwilling to provide the familial and social supports the child needs to develop a strong positive sense of self, then the child may become extremely vulnerable to self-injury.

The latchkey situation not only can serve to increase stress and heighten the child's sense of being less wanted, but also offers uninterrupted time to execute self-destructive ideas. Sometimes these situations provide just the right combination of elements to produce headline stories.

In Phoenix, Arizona, an eighth grade boy and his younger brother were latchkey children. Their house was an interior decorator's delight. As reported in the local paper, one afternoon, while both boys were home alone, the older boy stabbed the younger one to death in the living room of his house. He pulled his brother's body from the living room into the kitchen so that the blood would not soil the white carpet. He then calmly called the police to report that he had done something bad. Subsequent conversations with the boy's school counselor and personnel from the state juvenile division revealed that not only had the boy given indications of what he intended to do, for those who were able to interpret his school drawings, but that he carried out his plan to rid his parents of the burden of both boys with apparent calm. The boy had reasoned that since both children were not only irrelevent to their parents but a real burden, everyone would be better off with the boys out of the picture. His action was a premeditated plan for self-destruction. It came as a shock to both parents who understood too late the price their son was paying for their careers and the family's affluent display.

Stress is a fact of life. It can lead to self-destruction or growth. Latchkey children face a variety of stressors daily, each an opportunity. With good guidance and in a loving environment latchkey children can make the challenges they face work for them. They can become more independent, develop more flexible strategies for coping with problems and learn to become good executive managers of people and situations at an earlier age by virtue of the problems they encounter and must solve.

The parents of latchkey children can help their children grow by communicating love, appreciation, respect and confidence to them. Parents can help their latchkey children manage with a minimum amount of unwanted stress by preparing them to cope with the demands of latchkey life. And parents can let their latchkey children know that income and career are not more important than children by going out of their way to spend time with their children, involving them in as many parental activities as possible.

The latchkey arrangement often seems the only care arrangement available for many parents, especially those with handicapped children. For most parents concern and guilt are already high. Rather than massage one's guilt, keep close check on how your children are faring in the latchkey arrangement. If you observe stress or anxiety rising and even with your best efforts you can't alleviate it, be prepared to change care arrangements. If you cannot handle your own anxiety or guilt, find a good day-care center or sitter, even if it wreaks havoc with your budget. There are inherent stresses in self-care for children. For those children who cannot master them they can become destructive; for those who can they can become hurdles on the pathway to personal growth.

# Chapter 6
# THE PARENTS' PERSPECTIVE

The latchkey experience not only affects the children who spend their afternoons alone; it also deeply touches the parents who have struggled with the decision to leave their children alone. Fortunately parents, too, can reap benefits from their children's self-care arrangement. This chapter presents the parents' perspective: why they choose to leave their children alone, the benefits and risks as they perceive them and the complex array of feelings that accompany their decision.

## Why Parents Choose Self-care for Their Children

For many latchkey parents, the decision to leave their children in self-care is not made with forethought. It is an abrupt decision, made because their current child-care arrangements are upset. When existing arrangements are disturbed and a satisfactory replacement isn't easily found, parents and school-age children often share in a decision to try self-care. Once self-care is tried temporarily, however, it usually becomes a permanent arrangement.

A family move is often the precipitator of self-care. In today's mobile society, two out of every five elementary school children move at least once every three years. This high level of mobility shatters child-care arrangements for many families. In many cases the family only moves to a new neighborhood in the same locale, but even this can dissolve existing care arrangements, forcing the family to look for a new sitter or day-care center. As one parent explained, "I used to send my children to a neighborhood babysitter, but when we moved to Virginia I couldn't find a competent substitute. Since my eldest son was twelve, I figured my eight-year-old daughter and he would be all right for an hour a day." Another woman who used to hire a neighborhood sitter also left her children alone after she moved to a new neighborhood. "When we first moved to this neighborhood of course I didn't know anyone and I just didn't feel right asking people to watch my children after school, even though I would have paid them . . . I guess for some reason I thought they'd think less of me . . . allowing my children to care for themselves was easier."

For other parents, child-care problems start when their babysitter moves. Some find it impossible to uncover any other arrangements; others find new arrangements too expensive, inconvenient or of poor quality. At that point it's not a hard step to begin believing that one's children are old enough to stay by themselves. "A neighbor used to watch my daughter," one woman said. "When she moved away my daughter was nine. I didn't bother to look for anyone else. I believed my daughter was mature enough to take care of herself." Another working mother couldn't find child care after her sitter moved: "I looked for quality child care that was close and that I could afford, but couldn't find anything. I don't drive and there was nothing my child could walk to. I tried filling in with high school kids, but that was a ragged arrangement at best. So I started leaving Gordon alone, first two, then three, then five days a week. Now he spends twenty hours a week alone, two hours each morning and two every afternoon. Of course, I don't prefer it, but this arrangement is certainly as good as wasting money on erratic care by high schoolers." For some, the person who moved was a relative who provided free child-care services. "My father lived with us and watched my daughter after school. When he moved to his own apartment, I felt I had no choice but to leave Kristin alone." The step from apparently free child care to a paid arrangement is often a large one. Many parents find that it is much easier to step from free child care into child self-care. Many times the somewhat hidden costs of room and board for a live-in relative are ignored when calculations are made as to how much impact the cost for day care or employing a nonrelative caretaker will have on the family's budget.

Other children are thrown into self-care because of the death of a relative. For many of these children, the fact that the family member didn't move away but died often places a double stress on the child—dealing with self-care and the death of a loved one. One mother of several latchkey children said, "My mother lived with our family and supervised the children after school. When she died, the children started staying on their own. I knew they were upset, but I attributed it to Nana's death." On further questioning, it became evident that the children were upset by their grandmother's death for more than the obvious reasons: their grandmother had died in the house and the children were frightened by thoughts of their grandmother's ghost prowling around.

In some families the caretaking relative lives with the family; in other cases families depend on relatives who live nearby for child care. "My mother died when my son was eleven," said one mother of a latchkey child. "Before that, he would walk two blocks to her house after school and I would pick him up there on my way home from work. Now that she's gone, he spends afternoons by himself."

In still other cases, children begin self-care because a parent dies. When the parent who dies is the wage earner, this parent's death often pushes the remaining parent into the work force and the children into self-care. For many women, the death of a husband means returning to the work force before they normally would have or, less frequently, they must begin a career. In these families, the children not only lose a significant family member, but they must redefine their mother as a working woman, and usually must adjust to a lower standard of living, in addition to spending their afternoons alone.

Separations and divorces, however, account for most single-parent families in America today. A working mother with a husband can share child-care obligations with him at least part of the time and can usually depend on the benefits of two incomes. Should the woman separate from her husband, the entire burden for child care often falls on her shoulders if she becomes the custodial parent. A woman who was not employed outside the home before a divorce often finds that she can't maintain herself and her children at even a subsistence level after the divorce unless she works. Alimony has all but become a thing of the past and child-support payments from the noncustodial parent, even when regularly made, are usually insufficient to maintain the household at preseparation levels. Even when the father accepts custody of his children, the burden of child care, in addition to maintaining a job, is a hefty one. The custodial partnership that perhaps was shaky before the separation is often completely destroyed after the divorce. It is true that some divorced couples do take their individual child-care responsibilities seriously, but all too often, as the two former parents drift farther apart, the majority of the responsibility for child care falls on the shoulders of only one of them. Custodial parents frequently complain that the noncustodial parent fails to carry his or her share of the responsibility of having brought offspring into the world. Such complaints include, but are not limited to, making adequate and regular child-support payments. Even when the noncustodial parent is trying to fulfill a parenting role, child custody is usually a situation of one partner providing routine care and then being given a respite on some evenings, weekends and/or holidays.

Many divorced but custodial parents also feel a great need to find work for their own fulfillment. "I don't intend to remain unmarried for the rest of my life," said one. "How many eligible men would I meet staying at home taking care of two kids?" Due to a combination of financial and personal needs many mothers continue or seek employment after a divorce. As one said, "My husband makes over $100,000 a year, yet he only gives me $350 a month combined alimony and child support. I couldn't live on that amount, so I had to start work. At first my daughter was only four, so I held three part-time jobs just to make ends meet and still have some time with her. Now that she's older, I work full-time and she spends her afternoons by herself." Another woman with an older child had the same story: "I got divorced when Kristen was in the fourth grade. I went back to work immediately. Kristen and I looked at the options we had and decided it would be o.k. for her to stay alone. Frankly, I encouraged this decision, because it was cheaper."

Fathers who have custody, though they are much smaller in number than custodial mothers, also have child-care problems. "I got a divorce last year," one man explained. "My children are eight and twelve, and felt strongly that they were too old to have a babysitter after school. I agreed, so they stay by themselves. They are both very responsible, so I don't worry about them doing anything wrong. It's just that I'm a college professor and my hours are irregular at best. Two days a week I come home soon after they do so we can spend some time in the afternoon together. But three days a week, I teach late afternoon and evening classes. At least once a week I don't get home until almost 11:00. The two of them have to cook dinner and eat by themselves. They're usually awake no matter when I arrive home . . . I think they're afraid to go to bed until I'm in the house."

For all these families, a dramatic change precipitated the latchkey experience. Either they moved or a death or divorce occurred, which resulted in a change in the family structure. Under the stress of change these parents temporarily chose the most convenient alternative possible: self-care. When this arrangement appeared benign, they continued to let their children stay alone. What most parents don't realize is that their children are also coping with change and need support. A time of intense emotion, stress or change is usually not the best time to start self-care.

There are also other less severe circumstances which may lead to leaving a child in self-care. Many parents who have depended on friends or relatives to babysit can't afford a regular sitter or child-care center when such caretakers are no longer available. And for larger families, anything other than home care is too costly or un-wieldly. Cost of child care is cited as an issue by the majority of parents: "I began leaving my children alone when the oldest was ten and the youngest six," explained a divorced woman. "I sent them to a day-care center until I thought they could make it on their own, but I really couldn't afford two children in day care . . . not on my income and not in this economy."

Some parents who cite money as a factor can't afford child care at any cost. Many female-headed single-parents families fall below the poverty level and barely have the resources to buy necessities. But most latchkey children live in dual-income families where the re-sources are not so limited. For these families, the question is not that they don't have money, but that they don't have extra money to spend on child care. In order to spend a considerable amount of money on child care, they would have to spend less money on clothes, food or recreation—which would precipitate a significant change in life-style.

Even if money is not the primary issue, it is a compounding factor that often influences a parent's decision to leave his or her children unsupervised. Parents for whom money is not an issue have reported that suitable child-care arrangements are not always available or acceptable. "I wanted to send my son to a county recreation program after school," said one mother, "but I couldn't find anything near my house. Those that I did find didn't provide transportation." Admittedly, finding after-school programs is difficult. There were approximately 19,000 licensed day-care centers in the United States in 1980. Even when all forms of family day-care arrangements are added to available center care slots, they only provide care for half of the children age thirteen and under in families in which all parents in the home are employed full-time and who, therefore, need some form of care during the day. To make matters worse, many of these programs accept children only in the primary grades. Children from the higher grades are refused because the centers don't have the recreational facilities older children need.

One woman who had children enrolled in a day-care center was bitter because she had to take them out once they reached a certain age; her only alternative was to leave them home alone. "When my children were younger, they stayed with a babysitter. But I got so frustrated with unreliable babysitters that I enrolled both children at a day-care center. When John reached ten, the day-care center said he couldn't go there anymore. He was hurt at first, but then said it was boring anyway and wanted to stay on his own."

Even when day care is unavailable or inappropriate, creative parents might find workable alternatives like employing a trusted high school student, a senior citizen or a neighbor to watch their children after school if they don't want them to be alone. Many families with limited resources exchange room and board with a college student or a senior citizen for child-care services.

Some parents still choose to leave their children at home because they're not satisfied with the care they get from a babysitter or at a day-care center. "When Brett was eight, I left him with the parent of another child in his class. But when I would go to pick him up, the sitter wouldn't know where he was or when he was coming back. I felt he would be safer at home. My son wanted to stay home, too, because the sitter had three other children and the noise bothered him." The quality of care by babysitters drew the most complaints from parents: "I pay the lady across the street $2 an hour to watch my son after school. All he does is sit over there and watch TV. He can watch TV at home for free."

Parents who left their children at a day-care center also experienced problems. "I had to put my name on a waiting list to get my children into a day-care center. But once they were in, I wasn't satisfied with the program. It seemed as though there was nothing constructive for them to do. When I picked them up at 6:00, they were upset and exhausted. My children are shy. They said that a lot of the kids at the center were rough and would tease them. I talked to the teacher about it but she said she didn't see a problem. They begged me to let them stay by themselves rather than at the day-care center. I finally gave in." Another parent, also dissatisfied with the day-care program in which her children were enrolled, decided self-care was better. "When I started work, I felt the best place for my children to stay after school was at a day-care center, but it turned out to be a very unhealthy place. My kids caught every virus and communicable disease possible. When they got head lice, I decided enough was enough and let them stay home."

These parents decided to leave their children at home alone because of an unpleasant experience at a particular day-care center. But the negative experiences of a few shouldn't serve as an indictment of every day-care program in America. The quality of care differs from center to center. These parents might have considered exploring other day-care centers before deciding to leave their children alone.

## How Children Affect the Decision for Self-care

In a substantial number of cases the precipitating factor to a change in child-care arrangements was the children themselves. By fourth grade many felt too old for a day-care center and asked to take care of themselves. "My daughter is eleven and spends four hours alone each day. I first started working when she started school five years ago, and enrolled her in a country day-care center which was located in her elementary school. For a couple of years it was fine but she simply outgrew it. My daughter argued that she would be o.k. by herself after school. I agreed, since she showed responsible behavior in many respects." It's common for children to feel at some point that they've outgrown day-care centers and prefer to stay alone. One child summed up the sentiments of many when he said, "I don't need a babysitter because I ain't no baby."

Those children who would rather spend their afternoons in a day-care center find peer pressure hard to deal with. They are often teased by their friends who stay alone. In order to look older and more mature, children who succumb to such pressure will ask their parents to let them stay home alone, even if they don't want to. Even very young children experience pressure from their peers. One father complained that his first grade son was teased and called "diaper pants" because he went to a day-care center after school where younger children were enrolled. When a child begins requesting self-care, parents should carefully explore the reasons why they want to stay alone. Before a decision is made to let the child do it, try letting him or her stay alone for a trial period. If it's understood that it's only a trial period, children are more apt to honestly discuss their reactions to it. Many children who request self-care are frightened once they begin to stay alone but fail to complain because they requested to do so.

It is evident that the reasons parents choose self-care are varied. For some, it is because current child-care arrangements abruptly ended and no other arrangements could be found. For others, it is because child care is unaffordable or unsuitable. And parents who can find and afford proper child care are often convinced by their children that they are too old for a babysitter. All of these children spend their afternoons alone, even though, ideally, their parents would prefer to have them supervised.

### Benefits to Parents

Although most parents would not choose self-care for their children if they had a choice, once it is initiated many parents find it convenient in some ways. It makes their lives less complicated and eases the burden of work and home responsibilities.

First, transportation is no longer a problem. While getting a child from school to a day-care center often involves public transportation, taxi cabs, private bus companies or favors from a friend, getting children from school to home is a matter of course. Although some children routinely take public transportation to and from school, most children walk or are delivered safely to their door free of charge by a school bus. "My son used to go to a babysitter's after school. His teacher would call a cab for him every day and tell the cab where to go. He was too young to take a bus by himself, besides which there was no direct route. Then I would pick him up on the way home from work. It was out of the way, but he knew the woman well; she's watched him from the time he was born, so it was worth it. Now that he stays home by himself after school, I don't have to worry about getting him to and from her house." The freedom from worrying about transportation is a benefit to this parent, though in contrast she must sacrifice the emotional benefits of having her child stay with a trusted and loved babysitter.

Second, parents of latchkey children no longer have to leave work at a specified hour and rush to a closing day-care center. "I used to have to pick up my daughter by 6:00 or pay a late penalty of $5 for the first ten minutes and $5 for every ten minutes after that. I remember frequently sitting in rush-hour traffic and anxiously looking at my watch as the minutes ticked by. I was late at least once a week and there was nothing I could do about it. I couldn't leave work until 5:30 and if traffic was bad I was late." Parents of latchkey children don't have the same problem. Unanticipated delays, either at work or in traffic, can be handled by a telephone call home. A parent who is in the midst of an important meeting doesn't have to leave in the middle of it or risk paying stiff penalty fees. Instead, he or she can leave work with a sense of accomplishment.

While it is more convenient for a working parent not to have to be home at a specified time, it is traumatic for children not to be able to count on their parents' arrival. Though the latchkey arrangement allows for some flexibility, on the whole parents should make the same effort to get home on time as they would to a day-care center where payment of a late fee threatens.

Third, children home alone after school can help with household chores and ease the burden for parents returning from work. Many working parents complain that evenings are rushed as they try to prepare dinner, help the children with homework, do household chores and run errands. Children who are home after school can help with some of these responsibilities. Many older latchkey children are responsible for straightening up the house, setting the table and starting dinner. As one mother commented, "Ever since my daughter started staying alone in the afternoons, our evenings are calmer. Her homework is done, the piano practiced and dinner started all before I get home. It takes a lot of pressure off me." Unfortunately, the pressure that is taken off parents is often placed on children. Parents under stress should be careful not to assign too much responsibility to children and rob them of the experience of being children.

Finally, self-care is without financial cost. Though the unavailability of child care might be the reason some parents choose self-care, all recognize the savings it allows. "The only thing good about leaving your kids alone," one mother explained, "is that it saves money. But saving money is not the reason my child is alone—I can't find anywhere to send him."

### Concerns of Parents

Although self-care is free, it is not completely without cost. Parents pay in the concern and guilt they feel about leaving their children alone. Most parents are worried about their children's safety. Many cite their major concerns as fears of danger from external sources. They see the world as increasingly violent and worry about their children's safe arrival home and security once there. Over and over, parental comments reflected fear from outside sources, and for many parents these fears are grounded in reality. "We've had numerous burglaries in my neighborhood," one latchkey parent remarked. "Why should I think my son's immune?"

The other major fears of parents involve accidents and fires. These fears, too, are not ungrounded. Children who are home alone do have accidents. Parents' fears are compounded since often there are few adults in the neighborhood available to help and the distance from work to home is often far. "I work a full sixty minutes away," one woman said. "If anything happened to my daughter, there is no way I could be of any help."

Parents also fear fires, and with good reason—many children die every year because of fires. Many more children play with fire to entertain themselves when home alone. "My son's in the fifth grade," one anxious mother said. "He's very bright but doesn't entertain himself very well when he's alone. One day while I was cleaning his room I found some burnt matches on the floor. After that we sat down and had a serious talk about the dangers of playing with fire. I really thought I had made my point until I came home early one afternoon and found candles burning on the dining room table. They were practically down to the table. I was shocked. My son was sitting in the living room totally absorbed in the afternoon cartoons. In another fifteen minutes, the whole table would have been coated with wax and a fire might have started. I don't know how to convince him that playing with fire is dangerous."

In order to cope with fires and accidents, most parents teach their children emergency phone numbers, but few teach them first aid or have fire drills. Even parents who take the time to teach their children what to do in case of a fire worry that their children would panic in an emergency.

The concern parents feel for their children becomes evident when parents discuss what happens when they are unable to reach them by telephone or don't receive a check-in telephone call. Many become frightened or anxious when they can't make immediate contact. "I tell my son to come home right after school," the mother of an eleven-year-old boy said. "When he doesn't call by 3:30, I get worried. The first thought that runs through my mind is that something has happened to him. So far nothing has, and it turns out that he was just hanging around with his friends. But it scares me just the same."

Parents of older children often complain that their children are constantly using the telephone for socializing and therefore inhibit contact. "I try to call my daughter from work to see if she's all right, but I can never get through. She's always on the telephone. I don't know what she could talk about all afternoon. Sometimes I want to call to tell her I'll be late, but I can't reach her."

In order to insure contact, most parents urge their children to keep their telephone conversations brief so that they can be reached. Others have set times their children cannot use the telephone so that they can call to check on their safety and give specific instructions. One parent, frustrated by her attempts to call her daughter, decided to fine her daughter every time she tried to call and got a busy signal. The money was subtracted from the girl's allowance on Saturday. Possibly the easiest solution is to install a second line that is for parents only. The nominal cost of a second line would be worth the anxiety it saves parents who have a problem keeping their children off the phone.

Parents are not only concerned about the physical safety of their children, but they worry about their emotional needs, too. The primary concern is that their children spend too many hours alone and need the added security of having someone there when they get home from school. Parents also worry that their children don't have enough time to play outside or spend time with their friends.

In order to help their children cope with their time alone, many parents try to entertain them from a distance. "I try to think of things to keep my son busy," shared the mother of a seven-year-old boy who spends two hours alone every afternoon. "But it's hard to think of things that are safe that he can do by himself. I don't want him sitting and watching television all afternoon."

Parents are generally sensitive to the problems of self-care and often spot trouble signs when the children are home alone too much, but many don't know what to do about it. "Jim and I got a divorce this year and as a result Mike has to spend his afternoons alone. I know he's bored because he's gained fifteen pounds in these past few months—he must spend his whole afternoon eating. When I nag him about it, he just gets more depressed." Many children eat as a way of coping with boredom and loneliness and as a result show rapid weight gains. Nagging them about this only tends to increase the isolation and loneliness they feel. Parents who find their children are overeating should try to control *what* they eat, rather than *how much,* by ridding the house of cookies, candy, cake and other fattening foods, and substituting low-caloried foods such as fruits and vegetables.

Parents also worry that their children will watch too much television or get into trouble. The mother of a sixth grade boy commented, "I'm afraid that because my son is bored he'll get involved with drugs or alcohol." Parents also fear that children who are bored will play with fire or experiment sexually.

In addition to the fears parents of latchkey children have, they are frustrated by their inability to control their children when they are home without adult supervision. Making rules is easy, but getting children to follow those rules is difficult. The mother of a girl in the sixth grade was frustrated by her daughter's actions: "I told my daughter that under no circumstances should she let anyone in the house. I found out that she's been letting her friends in the house all year, boys included." Many parents are concerned that their children watch too much TV and have difficulty enforcing restrictions. As one mother of an eight-year-old boy noted, "I tell my son he can watch one hour of TV after school and that's all. I know he's watching more because he doesn't do his chores or homework, but there is no way I can check on what he's actually doing."

Parents with more than one child have additional trouble controlling their children from a distance. Fights are constant problems for most siblings and parents are frequently frustrated in their attempts to stop them. One mother described what appears to be a common scene in families with siblings in self-care: "My eleven-year-old daughter watches my six-year-old son after school. I tell her if he does anything wrong to call me at work, that she shouldn't try to discipline him herself. Yet when I walk in the door, three days out of five, the first words out of Jimmy's mouth are 'Linda hit me, Linda hit me!' "

Many parents of latchkey children are also concerned about the effect leaving their children alone has on their school performance. While many parents see no difference in school performance since self-care was initiated, a significant number think that leaving their children alone in the morning or afternoon has a negative effect on school achievement. Parents who leave their children alone in the morning worry that not helping them to prepare for school might affect their school work: "My son skips breakfast, which I'm sure affects his stamina and school performance. When I'm home in the morning he eats a good breakfast. Now, because I'm not there I can't make him eat. Sometimes I wake him up at five-thirty just to make sure he eats a hot breakfast." Another mother worries about her daughter's attitude in school: "I wish I could be with my daughter in the morning to make sure she leaves for school contented and in a good frame of mind. I think it's the key to having a good day at school."

Parents whose children are alone in the afternoon also have their concerns about the effect of self-care on school performance and homework is at the top of the list. Many parents wish they had more time to help their children with their homework, while others blame their children's poor performance in school on their working but don't blame homework specifically. "Sometimes I feel that my working is the reason my son's schoolwork has dropped. When I was home he used to be a good student with awards for grades, behavior and attendance. Now his teacher says he's not doing his best. I know he can do better, but I don't know how I can help him."

## Parents' Feelings

While some parents of latchkey children see the experience as a positive one, most feel some degree of guilt about leaving their children alone. This guilt is caused by a difference between their beliefs in what they should do and their actual behavior. Most parents of latchkey children today come from families in which their mothers didn't work. "I was raised in the old school that mothers shouldn't work, but should stay home with their children," one woman explained. "When I came home from school my mother was there to meet me. I should be there to meet my children." It is this myriad of "shoulds" that produces guilt in the parents of latchkey children. Even adults who didn't have the model of a parent meeting them at the door feel guilty about leaving their children alone: "I'm a former latchkey child myself and I know the loneliness of staying alone. I always wished my mother would be there when I got home from school, and now I'm doing the same thing to my daughter."

Parents who are ashamed of their behavior often urge their children to be discreet about their arrangement, since telling parents and friends would only reap more pressure and criticism. Women especially feel responsible, particularly those who view themselves as the primary caretakers. When that role isn't filled, regardless of the reason, it produces guilt.

But pressure on parents comes from internal as well as external sources. Most parents interviewed felt that children under twelve shouldn't be left alone, yet many admitted to leaving children as young as seven years old to care for themselves. One woman who called herself old-fashioned didn't think children under eighteen should be left alone. Still, her eight-year-old son spends three hours alone every day. This type of dichotomy between beliefs and behavior produces a tremendous amount of guilt. In addition, parents are ever fearful that something might happen to their children and if it did, the increased guilt would be unmanageable.

## Other Sources of Guilt

Parents of latchkey children feel guilty about not being home to meet their children after school as well as not having time to spend with their children once they get home from work. They try to act interested in their children's day, but find themselves both busy and exhausted. Many parents feel that not spending time after school cheats the child out of some of the joys of childhood. "My son always wants me to play a game with him and read him a story before bed," the mother of an eight-year-old latchkey child explained. "But by the time we have dinner and clean up, do homework and take a bath, it's 8:30 and time for George to get to bed since he has to get up early for school the next morning. We never have any time during the week to relax together." Children often reinforce this guilt or use it to get what they want by making statements like, "You never spend any time with me" or "You don't care about me." Statements like this are unnerving for any parent, but are especially painful to the parents of latchkey children.

Women who work solely for personal achievement and satisfaction generally feel guilty because they feel responsible for their children's having to stay alone. Women who must work because of their financial circumstances are often angry and frustrated by their inability to change the situation. They feel compelled to leave their children alone, either because they can't afford or can't find child care. "I have to work," one single parent commented. "For me it's not a matter of buying designer jeans for my kids, it's a matter of putting a roof over our heads and food on the table. I have to leave my children alone and nobody cares." The anger these women experience is often directed at government agencies which they feel are unresponsive to their needs.

Many parents feel so guilty about leaving their children alone that they search for ways to rationalize or minimize the arrangement: "My children aren't really latchkey children," a teacher remarked. "I get home shortly after they do . . . a half hour to an hour. Leaving children alone for less than an hour is certainly better than spending several hours alone." Leaving children alone for a half hour is certainly better than leaving children alone for several hours. But children alone for even an hour can experience fear, fights between siblings can develop or their safety can be endangered. Another parent was also quick to deny that his son was a latchkey child: "My wife works at a store a few minutes from home. My son is alone in the afternoons for about two hours, but I wouldn't consider him a latchkey child . . . he can ride his bike down to the store and talk to his mom if he has a problem." Although having a mother nearby does provide this boy with added security and reduces the stress he experiences when alone, he is still a latchkey child. Another parent explained that her fourth grade daughter was not a latchkey child because she checks in at the neighbor's. "When Belinda gets home from school she checks in at Mrs. Reynolds', who lives two doors down from us. If she's not there by a certain time, Mrs. Reynolds tries to get in touch with me as well as the school to see what the problem is. After checking in, Belinda goes home and waits for me. I get home between 5:30 and 6:00. If anything goes wrong, Belinda is supposed to go to Mrs. Reynolds for help." Belinda is fortunate to have Mrs. Reynolds as a resource, but she still spends her afternoons alone, without immediate adult supervision or companionship. Belinda is still vulnerable to the problems that affect most latchkey children.

Many parents acknowledge that having latchkey children interferes with work performance. For some the interference is the constant phone calls from bored and lonely children, or fighting siblings. "My daughter calls two or three times every afternoon and she wants to talk. These calls are regarded by the office staff as a nuisance. I resent their attitude. I know I don't work when I talk to my daughter but I'm her only relative and sometimes she needs to talk to me. I can't tell her to hang up, not when she's frightened or lonely."

Some parents remarked that it's not their children's calls that interfere with their productivity, but their own fears. "I hardly do anything from the time my daughter leaves school at 3:00 until I hear from her at 3:30. After she calls and I know she's safe, I'm o.k. until 5:00." Many parents feel uncomfortable as soon as they know their children are home alone: "Once my son is home I notice a definite loss of concentration. I worry about his whereabouts, especially if he doesn't answer the phone when I call."

Parents who leave their children alone before school also worry about their safety and complain about decreased productivity. A woman who leaves home when her daughter is still asleep explained that she doesn't get much work done in the morning because she worries about her daughter getting to school prepared. "I'm not worth much in the morning until my daughter is picked up and safely on her way to school," she said. "I worry about her and can't seem to concentrate on anything else."

As stated before, employers, too, notice the effects on parents of children who are left in self-care. Many reported decrease in productivity after 3:00 and the reluctance to stay past 5:00 among working mothers. "Three months ago my secretary started leaving her son alone in the afternoons," one man explained. "Before that he stayed at a friend's house. Once he started staying alone, I noticed a definite change in her behavior. Before, if we were in the middle of something or I needed some data that was important for a meeting, she would stay a few minutes late and get things together. Now when five o'clock comes she's out of the door no matter what's happening. In fact, she starts cleaning up before five, so that at five o'clock she leaves!"

Despite the benefits that can be gained, the latchkey experience is also a difficult one for parents. It adds additional stress to the job of parenting and guilt to parents who already worry that they are not doing an adequate job of raising their children. It forces parents to reassess their values and struggle to balance the priorities of work and home.

The task isn't easy, but thoughtful parents can come to terms with their feelings about leaving their children alone if they'll honestly face their reasons for doing so. Parents who are confident that they've exhausted all of the alternatives and feel they've adequately prepared their children for self-care need not make excuses, nor feel an inordinate amount of guilt for what is their rightful decision.

# Chapter 7
# LIFE BEFORE SCHOOL

Thousands of American children spend part of each weekday morning alone. The exact number or average amount of time alone is not known. What is known is that as more and more mothers enter or re-enter the labor force, more and more children must get themselves off to school. Some of these children are also in self-care after school.

The amount of time children spend alone in the morning is based on the difference between work schedules and school schedules. Work schedules vary according to the type of work and the employer. Secretaries usually start work between 8:00 and 9:00 A.M.; nurses work shifts twenty-four hours a day, but the morning shift usually starts at 7:00. Factory workers and sales persons work variable hours, depending on the hours of operation of the store or factory shift the person is expected to work.

Schools start at different times, too. Each school district or independent school is allowed by law to set its own hours of operation as long as school is in session for a predetermined number of hours per day. The number of hours required to constitute a full day of school is determined by the state and varies according to grade level. Most schools open between 8:00 and 9:00 A.M., but it is not unusual to find schools that open as early as 7:00 or as late as 9:30. In urban areas, where most children walk to school, all schools in the same district will start at the same time. But in suburban areas where children are bused to school, schools within the same district are often on a staggered schedule so that the same buses can be used to transport high school, junior high and elementary school children. Typically, high school students start school the earliest, junior high students next and elementary school students last. This means that in most districts, the youngest children spend the most time alone before school begins.

For parents who are expected at work before school begins, child care is a problem. Some parents arrange for another adult to get their children ready before school, but for most parents this is not an easily available option. "I hate to leave my children alone in the morning," said one young mother, "but what can I do? Everyone I know is rushing around in the morning, trying to get ready for school or work themselves. No one I know has the time to watch my children." With the demise of the extended family, few people have relatives living nearby they can call on for help. And hiring a babysitter early in the morning is difficult and expensive—or both. High school students are getting ready for school themselves, and professional babysitting services generally don't want to send a licensed babysitter to watch one or two children for only an hour. Most parents patch together arrangements with friends or neighbors and, if they can't, must leave children to get ready for school on their own.

Karlos is a single parent. He is a carpenter for a construction company, and must be at work at 7:00 A.M. "When I moved to Washington a year ago, the first thing I did was look for a school. I mean, even before I looked for a place to live. I figured after I found a school I liked, I'd find an apartment near the school so transportation wouldn't be a problem. My son Andrus was four, so I wanted a good preschool with an after-school program, also. The one I found is very expensive but worth it. Andrus can stay there as late as six o'clock. I try to pick him up by 4:30, but if I'm late I don't have to worry." Karlos also has to make arrangements for Andrus in the morning. "I have to leave for work at 6:30. Luckily I found an Italian woman who lives downstairs who can watch him. She's sixty-three and doesn't work. She comes up in the morning, has a cup of coffee, and reads the paper. At 7:30 she wakes Andrus up, gets him dressed, and makes him a nice hot breakfast. At 8:30, she walks him across the street to school. It's nice for Andrus, since he has no other relatives here; she's like a grandmother to him. It's nice for her, too. It gives her a little extra money, and a sense of being needed. I'm lucky she's reliable. If she wasn't, I don't know what I'd do." Karlos has gone to a great deal of trouble to provide his son with constant supervision, but it is expensive. "I pay over $100 a week for child care. Except for the rent, it's my biggest single expense."

Many children in kindergarten, first or second grade spend their mornings in day-care centers. Most of these centers open at 7:00 A.M.; a few open as early as 6:00. Parents drop their children at these centers on the way to work and then the children walk or take a bus to school. Many day-care centers in urban areas that have before- and after-school programs are located near schools so that transportation is not a problem. Others, in suburban areas, rely on school buses to transport children, or parents must contract with a private bus company to transport their children to school and often back to the day-care center at the end of the school day.

Some children spend their mornings at a friend's or neighbor's home before school. Lisa is five, a kindergarten student at a private school. Her mother, a single parent, is a teacher at a public high school. In order to accommodate the difference in work and school schedules, Lisa spends her mornings at a friend's. "I get up at five o'clock and get ready for school," Lisa's mother explains. "At 5:30, I wake up Lisa. Our mornings are very rushed. We have to leave the house by 6:00. I feel terrible that we can't spend time in the morning the way my mother and I did. All I keep saying to Lisa is, 'Hurry up, I love you. Hurry up, I love you.' Sometimes she has to eat her breakfast in the car. Toast and juice—some breakfast. She doesn't even feel like eating yet; she's still half asleep." When Lisa's mother drops her off at a friend's house at 6:20, everyone is still asleep. Lisa just cuddles up on the sofa and watches cartoons or naps until it's time to go to school at 8:30. Lisa's mother feels very uncomfortable about the whole arrangement, but is unable to come up with an alternative.

Whether children spend their mornings at a day-care center or the home of a friend, the problems are the same. Many of these children are up very early to accommodate the parents' work schedule. They might watch two or three hours of television before the school day begins. Breakfast is often rushed or eaten so early that the children are hungry by mid-morning.

Teachers are quick to point to the problems that disjointed care before school causes in the classroom. "I teach first grade," one teacher explained. "By the time I started reading at 9:00, supposedly the best learning time of the day, a lot of my students are too tired to listen. They have already spent an hour or more being shuttled from home to a day-care center and from a day-care center to school. Some have watched as much as two hours of cartoons. It's nine o'clock and they've been up for hours. Last week a little girl in my class was obviously upset; when I asked her what the matter was, she said she was mad because Jimmy hit her. I was confused since there was no Jimmy in my class. Then she explained that Jimmy is a little boy at the day-care center who always picks on her. What could I do?"

Another option for parents who must leave for work before school begins is to drop their children off at school. "My son, Tom, is a fifth grader at a Catholic school," one parent explained. "We get ready in the morning together. Then on my way to work I drop him off at school; otherwise he would have to take a public bus. He gets there a half-hour early because I have to be at work by eight o'clock, but this way, at least I'm sure he gets there on time." After school, Tom takes a public bus home. The riding, including one transfer, takes him an hour. Tom stays at home by himself in the afternoon from 4:00 until 5:30 when his parents get home.

The reasons parents drop their children off at school in the morning vary. One woman who has a daughter in the first grade doesn't like to leave her daughter alone in the house. "When I leave for work in the morning, I drop my daughter at school. Usually her teacher is there and she lets her come into the classroom and read a book. If her teacher isn't there, Cindy has to wait outside for a few minutes until she gets there. I don't know what I'm going to do in the winter when it's cold. I can't leave her standing on the school steps in the snow, but I can't leave her home alone either."

Although many parents realize the problems of dropping students off at school early, they still do it. Most claim they find it reassuring to know the children are somewhat supervised and that they made it to school on time. As one mother put it, "Although no one is outside watching the children when they get there early, I know that if my daughter got hurt, someone would come outside and help."

The problems that children who come to school early pose for school personnel are serious and the solutions are not simple ones. Teachers and administrators are split on how to handle the problem. They are torn between legal and moral responsibilities as well as their own personal interests. A discussion with the staff of a small urban Catholic school highlighted many of the problems: "School starts at 8:30," commented the principal. "We open the doors at 8:00. Yet when I get here at 7:00, there are children waiting outside. Their parents drop them off on the way to work. I constantly send messages home reminding parents not to send their children to school early. I stress that they will not be admitted into the building until eight o'clock. But it doesn't seem to make a difference; they send them anyway. Having children wait outside is upsetting. The biggest problem is the weather," the principal continued. "In the winter it's not uncommon to find that many children are sent to school an hour before it opens, even when temperatures are below freezing. When the weather isn't that cold, there is still the possibility of rain. There really is no shelter outside, so if it rains many children get wet. There are problems even in nice weather. The parking lot is a safety hazard. Cars are pulling up to let children out, while the early arrivals are playing football in the traffic. Fights and arguments are frequent, and someone is always pulling on the doors or banging on the windows yelling 'Let us in.' There are other problems parents don't think of. This is an elementary school, yet before school, junior high and high school students hang out on the playground and harass the younger students."

The teachers at this school are torn about how to handle the problem. Discussions often result in heated arguments. "I feel guilty not opening the door in the morning, especially in the winter," commented a third grade teacher. "I see a lot of my students standing there, obviously cold, and they beg me to let them in. 'Please let us come in and help you,' they say. It really pulls at my insides." This teacher would like to let her students in the room, but current school policy forbids teachers from allowing students to enter the classroom. "It's just not fair to let some students in and not others," explained the principal. "Most teachers are not like this one. They don't want their students inside before school opens."

One second grade teacher echoed the sentiments of much of the staff: "I get to school early in the morning to work, not to babysit. I need at least an hour in the morning to get ready for the school day—to be ready to teach these kids. Besides, I see enough of my students all day long. I don't want to see them for another hour in the morning." Another teacher agreed: "We're paid to start work at eight o'clock. Before then these kids are their parents' responsibility. I have my own kids, and I hire a babysitter in the mornings so I can do my work, not to watch someone else's kids."

After much debate this school arrived at a temporary solution on what to do about before-school care. "If it's cold or raining, the children are allowed to come inside and sit on the floor in the hallway. The janitor has agreed to watch them during that time. It's not the best solution, but it doesn't place any additional burden on the teachers and it gets the children out of the rain and cold. I'm lucky I have a cooperative janitor."

Increasingly, schools are being forced to deal with the problems of life before school. Some use the cafeteria as a holding pen and assign aides or the assistant principal to supervise the children. Thirty thousand schools participate in the school breakfast program, which hires staff to supervise children and provide a nutritious breakfast. Where no formal school arrangement exists, sympathetic teachers create jobs in the classroom to allow early admission of students.

Snow days and late openings also pose a problem. Teachers complain that even when school opens an hour or two late because of snow, parents still send their children at the regular time. Instead of having to wait an hour outside as usual, the children must wait two or three hours until school opens. "It makes no sense," one teacher said. "The reason school is opening late is because of inclement weather, and obviously that is no time for children to wait outside." A city principal echoed the teacher's feelings. "Sometimes I feel as though we don't have a communication system at all. Why bother to open school an hour late, if a large number of the students are going to show up at the same time anyway?"

When school is closed because of snow, administrators voice similar complaints. Even during a blizzard when it's obvious that school is closed, parents still drop their children at the school steps. In one district it was common practice for administrators to announce over the radio that school was closed, but teachers should report for work. That was stopped because so many parents would send their children to school knowing that someone would let them in and watch them until their parents could be reached—if they could be reached at all. One principal was quick to complain, "Even if school is closed, parents still drop their children at the door. I know this sounds unbelievable, but they wait until they see my car pull up and then they leave them. They know I won't leave their children outside to freeze. I have children of my own. After the child is in the building, I try to call the parents. They seem to be conveniently unavailable, out of the office, or in a meeting all day."

In defense of parents, many are left with few options when schools close because of snow. As one parent put it, "I never realized how often schools closed until I started to work. I feel like I'm always scurrying around trying to find someone to watch my children. If it's not a teachers' meeting, then it's a snow day." Snow days are especially difficult for parents because the decision that school will be closed is usually made at five or six in the morning, leaving most parents an hour or two at most to find someone to watch their children. Working parents with older children usually leave them home alone on snow days, but parents with younger children—those in kindergarten, first, second or third grade—generally try to find someone to stay with them. Many parents see their options as this woman did, who shyly admitted to leaving her six-year-old son at school on a snow day. "I didn't want to leave Mike alone all day. He's not old enough. He can stay home alone for an hour or two, but not for ten hours. I couldn't take another day off from work. I just couldn't. I've already missed a lot of work because Mike's been sick. I'm afraid if I miss much more work I'll lose my job. Leaving him at school was my only choice. I knew they'd take care of him." As an afterthought, she added, "They shouldn't have closed school anyway. There was only an inch of snow on the ground . . . The superintendent seems to forget that women work, too. It's not easy to find someone to watch your child at a moment's notice."

This parent's anger is not unusual. Working parents depend on school not only to educate their children, but also for child-care services. When school is cancelled, a contract for services is broken, and working parents are left without alternative child care arrangements. When school is cancelled because of snow, there is a hidden power struggle between parents and schools. Schools operate on the premise that parents are ultimately responsible for the care of their children. Parents believe it is the responsibility of schools to care for children on school days. In a sense the issue is between two groups fighting over the children—not who wants them, but who will watch them for the day.

For every parent who pays for a babysitter or takes a child to a day-care center or imposes on a friend, there is a parent who leaves a child alone in the morning. Other arrangements are not always possible. The classic picture of a mother standing at the door, handing her child a lunchbox and giving him a kiss goodbye is more a fantasy than a reality today. Some children wait as little as fifteen minutes before the school bus arrives or before they have to walk to school, but many children don't see their parents at all in the morning. These children get ready for school by themselves or with their siblings. Some parents do a great deal of planning and preparing for their children for school. Others leave their children to take care of the details by themselves.

Lisa, six, and Laurie, eight, are alone for over an hour before they have to leave for school. Their mother explains how she prepares the girls for school in the morning: "I have to leave for work at 7:30, so I'm not home when the children leave for school. I get them up at 6:30 and serve them breakfast. While I pack their lunches, they get dressed. By the time I leave for work, they're ready for school. I leave them on the couch in the living room watching TV . . . After I get to work, I call to tell them it's time to leave. They walk about four blocks to school." This mother goes to a lot of trouble to make sure her children are ready for school in the morning. "I have to get up at 5:00 every day. It takes me that long to get ready for work, make them a hot breakfast, make their lunches, pack their things and get them both ready for school in the morning. Don't think I'm not tired by the end of the day, but I think it's important that they start the day out right."

But even children like Lisa and Laurie, who are prepared by parents for the school day, pay a price being alone in the morning. They have to get up earlier than they normally would if either their mother or father didn't work, and at times the children get to school tired. In addition, they start the day watching cartoons. The only responsibility Lisa and Laurie have in the morning is getting to school and occasionally they don't make it. "Once I called to tell Lisa and Laurie it was time to leave for school but they didn't answer. I let the phone ring and ring and ring, but they still didn't answer. I figured maybe they left for school, or something happened to them. I didn't know what to think. So I waited a few minutes and called their school. They weren't there either. That's when I really started to panic. I left work in a hurry and headed straight home. When I got there, I found Lisa and Laurie exactly where I had left them— sound asleep on the couch." Lisa and Laurie are not unusual. Parents say that no matter how well they prepare their children, sometimes they don't make it to school on time or at all.

Some children don't see their parents at all in the morning. When they wake up their parents are gone and they get themselves ready for school. "My mother is a nurse," explained eleven-year-old Tracy, who lives alone with her mother. "She works the early shift, so when I get up for school in the morning, she's already left for work. I make my own breakfast, get dressed and get ready all by myself. I don't mind it. It makes me feel grown-up." Parents give their children varying amounts of assistance in the morning. Some call from work to wake them up; others set an alarm, while a few expect their children to get up by themselves.

Some parents lay out their children's clothes the night before; others let their children wear anything they choose. Some parents make their children's lunches before they leave for work; others leave money or give their children that responsibility. Some parents prepare their children's breakfast before they leave, so when the children wake up the table is set and breakfast is waiting; others expect their children to fend for themselves. Some parents call their children from work to tell them it's time to leave for school or to go outside to catch the bus. Others tell their children to leave at a prearranged time, or at the end of a certain TV program.

One mother said that she feels very guilty about leaving her daughter, Susan, alone in the mornings, so she does everything possible to make her daughter's mornings as pleasant as possible. "Susan is eight; in my mind she's still a baby, too young to be alone in the morning. But I work the early shift so we can have our afternoons together. I know it's depressing for her to wake up to an empty house, but it would be ridiculous to wake her up before I leave and then have her sit around alone for a couple of hours, waiting for school to start . . . I do what I can for her before I go to work in the morning. I lay out her clothes and make her breakfast, so I'm sure she's eating something healthy. I even write a little note that reminds her what she has to take to school and tells her that I miss her. Then when I get to work I call to wake her up. I don't like to wake her up too early, though, so she doesn't have a chance to be lonely. This way, she has just enough time, to eat, get dressed, get outside and catch the bus."

Many parents feel uncomfortable about leaving their children alone before school. Most of the concerns expressed by parents revolve around the responsibility of getting ready for school rather than their child's safety. "Of course I worry about leaving my child alone in the morning," the parent of a twelve-year-old girl said. "There's so much for her to remember: books, lunch, carfare, homework, gym shoes and flute. Who wouldn't worry?"

Children who are left to care for themselves in the morning are generally not left alone as long or at all in the afternoon. And the problems of life alone before school are somewhat different from the problems experienced by children who spend their afternoons alone. The morning is not a time filled with boredom or fear, nor is it a time when children spend most of their time watching TV, as those do who wait for their parents to come home from work. Instead, the morning is a busy time, filled with activity as children get ready for the school day, and it's an important time. The successful completion of morning tasks is essential to a successful school day. But without the help of parents, many times the child doesn't eat a good breakfast, or gets to school late, or goes unprepared, or doesn't make it to school at all.

### Breakfast

A good breakfast is critically important both physically and intellectually. A series of famous experiments, popularly called the Iowa Breakfast Studies, found that skipping breakfast resulted in decreased efficiency in the late morning hours, a reduced work output, slower mental reactions, increased muscular fatigue and a poor attitude toward schoolwork. Yet according to the Department of

Health, Education and Welfare, up to one-fourth of American children go to school without eating breakfast and even those children who have breakfast don't necessarily have a nutritional breakfast. Many eat empty-calorie foods such as soda pop, potato chips, cupcakes or candy bars. Studies that compare the breakfasts eaten by children of working mothers and nonworking mothers are unavailable, but it is clear that one of the problems children who spend their mornings alone must cope with is that of securing an adequate breakfast. How well children do this is debatable.

While many parents expect their children to make their own breakfast in the morning, they forbid them to use the stove. These children eat foods that are quick and easy to prepare such as cold cereal, toast or Pop Tarts. Parents who leave the house before their children are awake are never sure what their children eat for breakfast or if they eat at all. Even preparing breakfast ahead of time is no guarantee that children will eat it, as one former latchkey child explained. "When I was little, my grandmother raised me. She was very old-fashioned, an old Italian woman. Every morning she made me breakfast before she left for work—eggs, toast, milk and juice. When I woke up she was gone, but there sat these two sunny-side-up eggs looking at me. I don't know how long that breakfast sat there every morning, but the milk and juice were warm and the eggs were ice cold. I never ate it. Instead I put the eggs down the incinerator after I broke the yolks and smeared them around on my plate so it was sufficiently dirty to look like I ate them. Then I poured the milk down the sink and rinsed the glass so she couldn't tell. I did drink the juice and eat the toast. It was almost like a little ritual. Every night my grandmother asked me if I ate my breakfast, and every night I said yes. This went on for years."

Many children who walk to school either carry their breakfasts with them or use their lunch money or allowance to buy breakfast at a fast-food store. Some parents even give their children lunch money and breakfast money. It is not uncommon to find groups of children sitting in the schoolyard before school, eating their breakfasts. Breakfasts for these children who don't want to eat at home alone is a bag of dry cereal or potato chips, pastries and soft drinks. All of these foods can be transported easily and eaten while talking to friends. The family breakfast table no longer exists so children create their own family group at school.

When questioned about what children eat for breakfast, a Seven-Eleven supermarket buyer stated that the most frequent breakfast items purchased by children are loose doughnuts and prepacked pastries, such as Twinkies or cupcakes. To drink, some children buy ten-ounce bottles of orange juice, but more children buy soft drinks. The owner of a small dairy store across the street from a school says he serves the same children breakfast every day. "I see the same maybe forty or fifty kids every day. They live in the neighborhood and stop in on their way to school. They buy cupcakes, doughnuts and pastries to eat; and milk, orange juice or soda to drink. This store could do a larger before-school business, but the school across the street forbids the kids to leave school grounds once they have arrived, so the ones who take the bus can't come into the store."

Larger fast-food chains, like McDonald's, have not capitalized on the large children's breakfast market. According to an advertising executive, most of the people who have breakfast at McDonald's are adult males. But stop at a McDonald's located near a school early in the morning, and you are guaranteed to find school children there eating breakfast. What do they eat? "A little of everything," commented one McDonald's store manager: "Hash browns, sweet rolls, Egg McMuffins."

Children who take the bus to school can't stop at a fast-food store on the way to school. Instead, they must eat breakfast at home or not at all, unless they buy something to eat on the school bus from other children. Children routinely sell and trade food on the school bus. Once off the bus, some children sneak to a fast-food store to buy something to eat before the day begins.

Teachers are quick to point out the link between a poor breakfast and a poor school performance. Teachers complain that the diet of children before school begins—sugar-coated cereals, doughnuts and drinks—are high in sugar content and give students only temporary energy. As one teacher put it, "These kids come to school on a sugar high. Some are so pumped up that they're impossible to teach. Then about ten o'clock they're exhausted as their blood sugar drops. It's almost as if you can see the energy pour out of them." Those who don't eat breakfast come to school hungry, far from an optimal condition for learning. Hungry children often leave the classroom under the pretense of going to the bathroom in order to look for something to eat. One teacher said, "I had a little boy in my class last year, Rex, who would always ask to go to the bathroom early in the morning. I never thought anything of it until one morning another boy, Mike, had to go to the bathroom, too. We have a rule, only one child out of the room at a time. But since it was an emergency, I let Mike go anyway. When he came back, he told me Rex was in the bathroom eating his lunch. Upon investigation, I found out that Rex wasn't eating his lunch, but the lunch of another child that he had removed from a convenient locker."

Administrators have long been aware of the problems of children coming to school without a nutritional breakfast or without breakfast at all. Twenty years ago, a Catholic school principal opened her school early in the morning and began a breakfast program of milk and doughnuts for a nominal fee. Soon there was enough concern about the nutrition of American children to start a pilot program in 1966 under the Child Nutrition Act, where breakfast was served to needy children or in areas where children had to travel long distances to school. The program has expanded and now any school in the country can apply for the federal breakfast program. The program, currently in 30,000 schools, serves 3.4 million breakfasts a day to school children mostly in the elementary grades. This program costs American taxpayers $335 million at present, and in its fiscal 1984 budget the United States Department of Agriculture proposed spending $353 million for children's food programs. Ninety percent of the children involved receive breakfast free or at a reduced price. Only ten percent of the children involved pay the full price. Determination of whether a child pays the full price, the reduced price or obtains breakfast free is based on family income. The same guidelines are used that determine free lunch qualification. For breakfast children in the program receive one-half pint of milk, one-half cup of fruit or vegetables or juice and one slice of whole grain or enriched bread, or its equivalent in cereal, rolls or muffins; and as often as possible, protein-rich foods such as cheese, peanut butter, eggs or meat. A typical breakfast might be a banana, granola and milk, or orange wedges, bread with peanut butter and milk.

Although every school in the United States, private as well as public, is eligible for the federal breakfast program, only one-third participate in it. Full participation might meet the nutritional needs and even some of the psychological needs of the growing number of children who spend their mornings alone before school, yet many administrators are hesitant to participate in the program. A report from the Children's Foundation, entitled *Barriers to School Breakfast,* outlines some of the reasons schools cite for not participating in the program. They include scheduling buses and space, obtaining adequate supervision and having an adequate facility. Financial concerns, although stated by many administrators, are largely unwarranted since the program receives almost one-hundred-percent funding from the government. The real barriers to school breakfasts are not logistical, but attitudinal. Many administrators are opposed to school breakfast because of the additional responsibility and work it implies. Others are opposed because they see the role of the school as educating children, not feeding them. They argue that the home is responsible for providing breakfast and that school breakfasts weaken the family unit.

But most administrators who have used the program support it. A principal from South Carolina commented, "Breakfast is one of the single best things the government has done. I totally support it. You can tell the difference. The kids are more alert and it pays dividends in the curriculum areas of the school." A nutritionist from Maryland pointed to the psychological benefits of the program: "The school breakfast program supplies more than nutrition. It is a warm and stable influence in the life of a child who lives in a cold and unstable world."

Many schools that do not participate in the federal breakfast program still serve food to children in the mornings. Many private schools serve snacks in the morning, or tell children to bring a snack to eat mid-morning. Some public schools have machines from which children can buy food during the day and others open the cafeteria in the morning or during study halls so that children can buy something to eat.

## Lunch

Breakfast is not the only nutritional concern of school personnel. Lunch presents another problem. There are approximately forty-six million children in grades kindergarten through twelve in the United States. Approximately twenty-three million participate in the federal lunch program. The remaining twenty-three million children bring lunches from home or don't eat at all. Increasing numbers of children skip lunch and save their money to buy candy or play electronic games after school. Others spend their lunch money before they get to school. And just because a child buys a lunch is no guarantee that it will be eaten. Any cafeteria worker can testify to the large amount of food thrown away daily.

It is most often the responsibility of the latchkey child to prepare his or her own lunch. Many parents are too busy in the morning to pack a lunch. Some of these children make lunch while their parents supervise them, or at least check on the contents. But most pack their own lunches after their parents have left for work and receive no supervision. Teachers who have cafeteria duty are quick to spot student-made lunches. "Students usually make lunches that are quick and easy. Often they are not very well-balanced. "When I have cafeteria duty I see ketchup sandwiches or butter sandwiches for lunch. Some children bring just plain bread. Prepacked foods are very popular. Chips, Pop Tarts, candy bars, anything they can grab out of the refrigerator and put in a paper bag quickly. Raw hot dogs. I mean anything!" Many parents who work have no idea of the quality or the quantity of the lunch their children pack for themselves. Even children who know about nutrition will pack lunches that are less than healthy.

Sabrina was a fifth grade student who lived with her mother and younger brother. Her father, who had been a physician, died two years earlier. Sabrina's mother worked to support the family. She left early in the morning. Sabrina, who packed her own lunch, routinely brought a sandwich, an apple and several candy bars to school. During a parent-teacher conference the teacher mentioned to Sabrina's mother that Sabrina should cut down on the amount of candy she eats. Sabrina's mother was startled. "Sabrina's father was a doctor and kept the children on a low-sugar diet," she said. "We don't even have sugar in the house, much less candy. We sweeten everything with honey." Sabrina was buying candy on the way to school to add to her lunch.

Lunch was also a problem for another seventh grade boy who was expected to care for himself. One principal explained, "I was walking down the hall and I accidently bumped into a student and knocked his lunch out of his hand. I picked up the lunch and noticed it was suspiciously light so I looked inside. There I saw two miniature doughnuts. I immediately questioned the student and asked whether his mother was aware of what he brought for lunch. He told me that his mother was in Chile for two weeks and that he was completely on his own. Ramon had made his lunch himself."

## Absenteeism

Absenteeism is one of the major problems facing American schools today. The Bureau of Educational Statistics reports that on any one school day between six and seven percent of the nation's school children are absent, with some schools having an absentee rate as high as ten percent. And, although undocumented, observers note that children who are alone in the morning experience higher levels of absenteeism than their adult-watched counterparts. School personnel also notice higher levels of absenteeism beginning at about the third or fourth grade, when parents tend to begin leaving their children home alone.

Transportation is one reason why a child who is not sick but is alone in the morning might miss school. Fifty-seven percent of public school children are transported to school daily at public expense. Children in suburban and rural areas rely on school buses to transport them to school. A child who misses the bus has no way to get to school without the help of a parent. Few parents are able or willing to leave work, drive home, drive their child to school and then drive back to work. In most cases, when a child calls a parent at work to report that he or she missed the school bus, parents often tell the child to stay home that day. There are many reasons a child might miss the school bus. "I overslept," "I couldn't find my homework," or "I just didn't get ready in time" are frequent replies. Many children are home alone in the morning watching television. Engrossed in their favorite cartoons, they lose track of time or stay that extra minute to see the ending and miss the bus. One boy when asked why he missed the bus in the morning, responded, "My dogs." He said that every morning "I have to lock the dogs in the basement before I leave for school. Otherwise they tear up the place. Sometimes I can't catch them."

Children who live in an area where they can walk to school or take public transportation don't cite missing a school bus as their reason for being absent, but the consequences of being late are cited as a reason. Many schools insist on a late note for children arriving after a certain time. A child who is home alone and arrives late will often not be admitted to school because he lacks a note. To avoid the hassle this child will call his or her parent and explain that he or she is late and can't go to school now because he or she lacks the necessary note. The parent will often give the child permission to stay home and later write a note to excuse the child's absence. This note is an expression of the parent's guilt. Many parents feel partially responsible for their child's absences, since they aren't there to help their child get ready in the morning. One sixth grade boy was very candid about his manipulative behavior. "If I'm going to be late for school, I just stay home. I go to a Catholic school and if you're late even five minutes, you have to serve an hour of detention. Sometimes my mom gets mad at me for missing so much school. Then I tell her it's her fault for not helping me in the morning, that I'm doing the best I can. She doesn't say anything."

Children who are alone in the morning must remember to communicate with their parents regarding school business the night before. A child who wakes up to an empty house and suddenly remembers, "I was supposed to have this test signed," or "I need a note because I was absent from school yesterday," or "Today is the last day to bring the permission slip and money for the trip Friday," will often choose to stay home rather than go to school without the expected materials. In this situation, many parents will cooperate with the child's absence, especially if the parents feel partially responsible.

Other children might choose to stay home for a less than legitimate reason. Maybe they didn't have that critical homework assignment completed or failed to study for an important test, so instead of dealing with the consequences of not being prepared they decide to stay home. Children in this situation might honestly explain to their parents the reasons they want to stay home, but more than likely they'll call their parent at work and say "I don't feel well," "My stomach hurts" or "I have a headache." Parents, unable to make an adequate diagnosis over the telephone and feeling somewhat guilty anyway generally tell the child to stay home. Some children don't even bother to call their parents to ask them if they can stay home. During a discussion on the problems of latchkey children the teacher of a second grade student produced a note from a parent that said, "Please excuse Brandy's absence. She had a sore throat yesterday and neglected to call me at work to tell me." Later that morning the student must have had what educators jokingly call, "the miraculous nine o'clock cure," since many students who avoid school feel remarkably well as soon as the bus finishes their route.

At times several children of working parents will not go to school and then spend the day together. One school administrator reported more than one hundred phone calls during a year from neighbors complaining about groups of children in the next apartment or house. "Starting at about the fifth grade, students skip school and spend the day at a friend's with or without their parents' knowledge. We find out about it because they play the stereo loud, roughhouse, hang out windows and in general upset the neighbors. The people that call expect us to enter the house and take these children to school, but by law we are not allowed to do that."

Attendance, a problem on most school days, becomes even more drastic when school opens late because of transportation problems. Children typically get to school by one of four methods: they walk, are driven to school by their parents, take public transportation or ride school buses. Students who walk or take public transportation are not inconvenienced when school opens late. But parents who drive their children to school are faced with a problem. If schools open an hour late, they can either drop their children at school an hour early, or arrive at work themselves an hour late. Neither of these is an attractive option. Many parents don't want to leave their child at school an hour or two before school opens in inclement weather and they don't have the luxury of arriving at work an hour or two late. The easiest alternative is to let children stay home. The parent reasons that it's not a full day of school the children are missing.

Children who take the school bus also have higher levels of absenteeism when school opens late. Children who are alone in the morning are instructed to go outside at a certain time. When school opens late, children in the younger grades cannot make the adjustment to the new time they are supposed to go outside. Many children judge what time it is by the end of a certain TV program. Once school opens late regular cues are eliminated and children are late. Even children who know what time to go outside on a late opening day are often discouraged by the cold weather. "During the cold and snowy weather, buses don't run exactly on schedule," one administrator noted. "Many students go outside and wait a few minutes, get discouraged and go back inside. Then they take the day off. When their parents get home and ask why they missed school the response often is, "The bus didn't come."

Lateness for school is another problem parents aren't aware of that plagues children who are on their own in the morning. Children who walk or use public transportation can arrive at school whenever they get there. Sometimes children will go outside and play with their friends before school, get involved in a television program or oversleep because they are staying up too late at night. One day a sixth grade boy, Frank, arrived at school with a friend at ten o'clock. Frank had a note from his father that asked the teacher to excuse him. One teacher of an inner-city school complained about the problem of trying to teach when children come late. "I hate these students coming late. It disrupts the whole lesson and it's the same ones every day. Last week this boy in my class, Frank and his best friend Reggie, walked in at ten o'clock. They both had notes. But I was so angry, I called their parents anyway. As it turns out, the parents had no idea their boys were constantly late. They hadn't written any of the notes. Frank's mother was especially startled. She was home when Frank left the house that morning in plenty of time to get to school on time . . . it seems he was stopping at Reggie's house in the morning before school. No one else was at Reggie's house so the boys fooled around for a couple of hours.

## Getting Ready for School

Children who are alone in the morning also have the responsibility of dressing properly for school. Frequently they simply wear what they like. "It's not uncommon to see children wearing the same clothes two or three days in a row," one teacher remarked. "These are not poor children but children who are home alone in the morning, so they wear their favorite outfit day after day." Some children come to school looking as though they just got out of bed. No one is there to make sure they brushed their teeth or combed their hair, so they often forget. Sometimes teachers wonder how parents could send their children to school without even washing their faces, but they don't realize that the parents aren't home.

Proper dress for the weather is also a problem. Students who are home alone in the morning routinely go to school without hats, gloves, even coats in the middle of winter. It is not uncommon for children to go to school with tennis shoes on when there is snow on the ground, or to wear a sweater when it is pouring rain. These children have no concept of temperature and have difficulty selecting outerwear appropriately. They wear what they like or what they think looks "cool" regardless of the weather.

Children who are alone in the morning also have the responsibility of coming to school prepared for that day's work. This might mean homework, or the student might be expected to remember to have notes signed or to bring books, a gym suit, a musical instrument, a pocket calculator, library books, lunch money or other materials as requested by the teacher. It's easy for children to forget one of several things if they rush to prepare for school in the morning. Others don't forget, but they simply can't produce a signature or lunch money when they're on their own.

### Special Stresses of Children Who are Alone in the Morning

Latchkey children cope in the morning with a set of problems that are different from those that their afternoon counterparts deal with, and coping with these problems produces some degree of stress. Children who are home alone before school must complete certain tasks within a certain amount of time, and failure to complete one or several of them carries with it some natural consequences. Children who fail to prepare and eat an adequate breakfast must sit in class hungry. Children who fail to arrive at school on time will be reprimanded for their lateness. Students who don't dress appropriately for the weather risk getting cold or wet. Children who neglect to bring an adequate lunch or money for lunch will spend their afternoon hungry. Children who don't come to school prepared will be punished or reprimanded by the teacher. All of these possible consequences increase the anxiety level in children who must prepare themselves for school in the morning.

The stress on children is further increased if they have additional responsibilities to cope with in the morning. Many children are assigned the care of pets in the morning. Many parents don't realize that children are too busy getting ready for school themselves to accept the added responsibility of animal care. Dogs and cats can be less than cooperative, especially when a small child is trying to put them in the basement or bring them inside for the day. The stress of trying to deal with an uncooperative animal when under the time constraints imposed by a bus schedule is significant. In general it's better for parents to care for pets before they leave in the morning rather than add to the child's list of duties.

Watching younger siblings before school increases the stress older siblings experience. Having the responsibility not only of getting oneself to school on time but also a younger sibling is burdensome. All of the morning tasks are doubled, and all of the consequences for not completing those tasks successfully are increased. Because children don't have the control over their younger siblings that their parents have, the task becomes a difficult one. Ginny is in the fifth grade. She and her brother, Brad, a second grader at the same school, are awakened by a phone call from their mother who is at work. Ginny makes breakfast for the two of them. "Usually we have cereal for breakfast and watch cartoons while we eat. When I finish eating I get dressed and then help Brad get dressed. I watch the clock. We go outside and catch the bus at 8:15." Although it sounds simple enough, sometimes Ginny has trouble. "Brad doesn't want to listen to me. I tell him to hurry up, we have to go outside and catch the bus . . . he says 'just a minute.' I tell him to put his coat on, that it's cold outside . . . he says he doesn't need it. I tell him to eat his breakfast . . . he says he's not hungry. Then if we miss the bus, I have to call my mom at work. She comes home and takes us to school. But is she mad! She says it's my fault. I'm the one who can tell time so I should make sure we catch the bus. But it wasn't my fault. It's not fair."

Parents who expect older children to assist younger siblings in getting ready for school in the morning must be sensitive to the amount of responsibility they're giving them and help them in as many ways as feasible. Establishing a routine and doing as much preparation as possible will relieve the oldest child of some responsibility. Making decisions in advance, such as what each child will wear and have for breakfast, will decrease the stress the oldest child feels.

It seems that there may be advantages, if a parent has a choice, in leaving a child alone in the morning rather than in the afternoon.

More time is allowed between parent and child if the parent's work-day ends relatively soon after school is dismissed, and the child need not cope with bouts of fear, loneliness or boredom that empty after-noon hours can afford. But special care must be taken, if this arrangement is possible, to prepare the child to deal with the pressures he or she will have to cope with in order to get to school adequately prepared and on time.

# Chapter 8

# PARENT–CHILD RELATIONSHIPS AND THE LATCHKEY EXPERIENCE

The past thirty years have witnessed a sharp change in American child-rearing practices and the relationship between parents and children. Today, most American parents have limited contact with their children, unlike the way things were as recently as the 1950s when women thought of themselves largely in terms of their success as mothers first and wives second. Now the interests of women are more varied. Women still define themselves as mothers, but that image has been extended to include careers, their relationships with their husbands and friends and their personal interests. As a result, today's woman spends less time with her children than a mother of thirty years ago did. Fathers, the once absent parents of the past who defined their responsibility in terms of wage earning and providing material goods, have become more actively involved in the child-rearing process. But this gain in time fathers spend with their children is not enough to equal the amount of time mothers can't be with them. The end result is that parents on the whole are spending less time with their children. Latchkey children are the first to feel the effects when time is at a premium and will often complain about the lack of attention. "I haven't seen you all day," or "We never spend any time together," are echoed routinely.

Not only has the amount of time children spend with their parents changed, but the nature of that relationship is also different. Children frequently comment that the time they do spend with their parents is not as enjoyable as it might be. One boy complained, "All my mother and I ever do together is watch television . . . nothing fun." An eleven-year-old girl who was more articulate explained her relationship with her mother this way: "I cook dinner for me and my mom every night. She does the dishes while I do my homework and then we watch TV together until nine o'clock when I go to bed. On Saturdays we go shopping for groceries and maybe go to the mall. On Sundays we go to church and maybe visit my grandmother in the afternoon. The same thing every week. We never do anything special." What's striking about this girl's relationship with her mother is that during the week they have very little interaction. When they are together, they do parallel activities rather than things that can be shared. This could be changed if they did the dishes together and then the mother helped the girl with her homework. After all the necessary chores were completed they could play a game or get involved in an arts and crafts project together, which would help build a relationship that is strained because of the limited amount of time they have together.

Some families with latchkey children do manage to stay close and interact in a positive way. John, who is ten, has a real sense of family even though both his parents work. "My mother and father both work so I have to take care of myself after school. That's my way of helping the family because we can't afford a babysitter. Then when my mother comes home at 4:30, we talk about school and stuff and cook dinner together. When daddy comes home at 6:00 we all eat. After dinner we watch TV or play a game of cards or something."

It is important for parents to remember that maintaining a high-quality relationship while working does not come without effort. Research demonstrates that women who choose to pursue a career and strive to maintain a close relationship with their children must make personal sacrifices. They sleep less and have less time for the pursuit of personal interests. Time is spent with children on the weekends to compensate for the lack of time during the week and evening outings are limited. But these sacrifices are necessary when both parents work in order to help the children feel they are a wanted part of the family rather than a liability. A child who feels loved and needed will have a much easier time coping with self-care than a child who feels unloved and neglected.

Children in self-care often state that they don't see very much of their parents and as a result don't feel close to them. Latchkey children who spend their afternoons with older siblings often use their older brother or sister as a parent substitute. A six-year-old boy who stays home with his ten-year-old brother explained that he seldom sees his mother. "She works in the day and is always at meetings and stuff at night. If I need something I go to my brother . . . he takes care of me." An eleven-year-old girl who lives with both parents described the same problem. "The only time me and my sister see our parents is on weekends or when we go to my grand-mother's house for a vacation. Otherwise we're on our own."

Children who don't have siblings often lean on friends for compan-ionship. Karen is ten and the daughter of two working parents. Her best friend Linda, whose parents are divorced, lives with her mother. Every afternoon Linda visits Karen. "At 5:00 I go back home," explained Linda. "Karen's parents come home at 5:30, and I leave before they get there. But my mom doesn't get home until 6:30." Because of the time they spend together, Karen and Linda have become very close. "If I have a problem I talk to Karen," Linda said. "My mother's too tired and busy to listen to me when she gets home." Karen and Linda, like all children, need to be loved. They find warmth and support from each other since these needs are not now being met by their parents.

Children who are not allowed to have friends in the house or go outside and play use the telephone to make contact with others. These children learn to share school experiences and problems with friends in the absence of their parents. One common statement made by latchkey children is that they feel their parents are uninterested or unavailable, at best. In fairness to parents, there are few who can afford lengthy telephone conversations from the workplace with their children. Instead, working parents must wait until they get home to discuss relevant issues and school happenings. They are surprised when their children are reluctant to repeat what they've already discussed at length with a friend. Many parents also don't understand their children's need to talk to friends and attempt to limit their telephone contact with others. "Don't talk on the phone so much," is a common request from a parent with latchkey children. "What if I have to call you from work because of an emergency? I can never get through."

Parents find that even when they are home in the evening their children don't talk to them about daily events or problems. "I work in a grocery store," one woman explained, "so I can't call my daughter JoAnn from work. She's in the sixth grade so I figure she's all right until I get home at 5:30. When I get home, I try to spend time with her. I ask her what happened at school, but she always answers, 'Nothing.' After dinner she doesn't want to spend time with me. Instead, she spends hours talking to her friends about what happened at school. I don't understand it. When I ask her what happened at school, she says, 'Nothing,' yet she spends hours talking to her friends about 'nothing.' " This woman's problem with her daughter is neither unusual nor difficult to understand. JoAnn, like many latchkey children, sees her friends, not her mother, as confidants. She shares a common experience with them and they are there when she needs them. Latchkey children learn to trust and depend on their friends. They establish a pattern of sharing problems and that pattern is not broken when a parent walks through the door. In fact it continues, to the frustration of this mother and many parents like her.

There is a larger group of latchkey children who don't express the problems they are experiencing with anyone, parents or friends. Stacy, who spends her afternoons alone hiding in a closet or under the covers of her parents' bed, runs downstairs and pretends everything is fine as soon as her mother walks in the front door and calls her name. Mike, who sits on the living room sofa watching TV with a baseball bat beside him to "beat up" intruders, too afraid to get up even to use the bathroom, says "Hi" and smiles as if everything's all right when his mother walks through the front door. Mike and Stacy are not unusual. Nor is Kevin, who finds the three hours he spends alone every afternoon "long and lonely," but doesn't complain about it either.

The reasons these children and millions like them don't complain are complex. Primarily, they want to please their parents, who praise them for staying alone and acting mature. Parents clearly and frequently express their expectations for their children with statements like, "You're big enough to take care of yourself until I get home from work." Although apparently harmless, this kind of statement pressures the child to cope, or at least pretend to. If the child complains that he is scared or lonely, he's admitting that he's not mature enough to take care of himself after school, making him feel much younger than his years.

Children also fail to tell their parents the problems they're having because they're hesitant to add more pressure to parents who already seem stressed and overwhelmed. Too often children hear and worry about the stress their mothers feel trying to juggle work and home responsibilities. Women who must shoulder these responsibilities often express their fatigue, exhaustion and frustration indirectly to the children. Comments like "I have to work all day and then come home and clean up after you" make children feel like a burden. In order not to seem like a burden to their parents, these children withhold complaints and struggle to cope alone.

Children also view their problems with limited perspective—they see the problems but not the solutions. As one boy put it, "What good would it do to tell my mom I'm scared? What can she do about it? She tells me all the time we're broke, that she has to work. We don't have enough money to hire a babysitter. I have to stay alone." This mother apparently shares her financial concerns with her son. He worries about the family's finances, and with his limited perspective isn't able to see a solution to his problems. He knows babysitters cost money, so he doesn't talk about his fears—to him it's a hopeless situation.

Former latchkey children also remember a reluctance to discuss with their parents the problems of staying alone, many for the same reasons expressed by children today. Some explained that they didn't want to burden their parents with any more problems, like the woman who said, "I didn't want to add to the guilt I knew my mom was already feeling." Another woman felt the same way: "I know my mom wanted things to be different. I didn't want to give her anything else to worry about." Other former latchkey children didn't express their feelings to their parents because, as with the boy mentioned above, they felt as though talking about it wouldn't change anything.

Some former latchkey children are still angry with their parents for what they felt was their insensitivity to them, even though their latchkey experience ended over twenty years ago. One woman who had to watch her younger sisters from two in the afternoon until midnight because her mother worked nights after she divorced, is still evidently hostile. "The game was that I had to care for her ineptitude and guilt. A discussion wasn't worth it, because she swore she had to work nights." Unfortunately, this woman was never able to share her frustration with her mother. Had she been able to do so, some of the problems would probably have been worked out and their relationship would be better today.

For these former latchkey children, the major reason for the lack of discussion about their experiences was the lack of open lines of communication between parent and child. The parent was not the child's usual confidant, and problems regarding staying alone were no exception. One woman summed it up concisely when she said, "I just didn't tell my problems to my parents." Many felt their parents were too tired or too busy to listen. "It was always hard to discuss my feelings with them. I never felt like they cared," was a comment by another former latchkey child. Some were afraid to bring up the topic. "I was too full of highly-charged repressed feelings. Talking about how I felt staying alone would have been like opening Pandora's box, so I chose to keep quiet."

Those who did discuss the experience with their parents talked in terms of specific problems, and for many this meant specific complaints about their after-school responsibilities. Comments like, "I felt like the mother," were made by two former latchkey children. Another woman who lived alone with her father after her mother died had to take over all the responsibilities of maintaining their home. "Taking care of a whole house was too much for me," she recalls. "It wasn't my fault my mother died. I told my father to hire a maid, or if he wanted me to do all those chores, I should have more freedom." There were other specific complaints about staying alone after school. One man complained to his mother that he had missed after-school activities; another woman told her mother she was upset by the constant fighting between her brothers and sisters. But for some who felt very comfortable with their parents, conversations centered around nonspecific complaints, such as, "I don't like staying home" or "I want you to quit work and stay home in the afternoons." This type of complaint is difficult for parents to bear because it raises the level of guilt parents are already experiencing. But perhaps the most difficult statement for most parents to accept was recalled by a woman who started watching her three younger brothers and sisters at age eleven. "At times I felt like I was doing just fine, while other times I felt like nobody loved me."

Latchkey children who won't talk to their parents about their problems usually won't talk to other adults either. They have been trained by their parents to be cautious of adults for their own safety to the point where even a teacher can't be taken into confidence. As a result, most teachers have no idea how many latchkey children are in their classroom, and when pressed to guess, their estimates are grossly under actual figures. A sixth grade teacher in a wealthy Maryland suburb was appalled to find out that twenty-four out of the twenty-eight children in her class returned home to an empty house each day. A first grade teacher who knew she had two latchkey children in her classroom (because she had driven them home from school on a rainy day) was surprised to find out that there were several others. And an inner-city principal who claimed there were no latchkey children in her school because most of the parents were unemployed was embarrassed when a walk through her school found children in the halls with housekeys obviously displayed. Latchkey children are taught to be discreet. And adults are generally insensitive to the clues these children give regarding self-care.

But the silence of children runs deeper than the insensitivity of adults. Many children keep silent to protect their parents. Kandra, an eight-year-old girl, was asked if she discussed with her mother how she felt about staying alone in the afternoon. She responded, "Yes. Me and my mom are very close. I asked her if it was against the law for her to leave me alone after school since I was only eight. She said it wasn't since I was only alone for an hour." Many children like Kandra understand that their parents' behavior is frowned upon. They fear if they tell someone that they are home alone in the afternoon their parents will be arrested and wind up in jail. Then they would really be alone. So instead of risking losing a parent, many keep quiet. Marcel is eight years old. He lives with his father and spends several hours alone each day. Marcel is afraid that if anyone finds out that his father leaves him alone so much he will be taken away from his father and placed in a foster home. This fear was evident in our initial talks with him. When asked how he spends his afternoons, Marcel answered, "Are you from Children and Family Services?" He knew his father was neglecting him but he protected his father because he didn't want to live with anyone else. It was only after Marcel was assured that the interviewer was not from Children and Family Services and that nothing would happen to him or his father, that he would talk about his experiences after school.

Communication between parent and child also affects how the child perceives the self-care experience. Parents that feel positive about the experience will more likely have children who in turn also feel positive about the experience. Negative parental feelings and concerns are also directly and indirectly communicated to children.

Although it's important for parents to communicate with their children about safety precautions, such discussion can heighten fears indirectly. Statements like, "Be sure to lock the door when you come in," "Don't open the door for anyone," and "Don't tell anyone you are home alone," are intended to protect the child, but they also communicate danger. They tell the child it is unsafe for them to stay home alone. Rules like this, if given hastily and without explanation, can promote fears. Concerned parents need to share concerns with their children in a way that instills caution but does not heighten fear. Parents also should not intentionally frighten children into obeying rules by giving examples of what happened to children who didn't obey similar rules, or what might happen if rules aren't obeyed. One second grade boy was petrified when left alone. When questioned, he explained, "My mom said people are bad. 'If you let anyone in they'll hurt you. Be sure to keep the door locked all the time.' " This little boy's fears were intensified by his mother's statements. "I don't open the door for nobody," he went on. "A couple of times someone knocked at the door and I didn't answer it. I lay very still on the floor and pretended no one was home. But it scared me. I was afraid they would break a window and come in and hurt me."

Parents also express direct concerns for their child's safety when they make statements like "I worry about you. Are you sure you're going to be all right alone?" or "Call me as soon as you get home so I know that you got home safely." Voicing concerns in this way can also intensify fear. Frequently parents don't share their concerns directly with their children, but will do so in speaking with another adult which, all too often, the child overhears. The mother who discusses her guilt feelings and concerns with a friend when her child is in the room is maybe promoting fear. It's not good for children to overhear statements like "I'm worried about Johnny being alone. In fact, some days I can't do any work thinking about him in this house alone." When they hear these statements they know that their parents worry about them. Children then reason that if they're worried, they must not be totally safe. Even very young children are aware of their parents' concerns. A seven-year-old girl who stays home with her nine-year-old sister was aware of how her parents felt about self-care. "My parents worry about me and my sister fighting or about someone breaking into the house," she said. An eight-year-old boy who stays home with his ten-year-old sister was also quick to express his mother's fears. "My parents worry about me and my sister. They're scared someone will break in and me and Francine will be killed or raped." In this case, the boy not only internalizes his mother's fears, but also uses her specific phraseology. Adult fears can easily overwhelm young children and cause high levels of stress. It is important for parents to communicate concern to their children, but not to frighten them unduly with specific fears.

Communicating excessive concerns also causes children to be less open about expressing their own feelings. Children who know their parents are worried about them worry about their parents. "If I tell my mother all the things that happen when I'm home alone, she'll only worry more and I don't want to make her feel worse than she already does."

Former latchkey children are also quick to recall their parents' reaction to their latchkey experience. They remember their parents' fears, but they were also aware of the guilt their parents experienced. The vast majority of former latchkey children perceive their parents reaction to their experience as negative. Guilty and worried were the emotions most frequently cited. One woman who believed her mother felt a great deal of guilt said, "She would try to make it up to me on weekends by taking me out and buying me lots of things." Other words former latchkey children used to describe their parents' reaction were: "not happy, upset, nervous, difficult, apprehensive." One woman echoed the sentiments of many when she said, "My mother wished it could be different, but she had no choice. It was unavoidable."

Not only is the communication between the parent and the child critical, but the communication between parents also sets the tone of the experience. Parents who blame each other or argue in front of the children create an atmosphere that only interferes with the children's having a healthy experience. One woman went back to work as a nurse at a local hospital. As a result, her son, eight at the time, started spending his afternoons alone. "I felt guilty right from the start," she said. "Not only about Brad staying alone, but about not cooking dinner. My husband and son had to eat dinner by themselves five nights out of seven." Brad was aware of his mother's guilt and the strain her returning to work put on his parents' marraige since they often argued in front of him. "After I started back to work, I found myself always screaming at my husband. He always leaves work late and forces Brad to stay alone longer than necessary. I call him at work at 5:00 to remind him to leave, but it doesn't seem to do any good. Sometimes he gets home as late as 7:00, which means Brad is alone for four hours and has to wait till almost 8:00 for dinner. Dinner . . . they spend too many nights at McDonald's or Burger King because my husband is too lazy to cook. When I complain too much he gets angry and screams, 'Why don't you quit that job and stay home and take care of your son?' " Situations like this, where parents argue over whose responsibility it is to watch the child, again cause the child to feel like a burden rather than an integral member of the family. In this case Brad probably feels as though he is the cause of the fighting as well as interfering with his parents' careers. In his eyes, his father probably cares more about his job than his son, and his mother works unnecessarily. In order for this situation to improve, his parents need to stop arguing in front of Brad and agree on child-care arrangements that are mutually satisfying. Whatever arrangement they choose, self-care or an after-school program, both parents should make a commitment to make it work and stop blaming each other because of their own guilt.

For any family the decision to leave the children alone for even a short time before or after school will cause a change in the family dynamics. One of the greatest areas of change is the relationship between the parents and the children. Leaving children alone implies maturity and responsibility. By allowing a child to stay alone for an hour or two a day, the parent is indirectly communicating to that child, "I believe you are old enough to take care of yourself." During that time alone, the children are allowed to make decisions for themselves. For younger children, those decisions might be what to watch on television or what to have for a snack. Older children might be given the freedom to decide where and how to spend the afternoon and to come and go as they please.

This change in responsibility, from parental care to self-care, no matter how small, will cause a strain in the parent-child relationship if the parent doesn't adjust to the child's new perception of him/herself. During the initial stages of self-care the child is torn between feelings of anxiety and independence. The parent needs to recognize both these feelings and provide the child with more understanding and freedom when coming home from work. Failure to do so will only make the child's adjustment more difficult by causing frustration because he is expected to act like an adult part of the day and a child as soon as his parents walk through the door. "When I'm home alone after school, I can do whatever I want. I can watch whatever I want on TV and eat whatever I want out of the refrigerator," explained a fifth grade girl. "Then as soon as my mother gets home she starts in on me. 'Put that away, it's almost time for dinner.' 'Don't eat so many cookies. They're not good for you.' She treats me like a baby and I'm not one." Parents like this mother who leave their children on their own after school, and then control them once they get home from work, are expecting their children to give up their independence without reason. Sooner or later these children will resent their parents' interferences and rebel. Sensitivity on the part of parents to the double messages they are giving—"You're grown up; You're a child"—can help prevent this problem.

The changes that take place in a household when children are placed in self-care—more distance, less time together, resentment of controls—not only change the immediate relationship between parent and child, but may also have long-lasting effects. In fact, many adults that were once latchkey children point out the continuing effect it has had on them and their relationship with their parents. For over half of them there are still lingering issues and feelings that they would like to discuss with their parents even though they're now adults and the latchkey experience is twenty years behind them. While some would like to communicate positive feelings by explaining how much they benefited from self-care, others want to share resentment and make their parents aware of the pain they felt while staying alone.

A twenty-seven-year-old woman who grew up in New York and

saw her time spent alone as a positive experience put it this way: "I would like to tell my parents how much I respect them for being able to handle careers and be loving parents as well. If I could I'd like to dispel any feelings of guilt they may have. After all, I think I benefited a great deal from being on my own so early." Another woman who felt positive about being a latchkey child said, "I'd want my parents to know that they brought me up right. What was important was that they loved me, not that they were home all the time." Other former latchkey children felt that they matured from the experience. One said, "I'd tell them it was a valuable experience because I was forced to learn responsibility. My brothers and I learned that by doing our jobs, we had more time with our parents when they got home." A thirty-year-old woman who started staying alone when she was eleven also felt the experience was positive. "I'm sure it helped me to develop the sense of independence I now have. I can take care of myself. More importantly, my mother gave me a role model of a professional woman."

But the strongest statement about the positive aspects of the latchkey experience came from a twenty-eight-year-old woman who was outraged by the idea that the latchkey experience could be a negative one. She spent her afternoons alone with her older brothers and sisters in a poor Baltimore neighborhood for as long as she can remember. For her, her parents leaving to go to work wasn't equivalent to being abandoned. "Relationships with your parents aren't determined by how many times you're left alone," she said. "Parents leave children alone because of economic necessity, not because the relationship is bad or the child is unloved. I love my parents very deeply and I appreciate my mother having the motivation and foresight and determination to work so that we children could have the benefits other children had. Even after my father died my mother still raised five children with no outside help . . . The time we spent together was precious and valuable."

Although many adults have positive experiences to share with their parents, just as many have strong negative feelings. Many of the negative comments focused around a feeling of having had too much responsibility. These adults didn't like caring for themselves as children and wanted to be nurtured more than they were. One woman who started staying alone at age five for as many as nine hours a day and later was responsible for watching her younger sisters said frankly: "I would have appreciated being allowed to be a child—scared, protected, encouraged and minded—instead of a surrogate mother for my sisters." At first this might be attributed to the amount of time she spent alone, but another woman who started staying alone at age four for four hours a day also felt cheated. "Hell, all the responsibility was unfair. It robbed me of a lot of my youth and my carefree time." Many missed their parents and the experiences they thought parents and children should share together. One former latchkey child felt that his parents weren't there to teach him "how to cope with the world." Another man who started staying alone with his younger sister at age ten also felt cheated. "I needed someone to be more sensitive to my needs. They should have picked up the nonverbal clues that I needed them. I wasn't going to tell them."

Maintaining a close and trusting relationship between parent and child is critical in establishing a successful latchkey arrangement. But doing so when time together is limited and stresses are high is very difficult. Children who are left to care for themselves can very quickly begin to feel unloved if parents are not sensitive to their needs and problems. Parents must make sure they feel both loved and wanted. Convincing children of this when they're feeling rejected isn't easy. Consistency is critical. If parents want to maintain intimacy with their children, then it is important that they work regularly to develop a close and open relationship, taking the time to listen to both daily happenings and problems. A parent who listens four days in a row but comes home the fifth day and says, "Don't bother me now, I'm too tired," will be perceived by a child as lacking understanding. Children sometimes forget the positive things parents do, but will dwell on apparent rejections.

Affection and love should be communicated to a child daily, both verbally and nonverbally. A simple touch to say, "Hi, glad you're here," or an intense hug to say, "I missed you," or "I love you," will help any child feel wanted. Touch is a primary means of communication and is sometimes better understood by children than words or other gestures. Physical contact also communicates interest and can work to facilitate openness between parent and child. Verbal communication of affection should also not be neglected. Too often in the confusion of a day parents forget to tell their children that they love them, or they think that their children know they love them and they don't have to be told. To assure children that they are loved both actions and words are necessary.

Dependability is another way of communicating concern. A parent who says, "I'll be home at 5:30," but doesn't come home until 7:00, is likely to be misinterpreted as a sign of not caring about the child. Too often parents hear confirmation of this when their children say things like, "Your work is more important to you than I am," or "If you cared about me you'd come home from work sooner." Both of these statements indicate that the child is not feeling loved. Dependability can go a long way in assuring children that they are loved. Dependability applies not only to coming home on time but also to scheduling time to do things with the child and keeping those appointments.

It is also crucial that parents of latchkey children help their children to feel like contributing members of the family rather than a burden or a responsibility. One way to accomplish this is through the use of regularly scheduled family meetings, where all family members have an opportunity to freely voice concerns. Problems related to self-care, as well as to other areas, should be heard in a nonthreatening manner and discussed among family members so that changes in family policies and procedures can be made.

The family conference can be held on a regular basis, such as once a week or as often as needed. If conferences are held on a regular basis, a set time should be picked and maintained, though family round tables should not occur at the evening meal, which should be a family affair and tradition in itself. Family round tables can always be held after the evening meal. Whenever they're held, all family members should be present, and attendance should be considered as important as a meeting with the boss, the school basketball game or a favorite television program. An agenda box (an old shoe box with a slit in the top) could be placed in the kitchen where any family member could put problems or issues they would like to have discussed at the next meeting. If meetings are to be held on a crisis-only basis, each family member should have the power to call a conference.

Anything should be worthy of discussion at a family conference. Nothing should be considered too trivial to be included. The conference can be used to write up and discuss the house rules, to post the daily schedules of all family members, to divide chores evenly and settle disputes regarding the distribution of chores, to settle disputes between siblings regarding telephone and television privileges or to better prepare children to handle emergencies and crises. The purpose of the family conference is to help children feel better about their self-care experience and behave in a more responsible fashion.

Keeping any family together today is a real challenge. The pull of peers and the influence of television both serve to draw the child away from the family group. In families where both parents work, or in single-parent families where that parent works, the task is even more difficult. The stress on these families and the limited amount of time they spend together work to pull them apart. The magnitude of this problem and its effect on the nation's young people was recognized in 1964 when the Home School Institute (HSI) was formed to help families help their children to realize their potential through a variety of projects and programs. It publishes materials that all parents can use to develop their children's academic abilities and skills in coping with daily problems. Parents who wish to receive their publications may do so by writing to the Home School Institute at 1201 16th Street, N.W., Suite 228, Washington, D.C. 20036.

# Chapter 9
# THE CASUALTIES

The former latchkey children interviewed naturally differed in their reactions to the latchkey experience. A few found the experience positive, fostering independence and responsibility. Many said their experience was neutral but necessary. Some found the experience negative, full of fear, loneliness and conflict. Among these were the casualties, children who were overwhelmed by the experience of caring for themselves.

Among the former latchkey children interviewed, seventy-five in all, one in five was labeled a casualty. Casualties did not cope well with caring for themselves on a regular basis. They succumbed to high levels of fear, intense feelings of isolation or acceptance of too much responsibility. Fear levels were high enough to cause hiding, sleeplessness and nightmares. Isolation was intense enough to cause depression or strong feelings of rejection. The responsibility placed on them was overwhelming enough to cause bitterness, resentment and anger. Most of the casualties experienced two of these problems; some experienced all three. Casualties also reported that they thought the latchkey experience had a lasting negative effect. They look back and feel badly about their childhoods. They also feel that their experience as latchkey children has had a negative impact on them as adults. Many still have residual fears about staying alone. Others feel that their isolation inhibited the development of their interpersonal skills, while some still harbor a deep resentment against parents or siblings that interferes with present family relationships.

Casualties were also determined by the intensity of the experience. Instead of using phrases like "a little scared," these former latchkey children would say "terrified." Instead of not liking the latchkey experience, casualties "hated it." The intensity of their communications will be appreciated when their stories are read.

The experiences and reactions for five "latchkey casualties" are presented to illustrate the long-term negative impact of self-supervision on some children. Each of the cases presented is true. Each illustrates problems and reactions of individuals who did not cope well with the latchkey experience. The problems encountered illustrate the pressures latchkey children often experience, and may help some parents to avoid making similar mistakes.

Twenty percent of the adults interviewed were latchkey casualties. If they are representative of current latchkey children, then out of every million latchkey children in America two hundred thousand will experience long-term negative consequences. If there are five million latchkey children in the United States, twenty years from now one million will look back upon the experience as a negative one. Even if these figures are overestimates of the casualty rate, if only one child suffers in the way these adults report suffering, many would argue that the price is too high.

CASE 1

Linda grew up in Sacramento, California, with her parents and two sisters. During her childhood, she lived in a "nice" house in a suburban neighborhood she considered "safe." At age five she started school and her mother returned to work. Linda was expected to get herself ready for school and to care for herself from the time she arrived home from school at 2:15 until her mother arrived at 4:30. Her two sisters, seven and ten years older than she, went to private schools across town and arrived home after Linda's mother.

Compared to the lives of many latchkey children, Linda's experience was uneventful. During the thirteen years she cared for herself, there was never any reason for her to call the police or fire department. She was well-behaved and followed her mother's rules. She came home, locked the door and called her mother to tell her she was safe. She went outside to play but did not let friends in. About once a month Linda visited a friend.

Although Linda was physically safe, she had a difficult time dealing with the latchkey experience emotionally. "I felt abandoned. I didn't feel close to my parents at all. I felt like a little being . . . I got myself off to school; I took care of myself . . . The periods of time I spent taking care of myself felt so intense that the time I spent being with my parents couldn't compensate for the time I spent alone. When you spend a great deal of time alone, it's difficult to be with people."

Linda also felt hurt and angry. She interpreted her mother's going back to work as personal rejection. "Mom cared enough to stay home when my sisters were little but she didn't care enough to stay home with me. As soon as I started school, she started to work . . . I felt my mother loved my sisters more than me. I wasn't worth staying home for."

Linda was also very frightened staying alone. "The house was very large and I was so small . . . It made it seem even larger. There were lots of rooms connected by halls . . . lots of noises. I would turn on the TV to block out the noises. But I guess I was most frightened of myself. I was terrified of my own feelings. I wanted to be perfect and handle everything . . . I had to do things right and when I didn't I scolded myself. It's hard to be a child and a parent at the same time. I slipped back and forth between being the child I was and the parent I thought I should be to myself." In order to escape high levels of fear, Linda would spend a great deal of time playing in closets, where she felt safe. She would bring her toys with her and construct her own little world, much smaller and more manageable than the larger house in which she lived.

Even though her parents were home in the evening, Linda was still afraid to go to sleep at night. "I slept in a double bed. At night I would line up all my stuffed animals and sleep in the corner. That way, if anyone broke in, they would get the teddy bears and not me." Once asleep, Linda was plagued by nightmares which, unfortunately, only reinforced the distance between her and her mother. "In the dream I was walking along with my mother . . . then suddenly there was this open manhole and I fell in it. I entered another world. There was a city there and a gorilla that chased me . . ."

Some of Linda's childhood fears are still with her. Although she is thirty years old, she is unable to fall asleep easily, and has recurring nightmares of being chased by a man.

Linda stayed alone from age five until she started college. Her teenage years were rebellious, punctuated by acting out. She wanted to get her mother's attention and force her to stay home to control her, but it didn't work. "Being a latchkey child during my teenage years gave me a great deal of freedom. Starting at age thirteen, I frequently had boys visit my house. I became sexually active early. I think it was partly to show my mom I was angry at her for leaving me alone. She didn't like me having sex, but I could show her that I controlled my own body. I would leave obvious signs of my encounters with these boys for my mother to see, but she just ignored them. Sometimes I'd be walking out of my bedroom tucking in my shirt while mom was walking in the front door. I did some experimenting with drugs, too."

Being alone also had a serious effect on Linda's ability to interact with her peers, mainly because she felt different from her friends. "My friends' parents cared about them. Mine didn't. When I visited my friends' houses their mothers were always there. I was the exception. I didn't know anyone else who was a latchkey kid when I was growing up. I was ashamed, ashamed of my family, ashamed of my house. It was always a mess . . . I had to mature very early. I think childhood was taken away from me. I couldn't be a child and I wasn't an adult."

The fact that Linda spent so much time alone as a child still affects how she relates to others now. "Spending so much time alone created in me a real need for other people. I still have that need, but I'm ashamed of it. I think I should be able to handle or fill my needs myself. So when other people get close, I feel ashamed and vulnerable. I protect myself by turning them off before they hurt me. I still have trouble sustaining relationships."

Being alone also has affected how Linda views people in general. "It breeds a terror of other people. I spend time now maintaining the experience I had as a child even though I didn't like it. I seldom invite people to my house. I also tend to look for one person who can be a parent to me—a man, since I was so distant from my father. I can't stand a relationship that doesn't make me the central figure. I want to be taken care of."

Linda said that her mother felt a great deal of guilt over leaving her alone. "My mother dealt with the guilt by reading stories to me in bed and buying me things. She let me do anything I wanted to. When she first went to work, she spent a lot of time with me. But she says I wouldn't accept her attentions very well. I guess I thought she was being nice to me not because she wanted to, but because she felt guilty. When I got older my parents overcompensated with what they called trust. But it was more that they couldn't say no to me for anything. I wished they would have set limits for me . . . but I was so used to freedom that I would have resented the limits."

Throughout Linda's experience as a latchkey child she was physically afraid and psychologically lonely much of the time. Feeling abandoned and unloved, she tried to get her parents' attention by acting out, but never felt she had enough parental attention. There is still distance between Linda and her mother, and she continues to wonder if her mother loves her sisters more than her. Because she felt her mother abandoned her at such a young age, Linda remains suspicious of others, and has difficulty trusting people and maintaining relationships. Subconsciously she thinks the men with whom she has relationships will abandon her, so she doesn't let them get close enough to hurt her. Because of this she has to take care of herself, even though she doesn't like it.

Linda's problems as a latchkey child and consequently as an adult could have been avoided. Many of her problems stem from the fact that she became a latchkey child when she was only five years old. This is much too young to begin self-supervision. Children below the age of eight often have a poor sense of time. For Linda, knowing that her mother would be home at 4:30 or in two hours was very little comfort, since she had little concept of "4:30" or when two hours would be over. If Linda's mother wanted to begin her career when she did, she should have made arrangements for someone to care for her after school.

Linda also had a problem with staying alone because she never understood why her mother decided to begin work. At best she felt her mother loved her less than her sisters, and at worst she thought her mother was going to work to avoid her. Linda needed a clear explanation of why her mother was working and reassurance that her mother loved her as much as she did her sisters.

The other long-lasting effect of Linda's experience has to do with fear. Open discussion between Linda and her parents may have alleviated some of her fears. Having a close relationship with one's parents always facilitates such discussion, but Linda didn't feel she had such a relationship. In fact, rather than telephone her mother when she was afraid, Linda hid.

When Linda asked for help—her behavior during her high school years was clearly a plea for attention—her parents ignored her. This only reinforced her belief that her parents didn't love her. Had her parents responded with strict guidelines, more family time together, and professional counseling, Linda might have rejected these overtures, but they would have communicated her family's concern.

CASE 2

Jo Ann grew up in rural Maryland. She was an only child and lived with both parents. When she was nine, her father died suddenly. Her mother, who had never worked before, got a job at a local factory. Jo Ann's mother left for work when Jo Ann was still asleep and didn't return until at least 7:00 P.M. Jo Ann was usually alone seven hours a day, three hours every morning and four hours in the evening.

When Jo Ann was alone, she was totally alone. There were no neighbors she could go to for help in case of an emergency. She was not allowed to have friends visit and seldom visited them. In fact, Jo Ann's mother didn't even have a telephone. She couldn't talk to her friends or call her mother if she became frightened. Because there was no phone, Jo Ann never knew when her mother was going to be late. Sometimes her mother didn't return until midnight. On these nights, Jo Ann had to cook dinner and put herself to bed. She not only felt but truly was on her own.

Jo Ann frequently lost her key or forgot to take it with her in the morning. Consequently, she had to wait outside for her mother, sometimes for hours in all types of weather. She said there were no nearby neighbors with whom she could stay. Jo Ann said she hated those times. "I can remember standing outside or cuddling up on the front steps waiting for my mother to come home. My mother didn't get home until 7:00 and in the winter it was dark and cold. Sometimes it would be freezing and the time I waited seemed like an eternity . . . When she did get there, instead of feeling sorry for me, she'd yell at me for forgetting my key . . .

Before I wore my key, I would carry it in my coat pocket. I remember once, after I got home from school, I went outside to get the mail and the door slammed shut behind me. It locked automatically. It was November, and I was without a coat, hat, gloves or any of the necessities. I spent four hours outside freezing, afraid to knock on anyone's door to ask for help because my mother always told me to be wary of strangers. I remember walking the streets, trying to get my hands warm. I tried to pry the door off with a stick I found in the street but I was too small. I couldn't break a window because we lived on the second floor of a house and there was no way to get to our window. The lady who lived downstairs wasn't home. She never was." After this incident Jo Ann put the housekey on a string and started wearing it around her neck. "I never wanted to get locked outside again."

Jo Ann had a hard time adjusting to staying alone. "Everything happened so suddenly. One day my father was dead . . . gone forever," she said. "It was hard for me to accept that. I was daddy's little girl. I didn't get along with my mother at all when I was a child . . . then before I knew it my mother started working and I had to fend for myself. I hated it. I still try to avoid being alone at all costs."

Jo Ann also spoke of being frightened during the afternoons she spent alone. "Everything scared me—the dark, strange noises, the wind in the trees. I was petrified. I remember the first time I had to go to bed alone. The moon and the trees made shadows on the walls of my bedroom. The corners of my room were dark and I thought there was something there. I buried my head under the covers and tried to fall asleep . . ." Once asleep, Jo Ann often had nightmares. "I'd dream bugs and spiders were crawling all over me. Other times I'd walk in my sleep. I'd wake up and find myself in the living room in my pajamas. I'd hurry back to bed and get under the covers.

"I also had a terrible fear of thunderstorms. When I was alone in a thunderstorm I thought something terrible was going to happen, so I would hide in a closet with the door closed and put my hands over my head. I didn't want to see or hear anything. I remember one time, it was an extremely bad storm, I think the lightning hit a set of power lines and I saw it through the window . . . I bolted to my favorite closet and cuddled in the corner. I was screaming, crying, shaking, all at once. To this day, I'm still terrified of thunderstorms."

Jo Ann is also still afraid to stay alone. "I still have terrible nightmares," she said. "I dream my teeth are falling out and I wake up in a cold sweat . . . I don't like to be alone now either . . . especially at night I turn on all the lights and the television and I check under the beds and in the closets to make sure no one's there. If my husband isn't home, I have a real problem falling asleep. I wonder if I'll ever stop being afraid."

Jo Ann remained a latchkey child until she was twenty-one. During her teenage years she avoided going home after school for as long as possible, preferring instead to go to a friend's house or "hang out" after school.

Jo Ann spent many more hours a day alone than is common. Reflecting back on the experience, she feels it has affected her character. "Because I had to take care of myself, I'm strong-willed and independent. I make decisions very quickly, and I'm not used to waiting for anyone's approval . . . Sometimes my husband wishes I would wait for his, but he likes independence." But her strong sense of independence hasn't been without cost. "I feel totally disassociated from my mother. It's just the two of us and I'm not close to her at all. At times I don't even feel like I've ever had a family. But it's not just my mother from whom I'm distant. I have trouble forming strong relationships with other people, too. I've learned not to depend on others." Although Jo Ann is no longer a latchkey child, she is still isolated from others. Now, her isolation is self-imposed.

Jo Ann's problems with her self-care experience stem primarily from the amount of time she spent alone and the degree of isolation she experienced. Having a nine-year-old child care for herself after school is not unusual. Many do so successfully. But the amount of time Jo Ann was expected to spend alone and the limited amount of time she had to spend with her mother caused her problems. If Jo Ann's mother couldn't have returned home from work much earlier, then she should have taken some steps to reduce the amount of time Jo Ann remained in self-care each day. It's unreasonable to expect a child of that age to feed herself and put herself to bed even if it's only occasionally. Jo Ann's mother might have made arrangements for Jo Ann to spend a day or two each week at a friend's house, especially on those nights her mother thought she would be home late. Breaks like these can help to keep the week from seeming so long. Children today, in increasing numbers, complain that they spend too little time with their parents. Jo Ann actually averaged no more than ten working weekday hours with her mother. And even this time was often filled with household maintenance activities: cooking, cleaning, doing the laundry, paying bills.

Installing a telephone would have reduced the fear and isolation Jo Ann experienced by giving her social contact with her mother and friends and would have provided a link to emergency help should it ever have been needed. Without a telephone, Jo Ann was very vulnerable. She was aware of this and it heightened her anxiety about being alone. A phone also would have allowed her mother to contact Jo Ann if she were going to be late getting home from work. Whenever her mother was late, Jo Ann would imagine her in a car accident and would picture herself alone forever. To a child with only one parent the thought of losing that parent is very upsetting.

To take additional precautions against Jo Ann's being locked out, an extra key could have been hidden outside. Jo Ann, or any other child, should not have been expected to wait outside for a parent to return home—in addition to the dangers, waiting outside only makes a child feel unloved and abandoned. A parent today in a similar position could consider installing a push-button lock. These devices, more expensive than the usual dead bolt, are opened by pressing a combination of door-mounted push-buttons. They eliminate the need for a key but require the child to remember the combination. A forgotten combination, however, could be easily obtained by telephoning the parent.

After the death of her father, Jo Ann needed her mother more than ever, but it was at this point that their time together was sharply curtailed. One can hardly blame the remaining parent for the difficult circumstances Jo Ann found herself in. Unfortunately, working parents often find that important aspects of family or personal development must be squeezed into a much shorter time frame. Jo Ann's mother, after the death of her husband, had to carry out the tasks he used to contribute to family maintenance, bringing in income, repairing household items, paying the bills, filing the taxes, as well her own parental duties. And no matter how she struggled to devote the rest of her time to Jo Ann, if she didn't allow some time to herself she risked becoming resentful of her daughter or angry at her husband for dying—not an uncommon reaction for widows and widowers. Personal time was usually found on weekends. If she came home late on weeknights it was usually because she worked late. The time-and-a-half payment she received from overtime work was very important to Jo Ann's mother, who always seemed financially strapped. The result of all this time juggling was that no matter how much of the available time was spent with Jo Ann after work and household matters were taken care of, Jo Ann and her mother never found the time left over for their relationship adequate. This phenomenon is all too common for children of working parents, especially single working parents.

## CASE 3

Mike grew up in a small midwestern town. He was an only child and lived with his parents in a nice house in a safe suburban neighborhood. The summer before his freshman year in high school Mike's parents got a divorce. As part of the settlement, Mike went to live with his father. Beginning at age fourteen, Mike became a latchkey child.

Mike's father was a traveling salesman who took weekly business trips. Mike was often left alone for several days a week. Mike was acquainted with few neighbors, and had no relatives nearby to whom he could turn for help. Once when he lost his key, he broke a window to get in.

Mike was extremely frightened when he stayed home alone. He knew that with his father on a business trip, anything could happen. He related that he had trouble sleeping and often had nightmares. As frightened as Mike was, he never told his father how he felt about staying alone. Instead, he would turn on all the lights and the TV or stereo for companionship. When asked why he didn't tell his father how he felt, Mike replied, "I found it hard to express my feelings to dad . . . There's always been difficulty expressing feelings in my family."

Mike, now twenty-five, doesn't like being alone. "I find it hard to sleep," he says. "I begin to feel listless and find it hard to do anything constructive. Funny, but I think of a dog's behavior when he's left alone . . . chewing furniture, turning over garbage cans, things like that . . . Not that I ever do those things."

Spending many days alone as a teenager also had a strong impact on Mike socially. "I became introverted, and I spent a lot of time playing my guitar to amuse myself. I neglected schoolwork; there didn't seem to be a point to it. I easily got away with 'ditching school' or 'playing hooky' since no one was there to know about it. Since friends weren't always 'officially' welcome in my home, I felt guilty or sneaky having people over. I often drank beer or liquor for no reason at all. I became obsessed with TV shows like 'Kung Fu.' And I often did strange or unusual things for attention. Sometimes I would get so angry that I'd do things like punch my fist into the wall."

Mike clearly resented all the time he spent alone. "TV is not a good companion," he said. "Friends should always be welcome in the home. When my father was out of town on business, having friends stay over should have been o.k., or I should have been able to stay at someone's house."

Although Mike didn't start staying alone until he was fourteen, being a latchkey child was a destructive experience for him. Now, seven years after he left home to start college, Mike believes his experience has had long-lasting effects. He has difficulty being by himself, and often feels afraid and depressed. Partly as a result of those unhappy years during adolescence, Mike appears introverted and says he has difficulty making friends.

Since Mike's father traveled for a living, other arrangements should have been made for Mike when he was out of town although, as Mike points out, his father didn't know he was unhappy being alone. Ostensibly he had everything a teenager could want: stereo, color TV, electric guitar and freedom . . . everything, that is, except a family and friends. Teenage years are marked by a search for identity. Central in that search is one's relationships with others. Because of his isolation Mike missed the opportunity to find himself and to learn how to interact with others in a meaningful way.

The years before and after a divorce are usually very difficult ones for children. During this period children of divorce need solace, structure and security. Long periods spent alone are hard on any child, but the time Mike spent alone especially undermined his sense of security, which was especially low after his parents divorced.

CASE 4

Natalie grew up in Phoenix, Arizona. She lived with her father, mother and a sister, who is four years older than she. When Natalie's sister, Amy, was born, Natalie's mother quit working. When Natalie was ten, her mother returned to work, leaving Natalie and her sister to care for themselves. "My mom told me she had to go back to work because we didn't have any money for food. I thought this was bizarre. I didn't think we were that poor. It worried me . . . I mean . . . we were part of middle-class America. I thought my mother's working would help, but I didn't think it was a matter of survival."

Natalie subsequently spent three or four hours every day alone with her sister, until her mother returned home at about six o'clock. She was usually exhausted. "Two or three days each week I would cook dinner because my mother was too tired and my sister hated cooking. I was always trying to please my mother. The other two or three days we went out to dinner." Natalie also had to clean the house and iron her own clothes. Her sister was assigned chores but seldom did them. "I had a lot of work to do around the house, more than most of my friends. But I didn't mind. I did it just to stay on my mom's good side."

Natalie's sister was the source of most of Natalie's problems. "We never got along. When I was six, my sister was ten. We got in a fight one day and she ripped all my clothes off in a fit of anger." Natalie and her sister fought constantly and when they were alone, these fights often became intense. "My sister needed counseling desperately. At times she was very emotional, at other times very withdrawn. She was prone to having violent outbursts for no apparent reason." Natalie's sister was so violent that Natalie felt she would have been better off alone. "I never knew what Amy was going to do next. Sometimes she would get home first and not let me in the house. I would have to wait outside for my mother. When Amy got mad, and you never knew what would make her mad, she would scream and throw things or beat me. Once time she got my father's pickax and went into the backyard and just keep hitting the ground."

Natalie dreaded coming home after school. "I was nervous knowing my sister would be there. She was like a powder keg about to go off. My parents didn't know how to control her, either. They were as confused by my sister's irrational violent behavior as I was. Two or three days a week I would spend the afternoon at a friend's house.

We weren't close friends, but I just wanted to stay away. The days I was home I would often lock myself in my room just to get away from my sister."

Natalie had other problems at home besides her sister. "Living with my mother wasn't easy, either. She was a perfectionist, though I tried hard to please her. She would write notes every day for me and my sister telling us what to do." Natalie's mother was also very controlling. "My mom would wake my sister and me at six o'clock seven days a week and make us clean our rooms. By the time I went away to college it was such a habit that I still got up at 6:00 and cleaned my room. The rest of the girls in the dorm thought I was crazy."

"My mother would beat my sister several times a week. I mean beat her with a belt. I would feel sorry for Amy and try to protect her . . . I would grab my mother's arm or stand between my mom and my sister screaming for her to stop. Then mom would beat me, too. Dad never interfered either. He didn't hit us, but he never stopped my mom either. He would just go downstairs in his workshop and start sawing wood with his big electric saw. I guess that way he wouldn't have to hear the screams." In spite of all of this Natalie has forgiven her mother. "It's not my mom's fault. She was abused as a child by her father. It's my father I can't forgive; he should have stopped her."

When Natalie was twelve she began to rebel against her mother's control. "I felt fat and ugly, so I quit eating. I loved Seventeen magazine and wanted to look like the models. My mother was a force feeder. I felt great power by not eating. I remember my mother crying because I only weighed ninety-five pounds. Now I know I was anorexic."

Natalie describes her life as a latchkey child as "lonely." Because of all the work she had to do around the house she didn't have enough time to spend with her friends. In fact she doesn't recall having any real friends until her junior year in high school. "I remember feeling so isolated. I couldn't talk to my parents or my sister and I had no friends. I had difficulty relating to my peer group. I felt that I had to be responsible, that I couldn't fool around with the other kids. Plus, I had so many problems at home that I couldn't have any friends over."

Natalie was alone both physically and psychologically and she hated it. "I didn't realize how much I hated being alone until my husband walked out after five years of marriage. Even though there was psychological distance, he was present . . . Even though he was interested in other women and would punish me verbally, I wanted him with me . . . and even though he drank and was totally irresponsible, I needed him. When he left I finally realized what had kept us together all those years . . . I was terrified to be alone."

"Has being a latchkey kid affected me? Deeply . . . If I had children I would rather live in a little apartment in a lousy neighborhood and not work than leave my children alone. A lot of my friends feel the same way. They're trying to stay home with their children even though they're burying good careers to do so."

Natalie's was not a typical household. Her mother was an abusing parent, her father couldn't be counted on to stop the abuse. Natalie's sister was disturbed, or at least never learned how to act to keep from being abused. Even though Natalie learned how to be a "good" girl, thus avoiding much of her mother's wrath, every child in an abusing household is at risk. Natalie's biggest problem, as she saw it, was her sister, whose violence she didn't understand and always feared.

It is possible that Natalie's mother returned to work as a way of reducing her own propensity to abuse her children. Work put distance between mother and daughters for many hours each week. Sometimes children benefit from such arrangements as the lesser of two evils. But Natalie's mother's absence then left her younger daughter at risk with her sibling. Natalie would have been better off if she had friends to spend her afternoons with, but the family had few friends or neighborhood contacts.

The older sister needed help, but the frequency of her violent explosions wasn't noticed by her parents since they spent so much time out of the house. Natalie seldom mentioned her sister's bizarre behavior to her mother in order to protect Amy from being beaten. It was a relief for her when her sister finally moved out of the house to go to college, even though it left her alone.

Many siblings find themselves faced with the unpleasant choice of being alone or being with siblings who frighten and abuse them. Although Natalie feels sorry for her sister, she still feels she's disturbed and maintains no relationship with her. The two women live a continent apart.

Natalie's father could have improved his family's situation if he had been willing to get involved. He needed to challenge his wife and listen to his daughters, but preferred to retreat to his job or workshop. Although in Natalie's case her father's inattention didn't *create* the many problems this family was faced with (clearly the mother and older sister needed counseling), he should have stepped in to take control of a situation no one else could handle. Natalie's case is an example which illustrates the importance of having both parents involved in the family. Children in two-parent households who are left in self-care can especially benefit from and need the emotional involvement of mother and father, and their separate careers must be put in perspective with each other's needs and the needs of the family as a whole. Oftentimes the role of managing the household and parenting is still left largely to the woman, even though she may also work.

Since her divorce Natalie has not remarried. Now in her middle thirties, she is abandoning her thoughts of having children. She would like to remarry but in the meanwhile she is living alone. "I guess I learned to live with a certain amount of violence while growing up," she said, "but I also learned to survive by myself as well."

CASE 5

Margaret grew up in suburban Maryland with her mother, father and six siblings. She had one older brother, three younger brothers and two younger sisters. When Margaret was eleven, her mother accepted a job outside the home because the family needed the additional income. Margaret, the eldest daughter, was put in charge of her younger brothers and sisters for five hours each day—two hours before school and three hours after school. It is not uncommon for the eldest daughter to be given the major caretaking responsibility for younger siblings, even when there is an older male sibling present. Margaret's mother left for work at 6:30 A.M. Each morning Margaret helped dress her brothers and sisters, fed them breakfast and prepared their lunches before she went to school. After school she was responsible for everyone's safety. She helped her brothers and sisters with their homework and watched them while they played outside. Since her mother didn't arrive home until 5:30, Margaret sometimes cooked dinner. She also helped clean the house and she did the laundry.

Margaret didn't like all the responsibility. "I felt like I was the mother. I fed the kids twice a day, washed their clothes and made sure they did all their homework. I never had time to be with my friends. There was always work to be done." Margaret's occasional complaints to her mother fell on deaf ears. Her mother, already feeling guilty about leaving her children alone, would respond very defensively when Margaret suggested that she felt overworked.

Margaret was constantly with her siblings, but instead of satisfying companionship, they provided problems. "It was hard watching five kids, especially Joe and Tom. They wouldn't do their homework or their chores. They didn't want to listen to me. They fought all the time; I couldn't get them to stop. When they were bad I was supposed to make them sit on the couch or not let them play outside. Sometimes this worked and sometimes it didn't. When they didn't listen, I sometimes got in trouble. My mother would get mad because the house wasn't clean or dinner wasn't ready. I now realize that she became upset just because she was tired or frustrated or maybe guilty. At the time I thought she was picking on me."

Margaret became a latchkey casualty because she was given too much responsibility too soon. An eleven-year-old, even one who is mature and striving hard to please, isn't emotionally ready for the demands of extended self-care along with the care of several siblings. Although her parents saw the second income as being crucial to pay tuition for each child's intellectual advancement, their emotional well-being, Margaret's in particular, was sacrificed in the process.

Even though Margaret was seldom alone she was afraid when her parents weren't home. "I would hear noises outside, especially when it was dark . . . I remember once, everyone else was upstairs playing or doing their homework, and I was supposed to be hanging out the wash. As I went to open the back door, the porch screen snapped shut. I froze until I saw the cat out the window. I was convinced someone was waiting to get me." This wasn't the only time Margaret experienced fear. "I was afraid a lot. I'd often sit on the couch and watch TV with the other children when I was afraid. When my mother got home she'd be angry because the housework hadn't been done." Margaret is still fearful of being alone, particularly at night.

When Margaret was twelve, she underwent one of the most traumatic experiences possible for a latchkey child: fire broke out while she was watching her brothers and sisters. "It began outside," she said, "but quickly spread through the walls. As soon as I saw the flames I called the fire department. I tried to get everyone out, but my youngest sister was trapped in the room nearest to where the fire began and was killed. The fire wasn't my fault, but to this day I can't help feeling responsible. You don't know how many times I've wondered how I could have saved Bonnie." Overwhelmed by the responsibilities she shouldered and the fear she experienced, Margaret was also upset because she didn't feel her parents cared about them. They were gone early each morning "in order to let the children sleep later," but the impact on Margaret was that they weren't concerned about their well-being. Now as an adult she feels she was used and missed out on a significant part of her life.

Today Margaret is somewhat of an emotional misfit. She's developed habitual behavior that allows her to express caring in the material things she learned to do—cleaning, cooking, giving first aid—but has trouble demonstrating her feelings on an emotional level. "I very often don't feel emotionally concerned, even though I'll do things for people," she said. She resents her lost childhood, a feeling that grew during adolescence, and she continues to feel guilty about the death of her sister. To her friends she appears serious and mature beyond her years. She frequently wears a neck brace, and wonders if the tension of her childhood is responsible for her neck pain.

Margaret, like all little girls, needed the time and opportunity to be a child, to play, share with friends, be irresponsible. Margaret's parents might have hired a babysitter, or at least distributed responsibilities among all of their children, including the eldest son, who remained rather uninvolved with his siblings. Another possible solution might have been to put the two youngest children in day care or family home care, which would have greatly reduced the burden that was placed on their eldest daughter.

More importantly, Margaret needed her parents' support and understanding. When she tried to talk with them about her needs, however, she felt rebuffed. If a close relationship had been maintained, Margaret's parents would have had a better understanding of her problems that may have led to an adjustment in their care arrangements. Even if no other arrangements had been made, if Margaret could have spent some time each day talking with her parents openly, they might have helped her overcome the many frustrations she experienced.

Margaret's parents adequately met her material needs and always made sure she was well-dressed, which is reflected in her appearance today. They never blamed her for the death of her sister, in fact frequently consoled her that it wasn't her fault. "But," she says, "the burden of that death has never gone away."

Fortunately, not every latchkey child will be a casualty. Many parents make meaningful efforts that take time and energy to soften the negative impact of self-care on their children. These parents work at maintaining a close, warm, open and enduring relationship with each of their children by setting aside time to be with them. They listen when their children tell them something. They are as concerned about the emotional well-being of their children as they are about their intellectual progress and personal safety. Some parents will reason that unless the child is physically safe, materially provided for and intellectually capable, the softer qualities of a sense of emotional well-being, self-worth and security are inconsequential. Many children disagree with this analysis as the near epidemic number of suicides among adolescents will testify.

As we saw in the case of Linda, she never fully understood her mother's reasons for going back to work and felt abandoned, less loved, hurt and angry. Often parents, in an honest attempt to explain their plans to their youngsters, find that parental reasons fail to impress even the parents themselves. These efforts often pull parents up short as they discover that they are living in a generation that sees children as expendable, in fact, a burden to families. Some parents come to realize that they are generally unwilling to make sacrifices for their young, while others are challenged to reshape their values as they consider the importance of parent-child interactions on the total development of their children.

Each of these casualties experienced intense negative feelings, but in every case the child felt that he or she could not express the pain or that the parents wouldn't listen or that nothing could or would be done to alleviate it. Even if such feelings are only experienced infrequently children should know that they are experienced by other children and can be openly discussed with their parents. Often just expressing fear relieves the pain. At other times, as the parent hears a crescendo of fears, more direct interventions can be made. The important point in inviting your child to talk with you and planning time each day for this kind of sharing is that you let your child know that his well-being is important to you.

Children cannot be left in a self-care arrangement at too young an age. Children who have not matured developmentally also can't be expected to respond to emergencies beyond their capabilities. They can't explain phenomena that they are conceptually unable to understand. Part of Linda's problem was that she began as a latchkey child at age five. With other children the combination of a young age and other factors made the latchkey experience a destructive one. Jo Ann, at age nine, might have been able to manage if she were not so isolated and Margaret, at age twelve, could have done much better if she had not had to shoulder so many responsibilities.

Parents often ask what the minimum age for leaving a child alone might be. The answer depends not only on the developmental ability of the child but the circumstances that surround the self-care situation. Parents must examine each element in the equation from the child's point of view before deciding that the child can handle what even under the best of arrangements can be trying.

Some experts believe that children today are more resilient and better able to cope with life's hard knocks than children in other times and places. The argument goes that these children will be better able to cope with a society riddled with violence, marital breakups and financial and political insecurities. Surely all of the casualties presented here continue to function in society. But they do so painfully. There is no reason to increase childhood stress in order to toughen our children to a more hurried and unstable world. Every evidence is that warm, stable, low-stress environments better equip children to deal with a fragmenting adult world. Parents who are concerned about their children would do well to find a way out of the trap between adequate child care, self-fulfillment and a second income.

# Chapter 10
# REAPING THE BENEFITS

There are many ways to ensure that the latchkey experience isn't a negative one for a child. Many children, in fact, enjoy self-care and others are anxious to try it. The stigma of attending a day-care center, which frequently invites ridicule from a child's peers, is one of the most common reasons children give for wanting to stay alone. Also, children who do stay alone are quick to call those who don't "chicken." Some children feel too old for a day-care center, saying that it's "babyish." Because so few upper elementary school children are enrolled in day-care centers or after-school programs, most programs have adjusted accordingly and cater to the needs and interests of preschool or primary grade students. "I'm not interested in the things they do there," is a common reason elementary school students give for not wanting to go to an after-school program. "I did those things when I was in the third grade; I don't want to do them again." Others ask to stay alone because they want the freedom self-care provides. "Someone's been telling me what to do all day. I don't want to go to a day center where someone else will be telling me what to do," said one fourth grade girl. Her friend added, "I'm tired after a long day at school. I want to relax. They won't let you do that at a day-care center. They always want you to do something."

Some children ask to stay alone to please their parents. They struggle to live up to parental expectations and what they perceive to be hidden parental messages. "I know my mother doesn't have money to waste on a babysitter," explained a candid third grader, "so I told her I'd stay by myself."

But many children ask to stay alone to prove something to themselves. They see these short periods alone as excursions into adulthood. They get a chance to be their own bosses and take responsibility for themselves. They want to test their own competence and feel independent. Even children whose mothers don't work often ask to stay alone at times when their parents go out, rather than go with their parents or be supervised by a babysitter. "My son likes to stay alone," explained the mother of an eleven-year-old boy, "as long as he knows we're not going to be gone for long."

## Children Who Enjoy Independence

Many children ask to stay alone, or enjoy staying alone because of the freedom self-supervision provides. Very little freedom can be allowed in most elementary school programs. The structure of one teacher in charge of a large group of students means that individual freedom must often be denied. Students must participate in activities and complete assignments selected by the teacher. Where children sit, when they can move and when they can talk are all determined by group needs. In most classrooms, the teacher even determines when students can eat lunch, get a drink of water or go to the bathroom. Because most schools are so structured, many latchkey children cherish having some time to themselves.

Carolyn Sherman, in an article published in the Washington *Post*, described the luxury of coming home from school by herself and having the freedom to do what she wanted:

> First, of course, there was school. School all day. Bossy teachers. Noise. Lines. Hubbub. Pushing. Unending hassles . . . I liked school, but enough was enough. When I came home, when I opened my door,

I was in my kingdom. The house was cool and quiet and all mine. For the first time in the entire day, I was free.

But what did I do? What would you do? First I got comfortable. I flung off my hot shoes, tossed my coat and boots where I wanted. I could pick them up later. Then wandering from room to room, reveling in the pleasure of having the whole house to myself, I might survey myself in the mirror, rehearsing speeches or conversations for some future date, gesturing, arching an eyebrow, all inhibitions lost in the delicious freedom of being alone.

A sixth grade girl who stayed home with her sister also commented on the pleasure of staying alone. "I love the freedom to do what I want after school. Watch TV, play my stereo loud enough to hear, talk on the phone for over five minutes or play a game without being nagged. In fact, my sister and I got so used to being on our own after school that when my mother was home sick or having a holiday, we complained to each other. We knew that our mother would want to know where we were every minute, demand that we do our homework before going outside and not let us do some of the things we did when we were alone."

Many children who aren't in self-care will frequently ask their parents if they can stay alone on a regular basis. A child who makes such a request might be responding to peer pressure or the perceived needs of his/her parents, or might be expressing a maturity equal to the problems that may present themselves. A child who is required to stay alone who would prefer to stay elsewhere might not have the emotional strength or skills necessary to deal with self-care. How self-care is initiated and the readiness of the child are key factors in determining whether the experience will be a positive or painful experience for the child. Even children who initially request self-care may not subsequently find it a positive experience.

Staying alone begins the child's eventual separation from parents. It can teach children to be comfortable with themselves, and also prepares children emotionally and intellectually for the time when they will be on their own. Staying alone also teaches children to be responsible and independent people and to have confidence in their ability to care for themselves. It can provide parents with a unique opportunity to teach their children practical life skills such as cooking and cleaning, and gives children an opportunity to practice them.

Leaving children alone in the morning or afternoon often contributes to increased responsibility and maturity, particularly if younger siblings must be watched. Although latchkey children sometimes complain about the responsibility their parents place on them, former latchkey children often credit this early responsibility with traits they are glad to have as adults. One former latchkey child who spent her afternoons alone said, "I felt caring for myself was a valuable experience because it forced me to learn responsibility. It made me more mature and self-reliant, and I'm grateful for that now."

A woman who had to care for her younger brothers and sisters both before and after school felt the same way. "The experience of having to watch my younger brothers and sisters resulted in my reaching maturity at an earlier age than normal. This benefited my personal development in the long run." One man who was interviewed summarized the relationship between self-care and responsibility this way: "Being a latchkey kid forced me to act responsibly. Acting responsibly leads to being responsible, which is all part of the maturing process."

Part of responsibility is being able to solve problems or make decisions without adult assistance. These decisions, which millions of children make daily, might be as routine as "What should today's snack be?" or as critical as "Sally's arm is broken, what do I do?"

Being forced to make decisions and to suffer the consequences of those decisions is also a part of the maturing process. The child who is home alone learns to examine a situation and weigh the different possible outcomes before taking action, since that child knows he must live with the consequences of his behavior. The adage "you learn from your mistakes" aptly applies to latchkey children, but their problem-solving skills are developed in the process.

Adults who had a positive latchkey experience also frequently commented that self-care helped them to feel good about themselves. "It made me feel good that my mother trusted me to be alone. Staying alone fostered a sense of competence and trustworthiness that I wouldn't have without the experience," commented one former latchkey child, who echoed the sentiments of many. Jarrad, a fifth grade boy, expressed the same idea: "Taking care of myself makes me feel grown up. I know I can handle anything, and that makes me feel good." This confidence, apparent in many successful latchkey children, stems from their having behaved responsibly and coped successfully with the problems of self-care. These children see themselves no longer as children but as important members of the household. Successful latchkey children make comments like, "My mom says I have to help around the house because I'm not a baby anymore . . . I'm big." Children recognize that many of the tasks they are required to do when home alone, such as vacuuming or the laundry, are tasks that adults usually do. Successfully completing these tasks adds to the child's feeling of maturity and helps the child see himself as a contributing member of the family.

In caring for themselves, latchkey children also learn to be independent. They must be. "As a latchkey child, I learned to cope with any situation. I became tougher, wiser and more flexible. I also learned to be compassionate and empathetic to the needs of others," said one. "I wanted to prove to my parents and myself that I could handle staying by myself" was another frequently heard comment.

Many former latchkey children say that the independence they developed as children has stayed with them as adults. This willingness to act on one's own not only affects personal relationships, but professional development as well. "I never was a child," one woman said, "I had to take care of myself beginning at age seven. As a result, my academic and career accomplishments are phenomenal. I feel that my latchkey experience created a highly independent and successful career person." Another former latchkey child also felt that the latchkey experience was a major factor in his life: "It made me very independent. I'm more willing to take chances than most of my friends."

Older children who spend time alone learn skills that other children their age don't have. Many former latchkey children cite their ability to cook as an advantage of having spent their afternoons alone. Many parents instruct children who will spend time alone in basic household safety, phone-answering procedures, the use of appliances and cleaning procedures. Years of instruction and experience in household maintenance give many children a great deal of skill. "I'm only twenty-one but I'm capable of organizing and maintaining a household without too much difficulty," one young woman said. "I'm away at college now, but when I return home on weekends or vacations, I notice the house isn't as organized as when I was running it. Even my parents notice the difference."

Children alone not only learn practical skills but also learn how to use their time appropriately. Children who are alone before school must complete several tasks in a limited amount of time in order to arrive at school on time. Children who are alone after school must also learn how to budget their time; often they are expected to complete assigned chores and homework assignments before their parents return home. In addition, children have activities of their own they'd like to do—watch a TV show, have a snack, visit a friend —before their parents arrive home. But if the child spends too much time on personal activities, he may not complete his assigned chores or homework and may consequently have to deal with an angry or disappointed parent. In order to avoid conflicts with parents, many children learn to prioritize their afternoon activities, usually doing assigned chores and homework first and pleasurable activities second. Learning the value of time and how to use it appropriately was recognized by many former latchkey children as a valuable lesson. "I learned very early that my time was important and limited," explained John, who started staying alone at age eight for three hours a day. "I would arrange to play with certain people on certain days. I did what came natural to me. Sometimes I would spend the afternoon with friends; sometimes I would spend it by myself. I enjoyed the time I spent by myself. I never felt like I was really alone since I was always busy doing something."

Children who start staying alone when their mothers return to work often learn to view women differently. They learn that their mothers, too, have career aspirations and are capable of financial independence. Boys who have mothers who work relate differently to women in the work force when they reach adulthood. The firsthand experience of having a working mother may also affect any significant heterosexual relationship they might have later. For a girl growing up, viewing her mother as financially independent and as a contributing member of society is a positive role model. It also teaches children to exercise a choice between working, raising a family or both. One woman commented on the impact having a working mother had on her: "Being a latchkey child taught me that a woman could make it on her own. My mother did." Other former latchkey children commented that they viewed their mothers differently once they started to work, and that they valued the contributions their mothers made to their families. "I learned the financial realities of life," one woman said. "In order for my family to have everything we wanted, both my mother and my father had to work. My mother's income made a real difference in our life-style." Another woman also appreciated her mother more after she started to work. "I saw my mother as a vital woman. She was doing something she wanted. I really feel that it made her more valuable to me when she was at home. Many of my childhood friends whose mothers were home saw them as bored people who really didn't take part in life. I know, because I used to talk to them about it. I never saw my mother that way. I respected her as a person, not only as my mother."

Another potential benefit of being a latchkey child is that the opportunity is there to learn to spend time by oneself. Many children are never alone and as adults aren't comfortable by themselves. Many former latchkey children mentioned their ability to stay alone as a plus resulting from their latchkey experience. One man who spent a great deal of time alone said, "I tend to be a private person. I enjoy time to myself and the privacy of being alone with my own thoughts. It taught me to be self-sufficient, to entertain myself." Another man realized his ability to enjoy time by himself was a rare trait. "I am one of the few people I know who can go into the wilderness for three or four days at a time and enjoy the solitude. I know it's because I spent so much time alone as a kid."

Many former latchkey children said they enjoyed having time alone to reflect on the day's events or think about the future. "Being alone in the afternoon gave me time to think how I wanted to live and how I wanted to raise my kids when I got older." One woman mentioned that she still enjoys having time to herself: "I don't mind being alone, in fact there are certain things I prefer doing alone. I enjoy having the time to think and dream without feeling guilty for not always being busy."

While some enjoyed their time alone being introspective, a number of latchkey children said they used their afternoons to become skilled at a single hobby or activity. Hobbies are a popular way for latchkey children to pass the time. Apart from TV, the most popular afternoon activity for many latchkey children is reading. Many of them initially use reading as an escape, but as a result develop a fondness for books and literature.

Several former latchkey children indicated that they became very skilled in more active pursuits. "I spent a lot of my time alone listening to music and playing the guitar," one man recalls. "I became quite a good guitar player." One woman remembers spending her afternoons involved in craft projects, such as needlepoint and painting by number. Many children, too, spend their free time practicing a sport. "I wasn't allowed out of my yard, so I would spend hours practicing basketball in the driveway. I became a good shooter, and made the high school basketball team," recalled one man. Another used to practice lacrosse in the family garage. "My mother told me to stay in the house. I reasoned that the garage was part of the house, so I practiced throwing the ball against the wall of the garage and catching it." A third man, an engineer, recalled spending his afternoon hours building with his erector set. "I loved building. I still do. In fact, once in a while I take out my erector set and make something. I find it very relaxing."

What makes one latchkey experience a successful one and others less than positive seems to depend partly on the personality of the child himself: the intellectual and emotional makeup that the child brings to the experience. Children differ in their ability to solve problems and cope with fear and stress. Two children of the same age, living in the same neighborhood, asked to stay alone for the same amount of time, will respond differently. For one child it might seem unbearable to spend even half an hour alone daily, while another child might find two hours too short. Some children entertain themselves easily, others need constant adult attention. There are factors apart from the child's personality which help determine whether the experience will be a positive one: the maturity of the child, the amount of time he is expected to stay alone and how that time is structured are factors. The safety of the neighborhood and household, the availability of resource people and the relationship between parent and child all contribute. Even the most mature and well-adjusted child can be stressed if he or she is expected to stay alone for too long without appropriate guidance or preparation.

Parents must carefully assess their child's development and make clear plans before deciding to leave their child in self-care. A positive latchkey experience can occur only when parental expectations match the child's ability to cope. If parental expectations exceed the child's abilities, he or she will most likely have a negative experience.

## Latchkey Arrangements That Worked

Some parents manage to find the right combination of factors so that their children have a positive experience in self-care. Joe was one such person. He grew up in Pennsylvania with his parents and his younger sister. Joe's father was a coal miner and his mother a factory worker. When he was nine, his mother went back to work so that Joe had to take care of himself for an hour in the morning and an hour after school. His sister, Susan, was five at the time, and after school spent her afternoons at their grandmother's. Joe spent his afternoons playing outside in a nearby park. "I played there quite a bit in the summer and winter. Sometimes I was so involved with my friends that I would forget to go home and my mother would have to come and find me." Rainy or snowy afternoons were spent at a friend's house. "A lot of my friends had parents at home. They would let me play in their houses if the weather was bad. But most of the time we all played outside."

If Joe needed anything, he could depend on his grandmother, who lived a block away. "I carried a key to our house. If I lost it I was spanked, but I could always get another key from my grandmother so I never had to wait outside. We were very poor. We didn't have a TV or a telephone, so I had to keep myself busy. When my sister was eight, she started to spend her afternoons with me instead of at my grandmother's house. I had to watch over her. I didn't mind it, but I didn't love it either. We got along o.k. and it didn't make that much difference in my life. I still had time to go outside to play sports with my friends."

Joe didn't consider the fact that he was a latchkey child a significant part of his childhood. He still doesn't. It was simply an accepted fact of life. Joe understood that he had to stay alone because his family was very poor and needed the money. Fortunately, his experience as a latchkey child was uneventful. No emergencies ever occurred, nor was he ever frightened. Admittedly, though, Joe was seldom truly alone. He felt very safe since he knew everyone in his neighborhood, was constantly surrounded by people and could go outside or to his grandmother's house if he had a problem. As a consequence Joe doesn't feel he's suffered any negative effects from being a latchkey child. Today he continues to have a close relationship with his parents and sister, and feels good about his childhood, even though his family was poor. He comes across as an easygoing fellow who is bright, articulate and very likable. He has two master's degrees and is married with two small children. Joe presently works as a translator for a government office, and by anyone's standards would be considered personally and professionally successful.

Joe's parents made a less-than-perfect situation as positive as possible by not giving Joe more responsibility than he could handle. For Joe, the transition to staying alone was an easy one since he was used to playing outside with his friends even when his mother was home. Fortunately, his parents didn't demand that he stay inside and wait for them to come home. Had they done so, it would have isolated him from his friends, highlighted the fact that he stayed alone, and caused him to resent the time he spent alone. Joe's parents also didn't expect him to watch his sister after school when she was five and he was still adjusting to self-care himself. Requiring him to watch a five-year-old would have seriously limited his freedom, and perhaps have caused Joe to resent his sister. Furthermore, he was only expected to stay alone for an hour at a time, and had the added security of knowing that his grandmother was only a block away—something most latchkey children don't have.

Florence grew up in an apartment in Washington, D.C. Her parents divorced when she was eleven. After the divorce Florence and her mother moved in with her mother's younger sister, who was single at the time. Florence's mother accepted a job and since both adults in the household were working, Florence was left alone for two and one-half hours every afternoon, from the time she was eleven until she graduated from high school. Florence grew up in a safe neighborhood and was free to come and go as she pleased. She enjoyed spending time by herself, and used her spare time walking her dog, playing the piano and reading, since her family didn't own a television set.

Florence recalls few rules she had to follow when she was home alone. "Many things were not spelled out as rules, but I *knew* not to go out and get involved with strangers, leave the neighborhood, play with fire, or do anything else of which my mother would not approve. My husband and I often talk about the way my mother projected her expectations of me and my behavior when I was home alone. We never could figure out how she did it, but the high standard was there. My mother never *expected* that I would be anything less than mature, responsible, intelligent and moral while she was away. And by George, I was all that she expected."

Florence didn't have any difficulties staying alone. She had a close relationship with her mother and understood that, as a single parent, she had to work. "If anything went wrong I would go to the apartment manager, or call the switchboard operator who was a friend of my mother's," she explained.

Florence believes that being alone had a positive effect on her. "It made me mature and independent. It fostered a sense of competence and trustworthiness that I didn't have before. I was old enough to handle the responsibility my mother gave me." Florence was eleven when she started to stay alone, but she had the security of people nearby to whom she could turn for help and she felt comfortable with the amount of time she spent alone.

Even though Florence's experience was a positive one, she still offered advice to parents of latchkey children: "Children under eight are too young to be left alone. I might leave a nine- or ten-year-old for an hour if a neighbor were close by who could be depended upon for help, but I would never leave any child alone for over three hours, and there are some children I wouldn't leave alone at all. It's up to parents to know their children and not ask for more maturity than the child has.

"I also think it's important for parents to provide enrichment activities for children to complete in their spare time and encourage after-school extracurricular activities. Emotional closeness is the key. It worked for me because I had a close relationship with my mother. She shared her life with me and I shared mine with her. We were always honest with each other. She expected everything to be on the up and up, and it was. She trusted me and I lived up to that trust."

Beverly, an only child, also began staying alone after school when she was eleven. Her mother started working when Beverly was two. So she was used to having a working mother. Until Beverly was eleven, her mother had a variety of arrangements to make sure someone was with her daughter after school. Before age five, Beverly's family lived with her mother's mother, who watched Beverly while her mother worked. When Beverly began school her family moved into a house of their own. She then spent her afternoons at the home of a neighbor until her mother arrived from work. Later, her family moved into her great-grandmother's house, and Beverly spent her afternoons helping her great-grandmother with an antique business. It wasn't until her family moved to Cleveland, Ohio, that Beverly, then eleven, had to spend her mornings and afternoons alone.

"When we first moved my mother asked me if I wanted a babysitter to stay with me. I said 'no.' I was adamant. I felt I was old enough to stay by myself. My parents left at 7:30 in the morning and didn't return from work until 7:30 at night. They would wake me up for breakfast as they were leaving. I didn't have to be at school until nine o'clock. I ate, got dressed and caught the bus on my own. I was always afraid I wouldn't wake up in the morning because I had no way to get to school if I missed the bus. I missed the bus about once a month and when I did, my mom got really angry.

"After school I had to follow very specific rules: come directly home, call my mom to tell her I was o.k., finish my homework and do the housework. I was allowed to play outside in our yard, or visit a friend, but I always had to call my mother to tell her where I was going. I had a special friend at that time, Ginger. I would spend one or two days a week at her house and she would come to my house once or twice a week. She was the *only* person I was allowed to have come in the house."

When Beverly wasn't with Ginger, she spent her free time reading or watching television. "The TV was very important to me. I turned it on as soon as I walked in the door, partly because I was bored. I would do a lot of crafts when I was home alone, too, while watching TV. I seldom did my homework. Sometimes I wonder what I would have done if the TV hadn't been around.

"During the summers I was never alone. My mother would send me away to camp for most of the vacation period, then I'd spend a week with one grandmother, then a week with my other grandmother, and another week or two with my mother's sister, who lived on a farm. I spent a lot of the summer away from my parents, because my mother didn't want me to be home alone during the day.

"At times during the year I was frustrated because I couldn't participate in after-school activities. Whenever I felt bad, my mother and I would sit down and have a long talk. We were very close. I was close to my father, too. They asked me if I minded being alone so much. I said I didn't think it was that bad.

"I'm sure being a latchkey child helped me to develop the kind of independence that I did. I feel confident that I can take care of myself in any situation. I don't think of it as a negative experience. It gave me a role model of a professional mother. As a professional woman myself, I think that's critical. I learned a lot being on my own. I love to read and when I was alone, I started to write. Both of those things I still do today. In fact, I just got an article published . . . I'm comfortable with myself. I can spend time alone and enjoy it. A lot of people I know can't do that.

"I would leave my children alone if I had to. In fact, I do. When I got a divorce, my son was ten and my daughter was eight. I had to work to support the three of us, so they were left to care for themselves for a couple of hours every afternoon. I try to stress the positive benefits: self-reliance and self-control. They've been able to adjust to a lot of the upsets they've experienced. We're very close and we talk about everything together."

Beverly spent a great deal of time alone, generally from five to six hours a day, but she still managed to have a positive experience. First, it was her decision to enter self-care, so she didn't feel trapped. She also knew that she could change her mind about it at any time. Secondly, most of her afternoons were spent in the company of her friend, Ginger, reducing the amount of time she was actually alone to three hours a day. Ginger made her long afternoons alone bearable. Being allowed to go to Ginger's house was a bonus, since it provided Beverly with a change of scenery and reduced her sense of isolation. When Beverly was alone, she was able to entertain herself with reading and crafts. Both helped her get through the day. Throughout her latchkey experience, Beverly's family remained intact and she received the support of both her parents. Beverly had fewer adjustments to make than Florence but, given the different personalities of the girls, the experience was positive for both.

Caroline was the youngest of three children. When she was eight, her mother returned to work, at which time Caroline, her eleven-year-old sister and her thirteen-year-old brother stayed home alone afternoons. Caroline described her neighborhood as being "very safe." Her mother hid a key outside, so whoever was the first one home would open the door. Caroline was often first, and although her sister and brother usually entered the house right after her, she didn't like being home by herself, even if it were only for a few minutes. Their mother arrived an hour later.

Caroline was allowed to go to a friend's house for the afternoon or play outside, since her sister was there to watch her. Having grown up in the neighborhood, she knew most of the neighbors by name. At that time there were quite a few neighborhood women who were at home during the day, and Caroline felt she could go to any one of them for help.

"The time we were alone was so short and there was so much to do that it was just an accepted part of life. My mother gave us each jobs to do and we knew that we had to have them done before she got home. When my sister and I finished our chores we would prepare a tea party for mom. We set the table, prepared little snacks and made the tea. Then when mom got home we would have a cup of tea and share the day's events. Mom always made a big fuss over it. Those were very special times.

"The presence of my older brother and sister made me feel safe. They didn't pull rank on me, either. We got along beautifully. When my brother finished his chores, he usually went outside to play so it was really just my sister and me. We were both good kids, and the time we were alone was so short there was no time to get into trouble. It was nice having sis there. She gave me companionship and a sense of security. I know if she hadn't been there, I would've been uncomfortable staying alone."

A number of factors contributed to Caroline's successful experience. First, her latchkey arrangement started very naturally when her mother returned to work. She wasn't upset by the death of either parent, a divorce or a move to a new neighborhood. Another important factor was that Caroline saw her neighborhood as being both safe and familiar, one in which there were a number of people she knew and trusted—people she felt she could call on for help. Caroline also didn't have to stay alone in the afternoons. Instead, she had the security and companionship of an older and well-liked sister.

Consequently, Caroline was neither afraid nor bored during her afternoons alone. She had the freedom to go outside or visit friends if she wished, which kept her from feeling isolated. The length of time these children were asked to care for themselves was limited. This played an important part in the success of their latchkey experience. Even a positive sibling relationship can deteriorate when long periods of time are spent without adult attention, especially when siblings then begin to compete for a severely limited amount of their parents' time. Perhaps the greatest factor contributing to the successful experience of Caroline and her siblings was the quality of the time they spent with their mother. "When mom returned from work, she never seemed too busy or too tired to be with us," Caroline said. These children anticipated their mother's return and prepared for it, saving the excitement and stories about the school day until mom returned from work.

Each of these four former latchkey children had very different experiences. Two were only children; two spent their afternoons with sisters and brothers. Each had a different situation and different problems, but in general all felt the experience was a positive one that was both pleasant at the time and contributed to their long-term personal development. And although the situations are different, there are a few striking similarities: none of these adults began staying alone below the age of eight, all lived in safe neighborhoods and were free to play outside with friends, and all had at least one person to whom they could turn for help. They each described their relationship with their parent or parents as a close one, and felt problems and experiences could be discussed in an open, nonjudgmental manner.

In listening to these former latchkey children speak, a picture begins to form of what it takes for all latchkey children to "reap the benefits" of their arrangement. We can learn from the past, and in the process create a better future for today's latchkey children.

# Chapter 11
# PROGRAMS THAT WORK

There is no single response to the latchkey phenomenon that assures a continuous, safe, quality environment for all children in every situation. Each family must develop its own care package. Each community must provide its own menu of resources based on its own needs and strengths.

The quiet revolution in family life that began when American women started entering the work force in increasing numbers left a gap between the needs of families and available resources. This gap is especially evident in the area of child care.

As public awareness grows, as society adjusts to the notion that child-rearing is not exclusively the responsibility of the child's immediate family, more community resources are being mustered to help families rear their children. Helpful programs are being developed in both the public and private sectors of many communities in for-profit and not-for-profit, charitable and governmental organizations. Individuals are volunteering their talents, time and money to respond to the needs of children. Progress is slow. At times, it seems that we are losing ground. But greater public awareness, cooperative efforts and changes in attitudes are causing the establishment of programs that work in more and more communities.

We have been gratified by the daily stream of calls from individuals and individuals representing organizations from across the country asking for advice as to how they might help children relegated to self-care. Working parents are coming to realize that child care is a responsibility increasingly shared by the community. When this reality is accepted, working parents may feel less reluctant in requesting help.

Following are examples of help models that are working in various communities throughout the nation. They might help stimulate your thinking as to what could be done in your community. It is up to individual parents, familiar with their own needs, to seek, demand and help develop solutions to their own problems. Working parents must begin a systematic and cooperative effort to make certain that all children are well cared for and supervised.

Some programs are designed to remove children from the self-care situation, while others are designed to help children feel safer, less lonely or bored or to reduce parental anxiety while their children remain in self-care.

## Employer-based Efforts in Support of Working Parents

The workplace exerts a powerful influence on American families. And many American families look to their place of employment to help with their child-care needs either by providing services or by making work hours, the workplace or job demands more compatible with family needs.

Business and industry need the family to service the work force, to produce and nurture future employees and to create and maintain a community in which it is possible to do business. Many company executives realize this ecological relationship between the workplace and the home and have set about assessing the problems this relationship creates in order to suggest solutions to them. Most people agree that employers should make it easier for working parents to balance their oftentimes conflicting responsibilities of work and child-rearing.

In 1960 company child care was dismissed as irrelevant or unworkable in most corporate circles. That is less the case today. Many companies struggle to determine how they can respond to the family needs of their employees and still maintain a competitive edge in the marketplace. For some industries child-care services for employees are very good business, indeed. For others it fits with their philosophy of how a responsible corporation should behave.

Every industry and company has its own special culture. What may be desirable in one setting may not be desirable or possible in another. Each employer must make decisions as to what policies or practices to follow, depending on the reality of his or her own environment. Despite all of these cautions, here are some employer-supported programs that are working.

### ON-SITE CHILD CARE

Of all the options available to employers for helping working parents with child care, the most visible is the establishment of a child-care center on or near company premises. According to National Employer Supported Child Care Project data collected by the Pasadena, California–based Child Care Information Service during 1981–1982, approximately 212 U.S. employers were directly supporting child-care centers. Only 43 U.S. corporations were providing on-site child care; fourteen centers were being sponsored by governmental agencies, four by trade unions; the rest were operated by health care organizations.

If there is a pattern characterizing employers with child-care centers, it is their demand for labor. Child-care centers aid in recruitment, especially in organizations heavily dependent on women. Often the existence of a company-owned and -maintained child-care center serves to recruit even employees without children because these employees see such a center as a symbol of a concerned company.

The existence of quality child care also reduces absenteeism and tardiness and greatly reduces turnover among employees with enrolled children, since most are reluctant to move from a job providing adequate child care to one which may even be providing somewhat more money or other benefits, but not child care.

The corporations that have chosen to initiate and maintain on-site child-care centers generally have done so for sound business reasons. It is a costly option and may be an inappropriate one where employees must travel long distances on public transportation. Many organizations, even when they choose to start a center, only provide care for toddlers or preschoolers. Infant care is very expensive because of the very high child-to-staff ratio demanded. Care for school-age children can cause such a transportation nightmare that many companies find offering school-age child care impractical.

New Jersey–based Hoffman LaRoche, a pharmaceutical manufacturer, is one company that provides day-care center care for both preschoolers and school-age children. Diane Keel, the center's director, sees real advantages that the center provides for the company and parents, as well as for the children. Since the child-care center follows the same calendar as the company, it provides for some consistency and stability for employees. "Family ties are strengthened," said Keel in a New York interview, "because kids can stay closer to their parents during the day and parents and children can spend more time together as they commute back and forth to work." Keel has helped some parents arrange to transfer their children to the school district in which Hoffman LaRoche is located, even though the family lives outside that school district, so that the children can take advantage of the school-age programs provided by the company when their school day is over. "Our center operates twelve months a year, whenever the company is in operation," said Keel. "Children who are enrolled here are assured of continuous quality care and their parents are spared the transportation hassles most other types of family care packages demand."

As far as corporate on-site care goes, many hospitals are good locations for child-care centers. Hospitals are often centrally located in communities and are usually served by public transportation. They are facilities that are routinely used by everyone in the community. They have established food, laundry and housekeeping services, provide medical care on the premises and are open twenty-four hours a day. While not perfect, their many resources have helped make hospitals the leading provider of company-sponsored child-care centers.

The great majority of hospital child-care centers serve only children of hospital employees, however. And even then fees are often so high that not all of the staff can afford the service, when available.

Most company-sponsored child-care centers charge employees for the services provided. Costs are usually held down because the company provides the space used by the center and frequently has underwritten center startup costs. Most companies don't prefer to subsidize day-to-day operating expenses. But the cost of sending a child to many company centers might still mean that not all employees could afford it, unless the company further chooses to subsidize their portion of operating costs in addition to startup, space and utility costs.

Company-sponsored centers generally strive to provide high quality services despite higher costs. Larry Honeywell, senior vice-president of Official Airline Guides, Oak Brook, Illinois, a company that sponsors a company-owned and -maintained center that includes infant care, said: "Most employees wanted a developmental care center rather than a place that warehoused their children, and they were prepared to pay more for such a program." Most companies that provide center care agree with this assessment. Current costs at the Official Airline Guides' center are between $45 and $65 per week, per child.

Some companies limit enrollment in their facilities to children of employees. Others, such as the Stride Rite Child Care Center, Boston, Massachusetts, also serve the community. In this case, arrangements were made with the Massachusetts Department of Public Welfare to fill a portion of the available spaces in the center with children from the community. Tuition for Stride Rite employees is ten percent of their salaries. A contract with the Massachusetts Department of Welfare holds costs for community children to an amount substantially under the actual cost of operating the center on a per-child, per-week basis.

Tax incentives are available for companies considering day care. If a corporation establishes a day-care center to increase productivity, then company-supplied startup and operating costs are fully deductible business expenses. Intermedics, a Texas manufacturer, established its center, the largest industry-based day-care facility in the United States, as a profit-making, wholly owned subsidiary that operates at a loss, for which the company receives a one-hundred percent tax deduction. Intermedics' executives estimate that since their center's beginning, in December, 1979, half of the company's outlay has been offset by the tax benefits. The center is therefore no more expensive to the company than a good health policy and saves the company thousands of hours in reduced absenteeism and decreased turnover.

A corporation may file for tax-exempt status if its child-care center is incorporated separately, is not for profit and is open to the community, such as the Corning Glass Works Children's Center, Corning, New York.

Corning, in response to the dissatisfaction of many of its employees with their day-care arrangements, established an all-day, high quality child-care program designed to serve both community and employee children. It is funded through the Corning Glass Works Foundation.

Corning spent a year and a half planning a response to the community's child-care needs. In the process it outlined some qualities that all successful corporate day-care centers seem to have included:

- Commitment from a major sponsor for long-term financial support
- Qualified, trained and adequately paid staff
- Parent and community involvement
- Realistic expectations about the profit-making potential of the center
- Realistic expectations about initial and long-term enrollment (only a fraction of families who indicate interest in these projects actually enroll their children, at least at the outset)
- Maintaining optimism that if a need exists and a quality response is being provided, corporate child-care programs will eventually be accepted as part of the community and pay tangible and intangible benefits to the corporation.

Child care in a company-operated facility is available in less than one percent of U.S. companies. But such centers are programs that work, if the right combination of factors are brought together. Employed parents who experience the need for child care to guarantee their children continuous safe supervision shouldn't be embarrassed to suggest a company-supported child-care center as a possible solution. Most centers began because employees made their needs known. Still, employed parents can't insist on this as the only solution.

### CONSORTIA SPONSORED CENTER CARE

One of the least used approaches for child care is the joining together of several organizations to use pooled resources to finance a child-care center. The potential for such arrangements is great.

Two-thirds of all employees work in small businesses. But special circumstances must arise to make such arrangements work. Corporate competitors anxious to gain a competitive edge generally will not cooperate. Companies too far separated geographically find transportation an obstacle. When circumstances are right, however, cooperative arrangements can help overcome cost obstacles and protect against unexpectedly low enrollment rates that can periodically result from changes in a single corporation.

Malls are good places for cooperative arrangements. Many malls are becoming the unorganized care centers of latchkey children anyhow, as unsupervised children gather in the arcades, attend the mall theaters, meet together in the open areas of malls or wander through the shops. Industrial complexes are also good places for employers to cooperate, by reason of the geographic proximity of a number of businesses. Frequently no one organization in an industrial complex would be able to support a child-care center on its own, but the combined resources of several businesses could. In more modern industrial complexes, open space which is allowed to make the complex more attractive can also serve as available outdoor play space for children.

The Northside Child Development Center in Minneapolis provides child-care services for Control Data, Pillsbury, Northwestern Bell, the Federal Reserve Bank of Minneapolis, and a number of other employers. A common geographic location brought these employers together.

Children's Village was established in 1976 to provide worksite child care, largely for the children of employees of Philadelphia's garment industry. The Philadelphia Council for Labor and Industry helped found Children's Village by establishing a governing board that included representatives from government, business and labor. Some startup funds were obtained from the State of Pennsylvania and contributing employers obtained tax deductions. The Council for Labor and Industry saw that long-term benefits of a child-care center would be realized by encouraging mothers to hold productive jobs and by revitalizing the garment industry in Philadelphia.

The Broadcasters Child Development Center in Washington, D.C., is a good example of a care center started entirely by industry employees in cooperation with seven TV and radio stations, the National Academy of Television Arts and Sciences and American

University. Forty percent of the available slots are filled by community children, the rest by children of employees involved in broadcasting.

## INFORMATION AND REFERRAL SERVICES

In some communities part of the problem for parents is matching existing child care with family need. Many parents would rather place their children in some type of day care than leave them in self-care, if they could find it available. Many times satisfactory adult care is available but parents, particularly those who have moved into a new neighborhood, are unaware of it. Because these parents are blind to an available solution, they opt for self-care. The self-care option usually also means making a mental adjustment to accept one's child as adequate to the task. Once this is done, unless some traumatic experience later occurs, self-care becomes a permanent fixture, even though the family later learns of other acceptable alternatives.

Some government agencies provide services to families in helping them identify licensed or certified child-care facilities. This is certainly a service, but the majority of school-age children are not cared for in licensed or certified facilities and consequently many potentially useful resources may be overlooked by such agencies.

Corporations can help fill the information gap. Many are equipped with sophisticated computer systems that could be adapted to provide the location, fees, limitations and hours of operation of existing community resources. One such service was begun with funding and technical assistance from more than ten companies located in Minneapolis, Minnesota, in cooperation with Hennepin County, the local political jurisdiction. The system was designed by three non-profit child-care resource agencies: the Greater Minneapolis Day Care Association, the Southside Child Care Resource Center and the North Suburban Child Care Association. These three agencies now also operate the system known as the Child Care Information Network. Once this system was in place, it supplanted a small manual retrieval system operated by Hennepin County.

The Child Care Information Network was established in 1981 with impetus provided by Honeywell, General Mills and other similar employers who saw child care and work-related family issues as concerns that they might help address. "Honeywell has approximately fifty locations in the Minneapolis–St. Paul area," said Sonia Cairns, program manager of Honeywell's Corporate and Community Responsibility Department, "so a central day-care facility didn't seem to be our company's best response to family needs for dependent care. Instead, we have developed programs that make use of private, public and community resources. These include strong support for a computerized information and referral system, working parents' seminars, and now Honeywell is considering implementing a flexible benefits plan that would include a dependent care option. Our belief is that Honeywell's package benefits our employees as well as the larger community and it encourages a sense of confidence in parents to use their own abilities to identify and use their own and other resources."

Bonnie Martin of General Mills and Cairns both agree that the success of the Child Care Information Network might result in some user fees in the future to offset the cost of increasingly heavy use of the system. "Many companies are willing to contribute to start-up costs," said Martin, "but are reluctant to continue to underwrite costs of such projects on a long-term basis." "If the system begins to charge a user fee," said Cairns, "it is likely that participating companies will purchase a certain number of referrals for use by their employees. I don't see this system as being in jeopardy; it's working too well."

Information and referral services not only provide child-care information, but become involved in increasing the supply of child care. One service begun by a group of parents in 1981, the Child Care Resource Center in Cambridge, Massachusetts, is subscribed to by many companies that find they can offer an immediate response to their employees' child-care needs with little start-up time or expense and use the information reported back to the company by the service to decide what further steps the company might wish to take in responding to the dependent-care needs of their employees and the community.

Some information and referral services use incoming information to assess unmet needs and then become advocates for getting these needs met. Working parents often call to ask which employers provide child care. That's where these parents will seek employment. Companies use these services to look for alternatives to on-site child care.

Community-based information and referral services such as that in Cambridge can serve many community organizations simultaneously. A small organization can simply subscribe to the service. Other organizations may want to employ an in-house coordinator to assist by providing on-site information and training in addition to making use of such information systems. Examples of companies that have hired in-house information and retrieval counselors are Steelcase, Incorporated, of Grand Rapids, Michigan, and Mountain Bell in Denver, Colorado.

Steelcase is a nonunion, family-owned business with 6,000 employees. Hugh Faulkner Jones, a clinical psychologist at Steelcase, said at a recent meeting in Racine, Wisconsin, that employees meet with a counselor to discuss child-care needs, among other issues, and the counselor helps them to develop a suitable child-care response. Information and referral counselors make referrals to registered family day-care providers, but also work to help nonregistered providers become registered. These counselors maintain contact with the child-care community because they realize they have to look everywhere for realistic answers to complex problems.

Companies like Steelcase, especially those that have special problems because their employees work shifts of ten or eleven hours, or that routinely employ many members of the same family, believe they make best use of their financial assistance by helping their employees become better consumers of the available services they purchase. But these companies are also aware that at times they must add to the available child-care supply because of special needs. Steelcase discovered by tabulating requests for child-care services that their employees experienced the greatest need for services for infants below the age of one, for school-age children and for special help during odd hours due to night shift work. Such information will help Steelcase determine what level and type of corporate child-care assistance might be further required.

## SUBSIDIES, VOUCHERS OR REIMBURSEMENT PROGRAMS

Some companies help their employees defray the cost of child care by way of subsidies, vouchers or reimbursement programs. Such programs offer the advantage of flexibility, but can also exclude employees who are not able to find acceptable child care.

The Polaroid Child Care Subsidy Program provides nationwide reimbursement for income-eligible employees' child care on a sliding scale. Polaroid is headquartered in Cambridge, Massachusetts, but operates from twenty-six locations. Polaroid decided that an on-site solution could not meet the needs of its employees and came to believe that an employer subsidy for child care could make it possible for their employee-parents to purchase services of higher quality and greater reliability. The Polaroid program has been in operation since 1971, paying subsidies of between five and eighty percent of child-care expenses for employees earning less than $25,000 per year. Polaroid will pay for care only in licensed child-care homes or centers or for care provided by relatives. The cost of Polaroid's subsidy program is considered a work-related business expense and is tax deductible.

Of course, many state and local governments provide subsidized child care or subsidies for child care. However, most publicly operated social service plans provide far too few spaces even for eligible children, especially school-age children. And the income ceiling for government child-care subsidies is usually so low that most working, especially two-income families, are ineligible. Corporate subsidies are usually more realistically targeted to the incomes of their employees.

The Ford Foundation in New York City operates a child-care subsidy program similar to Polaroid's and in addition provides payment for employees to consult with child-care specialists about their child's education. Organizations that provide subsidy programs often find that they must soon develop or begin to participate in an information and retrieval system in order for their employees to make the most informed choices about child care.

Other companies subsidize child care by reserving and paying for places for their employees' children in existing child-care programs. Or, as in the case of the Connecticut General Life Insurance of Bloomfield, Connecticut, they negotiate to have a privately operated center run on their property. The company, then, in return for a guarantee of the purchase of a certain number of child slots, obtains a discount in the fees charged its employees for child care.

Two programs in the state of Florida seem to be special in the way they have developed a partnership between the public and private sectors in providing child care. One program is Community Coordinated Child Care of Central Florida, located in Orlando, Florida.

This program is an assurance plan that brings together the resources of a managing agency, a network of local providers, the public day care subsidy program and employers whose employees need day-care services.

The management agency, called 4-C, determines the eligibility of employees for public child-care assistance, establishes the fee each employee will pay for needed child care and then determines the corporate subsidy that is needed after public funds and the family's ability to pay have been deducted from the total cost for child care. 4-C supplies, both directly and by referral, child health services, counseling and other services the family needs during the child-care placement process, including coordination with the public school system. 4-C takes care of all accounting, collecting fees, paying providers and reporting to each participating business.

The advantage of such a system is that many aspects of the child-care network can be coordinated and a child can continue in the same child-care environment despite changes in family circumstances. 4-C can also provide centralized support services to providers including training, resource depots, health clinics and communication systems that small individual providers are not able to afford on their own.

Such networks are better able to assure payment of fees through the establishment of a central trust, and allow parents to choose the most appropriate care-giver for their children because of centralized information and referral systems. The 4-C system includes for-profit and not-for-profit, church and secular related, academically and physically oriented services at every age level.

Another Florida cooperative that operates in Pinellas and Pasco counties is just beginning to expand its already sizable network to a corporate child-care system. This non-profit agency, called Latchkey, is headquartered in Largo, Florida, and currently serves nearly two thousand school-age children with working parents as well as programs for infants and preschoolers. Since Latchkey centers are largely operated in public schools, a more detailed description of the program will be given later.

Programs like 4-C and Latchkey can make use of not only center care but care in private homes that accept only a few children. This type of care, called family day care, is most preferred for very young children and for school-age children.

## FAMILY DAY CARE

Some employers become involved in family day care networks because of the lower startup costs, the flexibility provided by multiple sites that can service employees living in a widely distributed area, and the fact that many families prefer these more homelike environments that can keep all siblings together in one location.

The Massachusetts Institute of Technology Family Day Care Program is really a network of independent, self-employed family day care homes. In this case all providers are affiliated with MIT and largely serve MIT-affiliated families. The child-care office recruits providers, helps them become licensed by the Commonwealth of Massachusetts and monitors the level of service provided on a regular basis. The program then serves as a broker between those needing care and those willing to provide it.

Some other programs, such as the Family Day Care Network located in San Francisco, California, service many employers simultaneously. This network provides services to employees in eleven hospitals who need access to child care for various periods of time, twenty-four hours a day. Hospitals are special in that their employees demand child care around the clock and on weekends and holidays. Hospitals are also often reluctant to start on-site care centers for children that might interfere with their ability to carry out their health care business.

The San Francisco Family Day Care Network differs from that at MIT not only in that it is a cooperative but that, in addition to brokering and monitoring functions, it helps providers relieve space constraints by purchasing space. By buying property the network gets equity and is able to offer providers low-rent housing.

All providers are independent contractors but the network helps relieve the isolation usually experienced by such contractors by arranging training for providers, for which the provider is paid, and for substitutes so that providers can get a day off occasionally to carry out personal business.

The cooperating employers support the Family Day Care Network's staff, which in turn coordinates the network's involvement with federal, state and local programs. The staff also provides a sick-child-care component, monitors the individual homes, creates a benefits package for providers and offers them any other technical assistance requested. Participating hospitals refer their parent-employees to the network for placement and generally pay for a number of slots on an annual basis or are charged for each child of an employee using the service.

## EDUCATIONAL PROGRAMS

Working parents need additional information to help them successfully juggle job and family. Some employers are offering educational programs at the worksite to give working parents the information and additional parenting skills they need. Such programs tend to be preventative rather than problem-focused. Parents employed by the same organization offer support to one another, and can collaborate to advise their organization of other improvements it could make to ease employee parenting needs.

A series of seminars titled "Balancing Both Worlds—A Challenge for the Working Mother," developed through the Dayton Hudson Foundation, has been delivered through various United Ways at a number of employer sites during the work day. Control Data has developed a parent education curriculum that is available to employees through its Plato computer system. And the General Accounting Office of the U.S. government has developed a series of seminars on parenting and other family-related issues that is delivered to its employees, usually by its in-house counseling-center staff.

Such seminars help employees become aware of resources outside the company that can assist them in child-rearing and a supportive network of people inside the company, as well as of company benefits. Employees are also helped to become more aware of personal resources, better means of child-rearing, and more attentive to employer and community needs.

The Texas Institute for Families located in Houston, Texas, has had as a goal to establish a statewide program of brokering information and resources among parents, professionals, academics, civic, business and public leaders. Noontime seminars offered by this institute have been offered to employees in more than two dozen companies around Texas. And the Institute's involvement with a large number of companies has increased corporate awareness of family problems.

## WORKPLACE PRACTICES

The above programs largely focus on ways to help families find substitute care for their children. Many parents prefer to have at least one parent available during all of their children's waking hours to offer direct personal care. Some parents resent missing so much of their children's growing up because of work schedules, or are concerned that their children's personalities will be more influenced by a series of caretakers than by the parents themselves. Many parents who waited until their children began full days at school to return to work feel concerned that school-day schedules and work-day schedules so often seem incompatible.

One parent somewhat tearfully told us that she dropped her nine-year-old off at a day-care center at 7:15 each morning and picked her up there at 6:15 each evening. "It's a very good center and my daughter seems to like it," the mother said. "But then, because she has to get up at 6:15 each morning, she goes to bed about 7:30 each night. You know, my daughter's learned to ride a bicycle, but we didn't teach her, the day-care center teacher did."

This mother and her husband are both pursuing very rewarding careers, but there is no mistaking the pain she feels that their jobs allow so little time most work days to spend with their daughter.

As the nation's labor force approaches being staffed equally by men and women, attitudes about the responsibility for parenting are also changing. Despite the fact that among single-parent families ninety percent are headed by women, partially an artifact of the philosophy and intervention practices of the courts, there has been a marked attitudinal swing which now sees the responsibility for parenting as an equal obligation resting on both the mother and father.

Attitudes toward parenting are having an impact on workplace practices, just as are employee needs at various stages of development. Greater flexibility is being demanded from companies in benefit packages, in work schedules, in the location of the place work is carried out, in policies regarding sick days, personal leave days, maternity and paternity leave policies, in policies governing work-related travel and job relocation.

Some organizations are taking these demands for change seriously and have begun to rewrite workplace practices. Perhaps the most complex change is to be found in the rewriting of benefit plans.

FLEXIBLE BENEFITS

Most companies today still design their benefits plans as if every employee were a male head of household with children and a wife who stayed home to watch them. This image only accounts for a fraction of American families. By and large, corporate benefit structures have not caught up with changes in the American family and work force. One possible solution to changes in society is to create flexible or "cafeteria-style" benefit packages from which employees may choose a limited number of benefits, depending on the employee's current life circumstances.

Cafeteria-style benefits plans were pioneered by a company called TRW. A few other companies such as American Can and Pepsico have followed suit. While today such plans tend to cover only options in five benefit areas: retirement/savings, medical, disability and life insurance and vacation or leave days, newer plans are including dependent care options as part of the list of benefits from which employees may choose. Honeywell, Incorporated, is expected to implement such a plan in 1984.

There are problems with flexible benefit plans. They are more complex and usually demand more administrative costs. There is the possibility that some employees will make unwise choices that affect both the employer and employee—trading all vacation days for child-care benefits, for example.

Employees who use flexible benefit plans say that they find them satisfying. With such plans already in place, an employer can easily offer new benefits without adding costs. For the working parent, benefits that offer dependent care subsidies or more days off might be very attractive while their children are young.

## CHILD-CARE ALLOWANCES AS A FRINGE BENEFIT

Many people are not yet aware that the United States Congress authorized a new tax-free fringe benefit as part of the 1981 Economic Recovery Tax Act. This benefit, called the Dependent Care Assistance Program (D-CAP), could produce a real breakthrough in making quality child care affordable to parents. A Dependent Care Assistance Program may be added to any employer's benefit package and benefits can be applied to any day-care expenses for employees' children age fourteen or younger or for a disabled spouse or disabled dependent of any age. Benefits may be used to cover care in an employer-sponsored child-care center, in other licensed day-care centers, in family day-care homes, in after-school programs, day camps or in the employee's own home during the hours the employee is at work. First the employer must prepare a written D-CAP plan setting forth the eligibility requirements for the fringe benefit, and establishing a method of payment. These payments are tax deductible as a business expense for the employer. Employers interested in implementing such a program may receive further information regarding how to do so by contacting the I.R.S., a benefits specialist, their company's accounting firm or a local day-care organization which offers general child-care information or technical assistance.

There are two ways of financing this new child-care program. Benefits may be underwritten by the employer as a fringe benefit that is in addition to the employee's pay, and/or the Dependent Care Assistance Program allowance may be a salary "set-aside" where employees may designate a portion of their gross salary to be used for dependent care. Since this salary "set-aside" lowers the employee's taxable income, it reduces that individual's federal taxes, as well as Social Security taxes for both the employee and employer.

Dependent Care Assistant Programs underwritten by employers appear to be a relatively simple means to help workers afford child care, if employers choose to offer such an additional benefit. Since the United States Internal Revenue Service has yet to issue regulations on salary "set-aside" plans and there is no legislative history about such provisions, it is unclear how "set-asides" will be accepted by the I.R.S. At present, verbal communication from the I.R.S. is that they will not allow salary "set-asides" since no limits or regulations have yet been written into the law. Employees who, under the auspices of their employer, wish to set aside part of their salary at this time run some risk of having their claim denied by the I.R.S. for tax purposes until a provision for such a plan is made.

To understand the tax benefits of a Dependent Care Assistance Program consider the following: when such a program is offered as a fringe benefit, you would obtain more spendable income than an equivalent amount in straight salary. For example, if you are given a child-care allowance of $1,500 a year, the full $1,500 is available to pay for child care. However, if you're given $1,500 as additional taxable income, then you would receive only $1,200 of spendable income if you're in the 20 percent tax bracket and only $750 if you're in the 50 percent tax bracket.

If you were to shelter $1,500 as a salary "set-aside" under a Dependent Care Assistance Program, your taxable gross pay would be reduced by the amount used for the child-care allowance, resulting in significant tax savings.

In addition to tax benefits obtained from the federal government, some states add child-care tax credits at a percentage of the federal tax credit. New York, for example, offers a state child-care tax credit at 20 percent of the federal tax credit.

Few states offer child-care tax credits to employees, but eleven states currently give tax credits to employers who construct or renovate an on-site or near-site child-care center. Connecticut, for example, has a generous start-up tax credit for employers. To date, tax incentives for employers haven't produced many responses, but with increased need for child care and new federal initiatives, perhaps this record will change.

Associations—such as the Pre-School Association, Inc., in New York City, which addresses itself to child-care concerns—are working hard to gather information for both parents and employers regarding programs and policy issues affecting child care. Studies carried out by such local research groups as the Greater Washington (D.C.) Research Center and the Day Care Forum, also in New York City, are beginning to report statistics indicating that the *primary* arrangement for supplemental child care, at least for school-age children, is self-care by the child. The results of such studies should increase employer incentives to consider employer-facilitated childcare options and encourage schools to look at school-supported, extended-care alternatives.

## FLEXTIME

The work force has changed dramatically since 1940; the average work week has not. Today's working parents need less rigid work hours and job arrangements, but are often constrained by a standardization of worktime that was put in place when the country's economy depended on the manufacture of goods and men were the mainstay of the work force.

Flexible worktime options, or "flextime," are ways of scheduling work that permit employee options in determining arrival and departure times, even the number of days in which work hours will be carried out. Flextime does not usually reduce the total number of hours in the employee's work week, but it relaxes the routine of working 9:00 to 5:00, five days a week.

Flextime can allow the working partners in a marriage to arrange their individual work hours in order that at least one parent can be present whenever their children are at home. Even in single-parent families, the working parent can use flextime to work when children are otherwise occupied, as during school hours, or when child care is most likely to be available.

Flextime was introduced to the United States during the 1960s. It has spread gradually since then. Today about fifteen percent of all nongovernmental organizations with fifty or more employees use flextime. Surveys conducted by Better Homes and Gardens, the 1980 White House Conference on Families and General Mills all confirm that the majority of respondents would be interested in some form of flexible work scheduling.

Alternative work schedules currently include options ranging from staggered work shifts chosen by the employee through flexible starting times, flexible work hours and flexible work days. Following the options allowed, employees can choose their own work start times, vary their start times from day to day, vary the length of the hours worked from day to day or the length of the lunch hour, or can carry hours to be worked from one day to the next. Some options even allow compressing the work week to, for example, four ten-hour days or even three twelve- or thirteen-hour days.

Flexibility in work scheduling can often mean that parents can work full-time jobs and still have one or the other parent present during all or most of the hours their children would be otherwise unattended. Parents have found that flexible work schedules can completely eliminate self-care as an option for their school-age children, or at least reduce the time of self-care to only a fraction of an hour a day.

Working women and women planning to work are the groups most interested in employer policies that allow employees greater flexibility in work schedules. As women enter the labor force, and maintain attitudes about their responsibilities as mothers and wives, they find themselves with less personal discretionary time.

Flexible scheduling and other flexible company policies regarding work schedules will not in and of themselves increase the time workers spend with their families. Attitudes about family involvement will have to be improved in order for parents to use work schedule flexibility to increase the time parents spend with their children.

Because current evidence is that many workers do not spend more time on family life as a result of flexible scheduling, most companies instituting flextime are not doing so as a solution to family-work problems, but rather to reduce absenteeism, tardiness or commuter congestion. The important point here is that programs that can work won't unless parents cooperate with them. Flexible work schedules can have no impact on child-care arrangements if parents use flexible time to play golf or to undertake a second job instead.

### PERMANENT PART-TIME WORK

Other ways for working parents to increase the amount of time they have available for their families include part-time work and job sharing whereby two people share the responsibilities of one full-time job, usually with salary and fringe benefits prorated between the two employees.

About thirty percent of employed women work part-time. And polls indicate that a much larger percentage would prefer part-time work if it were available.

Workers who need a regular income avoid part-time work in many cases because it means sacrificing many of the benefits usually enjoyed by full-time workers, like accumulating seniority, job security and other benefits such as health insurance, vacations and paid sick leave.

There are problems in employing a part-time work force. Many companies believe that it is more costly to employ part-time people, even though benefits are prorated. And there are obviously personnel problems when the number of workers a company has to deal with is increased, even though the total number of hours they work is not.

But companies that have tried using permanent part-time employees, such as Connecticut General and Xerox, find that associated disadvantages can be overcome. Equitable Life Insurance Company of New York has developed a three-day work week as well as a system of paying employees only for the hours they work while prorating benefits. Working mothers seem to be especially happy to have the option of working flexible lengths of time. Part-time work seems an ideal way to allow for parental responsibilities while continuing to pursue a career or participate in the country's recognized labor force.

JOB SHARING

Job sharing is another way that allows parents to spend more time with their children while working. Many people see job sharing as a way for a husband and wife to split a single job so that both can participate in the labor force. If this were the extent of job sharing, it would not be workable for many people. Job sharing actually involves any two people sharing the responsibilities of one full-time job and dividing the salary and benefits. Job sharing allows coverage of a job that doesn't lend itself to part-time work. Job sharing reduces stress on the worker because each worker is able to share job tasks with someone else. Employers get a wider range of employee skills and one partner can cover for the other in case of an emergency.

Job sharing and permanent part-time work help parents to see an alternative to the all-or-nothing concept of work or parenting. These work options allow parents to cover most, if not all, hours their school-age children are at home while earning a salary, albeit a reduced one. Some companies using job sharing pair an older worker with a younger one to make child-care coverage possible and in many cases to foster a kind of job apprenticeship relationship.

As the available work force shrinks during the mid-1980s, it is likely that more companies will see some greater advantage to implementing job sharing and permanent part-time options. Increase in the available labor force will likely come from increasing the number of women in the labor force or from expanding the involvement of workers at either end of the work age spectrum. All of these work groups, women (usually mothers), senior citizens and adolescents appear even now to want to work, but often not on a full-time basis. This potential labor pool also seems willing to trade time for money, a characteristic less common in middle-age males. As more information becomes available about the workability of such options in the marketplace, the current reluctance of companies to implement them should diminish.

THE FLEXIBLE WORKPLACE

The increase of technology has opened another option for parents who need to accommodate work demands with home responsibilities. Many jobs can now be carried out with a computer and a telephone hookup that can be installed anywhere. Some companies are beginning to experiment with allowing employees to work at home. Experts in labor even foresee a great increase in cottage industries as the cost of transportation merges with a technology that allows work to be carried out without face-to-face contact.

The advantages to families of the option of the flexible workplace are not readily apparent. This work option is still in its infancy, although companies such as Atari, Lanier and Continental Bank of Chicago allow work-at-home options for some of their employees. Perhaps the greatest stumbling block to the widespread use of a flexplace option will be employee and employer attitude. Accepting the fact that work can be adequately carried out at home, especially with children present, runs counter to the common wisdom that parents can't get anything accomplished while their children are awake. Accommodations may well have to be made to intermingle work and parenting responsibilities loosely throughout the day, but this can only be accomplished if parents are readily accessible to their children as in a work-at-home situation.

## Community Efforts in Support of Working Parents

Even though many employees look to their place of employment to find answers for providing continuous care for their children, employers are not the sole resource. A growing number of alternatives are being initiated in communities across the nation, sometimes with corporate support, sometimes with governmental support, sometimes through personal cooperative and volunteer efforts of many people without any external support. The following sections will outline programs that are working, or models that give promise of working, to relieve problems associated with child self-care. As before, some models serve to remove children from the latchkey situation entirely, others try to help latchkey children and their parents establish the best self-care environment possible.

### SCHOOL-BASED CHILD CARE

Even though most corporate care is focused on preschool youth, latchkey children are largely of school age. They have entered an age during which their care is already shared between their parents and the school. School-based child-care programs are programs that supplement the care provided children during the normal school day.

Sharing the care of one's children does not mean removing responsibility from the child's parents. It is the result of the reality of American life that accepts mandated universal education; the necessity of a large work force now made up almost equally of men and women; the fact that America is no longer mainly a farming society and the dissolving of the extended family so common a century ago. Developing alternative ways of sharing the care of our children is a way of compensating for the loss of the extended family and can, if well done, develop kinship networks that do not depend upon blood relationships.

We do not wish to tell you here how to design, develop, initiate and operate school-based care programs for children. There is a book called *School Age Childcare: An Action Manual* (Auburn House Publishing Co., 1982) by Ruth Baden, Andrea Genser, James A. Levine and Michelle Seligson that does an adequate job of doing that. Instead we want to describe briefly some programs that seem to be working. Perhaps you can then elaborate on one of these themes in your own environment.

School-based child care makes sense nowadays. We have built more schools in many parts of the country than the current school-age population warrants. As a result classroom space is becoming more available, making school-based care a viable option in many areas. In addition, children are already transported to school for half of the year. And there is something positive to be said about allowing children to remain in a consistent environment, rather than being moved from one environment to another several times each day. School space often provides a lower cost option as a care facility than other forms of center care, since schools are already built and equipped for children.

*Madison, Wisconsin.* Some programs, such as that operated by the Afterschool Day Care Association, Incorporated, Madison, Wisconsin, came about as the result of a group of citizens identifying an unmet community need and then doing something about it. In Madison the Afterschool Day Care Association was formed in 1974 to service five after-school programs that were operating or about to open in the city. These programs, ironically, were partially spawned as a result of teacher union negotiations that resulted in shorter public school hours. This action drew attention to the growing number of families with school-age children in which all resident adults worked and which, as a consequence, had need of child-care services.

Some of the early Madison programs closed because of low enrollment. The Association was surprised to discover that some working parents did not see a need for continuous supervised care for seven-year-olds. The Association then set out to discover which parents did see a need for extended care for their school-age children and which neighborhoods had enough interested families to support such programs. A needs assessment done in 1978 determined that the kinds of families more likely to use an after-school care program were: headed by a single parent, had younger children, had mothers in professional or managerial jobs and had used preschool day-care programs with which they were satisfied.

Armed with data, the Association set up and now sponsors nine programs that operate three to four hours at the end of each school day. Eight of the programs operate in Madison public schools located in neighborhoods with families most likely to use the services. The ninth program is located in a former school building that also houses a variety of other child-related agencies. All nine programs are open all day during school vacations.

Initial funding for Association programs came from the University of Wisconsin and space was donated by the Madison public schools. The Association quickly found that public funding was unreliable. As a consequence, the Association determined that, in order to operate stable, high-quality programs, it had to rely on parent fees. Unsubsidized parents pay the full cost for the child-care slots used by their children, about $25.00 per week per child. Most low-income parents receive direct child-care subsidies through the county-run Social Services Block Grant. Other needy families obtain subsidies through the City of Madison Day Care Unit.

Costs for these programs are held down somewhat because the paid staff is assisted by volunteers from the University of Wisconsin Schools of Education and Family Studies. These student volunteers often obtain course credit or satisfy field work requirements while they help reduce the normal ten-to-one child-to-staff ratio.

The United Cerebral Palsy Association trains its After School Day Care staffs to facilitate mainstreaming of children with special needs into child-care centers. This cooperative effort helps relieve a serious child-care problem for many parents with exceptional children.

*Arlington, Virginia.* The Extended Day Program operated in the public elementary schools of Arlington County, Virginia, was one of the first programs established in the United States. It began in 1969 as the result of the concern of the Arlington Health and Welfare Council for a growing number of latchkey children.

The initial program served sixty-six children in three elementary schools. Today there is an extended day center in every elementary school in the county. These centers operate from 7:00 A.M. until 6:00 P.M. and serve over twelve hundred children, about equally divided between children from single parents and two-income families.

Arlington County pays for one-third of the cost to operate the program. The other two-thirds of program costs are obtained from parent fees. These fees are assessed on a sliding fee scale ranging from approximately $8 to $80 per child per month.

The extended day centers in Arlington County are staffed by paid child-care workers. The entire program is coordinated by Pat Rowland and one assistant and monitored by a countywide advisory committee. Rowland was careful to note that while the Extended Day Program operates in public elementary schools, its budget is not part of the county schools' budget.

*Suburban Minneapolis, Minnesota.* Other programs are administered by the school district. In the Robbinsdale Area schools an extended day program running from 6:45 A.M. until 6:00 P.M. is administered by the school district's community education department. The summer program is a collaborative effort between the YMCA and the school district's summer school.

Programs such as this one also manage to assure participating children hot breakfasts and lunches, involvement in programs sponsored by the parks and recreation department and even such benefits as special gymnastics and drama courses. Fees average about $25 per week per child. Low-income families are subsidized from community funds on a sliding fee scale.

*Nashville, Tennessee.* Many programs are initiated because of collaborative efforts on the part of citizens who may or may not personally need the use of the services they are helping to develop. Generally programs, whether citizen-initiated or not, are operated by people other than the users of the service. The Eakin Care Program is an exception. This school-based center is run by the parents who use it. They are accountable to the school principal and to the system that contributes the school space and utilities rent free, but they hire the staff, set policies and support all other costs.

*Columbia, Maryland.* The Columbia Public Schools sponsor an after-school program that can provide extended care for a limited number of children between the hours of 3:30 and 5:25, five days a week during the school year and a cafeteria package for children who may only need extended care a day or two each week. This cafeteria model allows children from kindergarten through sixth grade to be enrolled for one or two classes in a wide variety of areas of interest on any weekday they choose. Subjects include crafts, exercise, foreign languages, sewing, board games, storytelling, cooking, journalism, dancing and even archeology.

Were it not for the extended day component, such a program would not prove satisfactory for children needing adult supervision five days each week. But as a school-based option for children needing a limited amount of care each week, or as a regular break in the monotony of being in daily self-care, the Columbia After School Program offers a relatively inexpensive alternative that could operate even more inexpensively using a number of volunteer instructors, each teaching a two-week course one day a week, and a small number of paid supervisory personnel.

*Fairfax County, Virginia.* Perhaps the most common models of school-based school-age child-care programs are partnership models, such as that operated in Fairfax County, Virginia, and joint occupancy programs on a lease for a fee basis, such as that operated by adjoining Montgomery County, Maryland.

The Fairfax County program began in the early 1970s and is similar in structure to that in neighboring Arlington County, Virginia. In the intervening years it has grown from eight pilot programs to nearly thirty centers, including services for the handicapped. All centers are housed in public schools, but are administered by the Fairfax County Office for children. It is this partnership between a nonschool agency and the schools that helps reduce the burden of operation of extended care programs for school systems while still allowing services to be offered in public school buildings.

In order to be eligible for one of Fairfax's School Age Child Care Centers children must be enrolled in grades K through 6 in Fairfax County public schools. Children must attend the same school in which the center is located, and all adults living in the child's home must be:

a) working at least 30 hours a week and/or
b) attending employment-related educational or training programs at least 30 hours a week and/or
c) medically unable to care for the child.

While the Fairfax Centers operate both before and after school during all days schools are in session, children cannot register for before-school care only or for care on a temporary basis. These centers try to care for children whenever circumstances cause late school openings or early school closings, an all-too-common phenomenon for schools in the country's snow belt. These centers do not operate on school holidays or when the school is closed for a full day for other reasons. Parents must enroll their children in a separate program if care is wished during winter, spring and summer vacations.

The Fairfax County School Age Child Care system has been aided by a grant from the Wellesley School Age Child Care Project, a group operating from Wellesley College, Wellesley, Massachusetts. This group has been interested since its beginning in 1979 in the ways communities put collaborative child-care programs together. "For the most part public schools have been one of the partners in the programs we have studied," said Michelle Seligson, director of the project. The Wellesley School Age Child Care Project has also been providing technical assistance to anyone interested in getting a program started or in improving an existing program. The collaboration between Wellesley and Fairfax County has produced not only an improved way of delivering child-care services in Fairfax County, but also an able group in Virginia which can help others develop a working child-care partnership.

Although the Fairfax partnership represents a cooperative effort between two government agencies, community groups may also be successful in arranging a partnership with public schools. Many school systems are willing to enter into a lease agreement with for-profit or not-for-profit agencies which are interested in providing community child-care services.

*Montgomery County, Maryland.* The Montgomery County, Maryland, Public Schools system is one that is willing to lease school space to qualified users. Most of Montgomery County's tenants come from the private sector and not all operate child-care services, though many do.

Enrollment decline and the resulting classroom surplus often leads to school closings unless alternative uses for this surplus space can be found. Day-care programs are excellent public school tenants.

Joint occupancy with day-care programs has several advantages. School space designed for children continues to be used for children. And housing a day-care program in the school that day-care participants attend manages to maintain day-long consistency for these children.

Joint occupancy can lower day-care center costs by reducing or eliminating transportation costs between school and center, and enabling the day-care program to quickly comply with health and fire regulations. Such occupancy can also increase the regular enrollment in schools that accommodate an extended day program, since many parents, desirous of full-day care, would be likely to transfer their children to a school providing such care from a school that did not.

*Oak Park, Illinois.* Certain benefits have been achieved by a collaborative agreement between the Hephzibah Children's Association and the Oak Park, Illinois, public schools. Oak Park found that the presence of an in-school day-care facility drew parents from other parts of the school district to send their children to the school with the child center. During the first year of operation this school's enrollment increased by seventy children. The school district also found help in furthering school integration, since half of these new students were minority children they helped adjust the school's racial balance.

*Pinellas and Pasco Counties, Florida.* Latchkey is a private, nonprofit agency that operates its programs in the public elementary schools. The agency was incorporated in 1976 obtaining its initial support from the First United Methodist Church of St. Petersburg and the Pinellas County Juvenile Welfare Board (a public agency that funds children's programs through tax assessments). It has doubled its budget annually and despite federal social services cuts has become a nearly $3 million program that expects to serve 2000 children during the 1983–84 school year and about 4000 children during the summer. Forty-four percent of the children Latchkey serves are school age; ten percent are infants; the rest are preschoolers between the ages of two and five.

Approximately forty-five percent of the parents served by Latchkey are single, most are low-income and are working parents. "A survey conducted in 1976 in Pinellas County uncovered 15,500 five- to twelve-year-olds in need of child care," said Jean Cook, assistant executive director. "That was probably an underestimate of the real need then."

When the subject of starting the Latchkey program was taken to school and other agency officials, prevention was emphasized. "There was little disagreement that child care might help reduce crime among children and welfare dependency among parents," said Cook, "but there was flack from the principals of schools in neighborhoods that needed the Latchkey program the most." "Principals at some of these schools were facility-oriented," said Linda Morlock, the program's executive director. "They worried more about the wear and tear on their buildings than about the needs of children. They didn't want their water fountains used the extra four hours a day our program operates beyond regular school time."

Those principals willing to try the Latchkey program soon saw their enrollments go up when parents without such programs in their own schools requested special transfers for their children. The increased enrollments at these transfer schools meant increased school revenues. In addition, principals in schools housing Latchkey programs found that the Latchkey staff was willing to assist school staff during the school day in a variety of ways, from tutoring to serving as lunchroom monitors.

Morlock has been very successful in developing multiple funding sources for the Latchkey program. Latchkey obtains funds not only from the Juvenile Welfare Board, it is also funded by the State Department of Health and Rehabilitation Services, Pinellas County revenue sharing, Community Development Block Grants, the Law Enforcement Assistance Administration, the City of St. Petersburg and by private donations and foundations. Many in-kind services are donated by private and public organizations. And children using the service are charged about $20 per week during the school year and $30 a week during the summer, if their parents are able to pay. "Only thirty percent of our parents pay full fee," said Morlock, "the rest are subsidized from a variety of sources."

*Mohegan Lake, New York.* A rent-free school base, volunteers, parent fees and donations are the combination that go to make up the three in-school day-care centers operating in the Lakeland, New York, central school district. These centers serve children from kindergarten through grade five and, unlike many other day care facilities, accept drop-ins with a twenty-four-hour advance notice.

The centers receive no financial support from the Lakeland Board of Education other than the use of school space. They operate from 11:00 A.M. to 6:00 P.M. whenever school is in session, but are planning a cooperative agreement with neighboring churches to use church space to cover holidays and vacation periods during the school year.

"Every center has a paid teacher, director and aide," said Judith Shepherd, a center vice president, "but in order to meet the state's requirement of a one-to-nine staff-to-child ratio we must have volunteer help." A grant from Young Volunteers in Action, a federal agency, to another association of which Shepherd is a member, helps the Lakeland child-care centers recruit volunteers. "We couldn't operate without them," said Shepherd.

### HOME-BASED CARE

School-based child care is a workable, even a fiscally sound endeavor in many communities, though not all. Sometimes school-based care is not possible because of geographic or transportation limitations. At other times the philosophy of the school board about child care or concern about rising school costs by taxpayers limit the school's positive response to extended day programs. Another solution to care for the school-age child is home-based care.

Home-based care is divided into two broad categories: one is substitute care provided in the child's own home; the other is family day care. Family day care is child care provided in a private home other than the child's own. Encompassing a myriad of arrangements between families and their day-care providers, family day care constitutes the largest, most complex system of child care in the United States. Nearly half of the children in day care in the United States are cared for in family day care homes.

Family day care is made up of three major categories. The largest of these categories, accounting for ninety percent of all family day care in the United States, consists of unregulated providers who operate informally and independently of any regulatory system. A second category, accounting for about six percent of all family day care in the United States, consists of regulated care-givers who meet state and/or federal standards but, except for this link with the broader day-care community, operate independently. The third and smallest group consists of regulated homes that are operated as part of day-care systems or networks under the administrative auspices of a sponsoring agency.

Unregulated family day care historically was provided without charge by relatives or bartered between friends and neighbors in an informal exchange of services. Today the nature of informal family day care is changing with the disappearance of the extended family and the declining availability of mothers at home who are willing to care for their neighbors' children.

These personal care arrangements continue to exist in communities everywhere, and though relatives are no longer the providers, they are still valued because often similar family values, life-styles and child-rearing practices are used. At the same time, informal family day care is isolated from the resources available to the rest of the day-care community and usually is unknown to parents outside of the immediate neighborhood.

Certainly a good friend or relative providing care for your child can offer an arrangement that works. But because of its very unique nature, it's not one that can be easily categorized. In general, this type of family home care constitutes the largest number of child care sites taking care of the smallest number of children per site. The care-givers tend to have only limited family day care experience and generally don't rely on income from child care to meet their families' economic needs. Most of us understand this model and many working parents are grateful they have found "a wonderful neighbor" or that they have a terrific relative nearby to care for their children.

Regulated homes care for more children per home than un-regulated homes do, and care for fewer children than homes that are part of a regulated and sponsored system. Those that run regulated child-care centers are more likely to view child care as their permanent vocation. But on the whole, the National Day Care Home Study, published in 1981 by the U.S. Department of Health and Human Services, found little difference in the types of activities in unregulated and regulated homes. Family day care homes seem to be generally positive environments for children. These homes are generally safe, homelike environments that are less structured and more homogeneous with respect to children's ages than day-care centers.

Family day care homes that are part of sponsored systems tend to be slightly different: more structured, more academic, more professional. They constitute a small portion of all family day care homes, but they are important beyond their numbers because they provide care for most state and federally subsidized children in family day care settings. It is partially for this reason that we mention the two following programs.

*Reston, Virginia.* In 1978, the Fairfax County Office for Children obtained start-up funding for Reston Children's Center, a private non-profit child-care center located in Reston, Virginia, to establish a program called the Satellite Family Care Program. This program provides home-based care for school-age children. In this program a number of private homes are identified, each with a care-giver who is also the parent of a child. Then as many as five other school-age children are assigned to each care-giver who serves as a kind of substitute parent for all of them. The program offers home-based before- and after-school care to these children at a cost slightly below the cost of many center-based programs. The care-givers directly supervise the children at all times, plan activity-oriented schedules that can be carried out in the home environment, and also monitor children as they go to and from scout meetings, music lessons, athletic practices and the like. The children's center supervises the providers.

Such programs provide flexibility and an environment similar to the child's own home. But they depend on being able to identify care-giver homes that are in the child's neighborhood and a neighborhood that is reasonably safe. The Reston community is a planned community that is ideal for this type of child care.

*Planning a Check-in Program.* The County of Fairfax, Virginia, has been funded by the U.S. Department of Health and Human Services to design and pilot a satellite home/check-in care program for school-age children. The County of Fairfax, despite a large school-based child-care program, discovered that during the 1981–82 school year one-third of all complaints coming into the county's Child Protective Services Unit were regarding unattended or unsupervised elementary school-age children. Further, the Fairfax County Office for Children had determined in the fall of 1981 that there were 2,402 Fairfax families representing 3,241 children not then enrolled in the county's school-based child care program who were interested in, eligible for and in need of such care. During the 1982–83 school year the School-Age Child Care Program only accommodated 100 additional children.

Finances limit the rate of school-based child-care expansion. Many low- and moderate-income families find it hard to make ends meet if they are required to pay child-care costs, even with sliding fee schedules. And many school-age children do not want to be enrolled in center-care programs.

The Fairfax Office for Children staff is of the opinion that parents should have the right to choose child-care arrangements from a variety of acceptable alternatives. Further, that day-care plans that include leaving children alone for three or more hours a day, five days a week, are not acceptable. "We are convinced," said Judith Rosen, the Satellite Home/Check-In Care Project's principal investigator, "that the effects of such care are not apparent until loneliness, idleness and vulnerability affect emotions, lead to neglect and abuse or drive children to the streets and predelinquent behavior in an attempt to fill empty hours."

"Most programs that exist for the school-age child are either center-based or activity-oriented home care and require the same administrative and supervisory support that preschool child care requires," said Rosen. "What we want to do is develop a model that will offer parents of preadolescent children a responsible place for their children to check in, but which also provides for out-of-sight responsibility." Check-in care services would allow older children and children with older siblings to spend time in provider homes and, within the limits of the parent's guidelines, also spend time in their own homes, visiting friends, attending after-school activities or playing in defined neighborhood areas.

No similar models still in existence were found. Problems that include provider liability, ways to effectively restrict children to predefined areas and activities, and means for responding to the needs of several children in multiple areas of even one neighborhood have seemed insurmountable in establishing satellite home/check-in programs or keeping them in existence.

And yet, such programs may well be the most cost-effective means of child care in many communities. They may also bridge the gap between the choice of child self-care on one hand and complete center care on the other, allowing children a sense of freedom along with a feeling of security.

### CARE IN ONE'S OWN HOME

Because of the great differences in care-giver styles, reliability and ability, little comment needs to be made about child care delivered in one's own home. Horror stories are liberally mingled with praise for nannies who "do a better job at raising my children than I could do myself." Parents selecting such care for their children need to exercise due caution in choosing care-givers, should monitor their activities with frequent calls and listen carefully to any complaints their children make regarding the care-givers' treatment of them.

### SOCIAL AGENCY PROGRAMS

Many social agencies have become serious about providing school-age child care. Perhaps the group most involved in offering a great variety of service models is the YMCA. School-age child care is one of the fastest growing programs in YMCAs today and one of the Y's top priorities.

When the Dade County, Florida, public schools became aware of the great need in the county for school-age child care, they set out to establish nearly sixty centers throughout the school system. It didn't take long before reductions in funds, disappointing enrollments and high start-up costs nearly saw the whole program scuttled. The YMCA was in the wings ready to help, however, and in rapid succession has taken charge of nearly every extended day center envisioned by the public schools.

"The Y believes that it is the responsibility of parents to provide children with full-time care from birth through adolescence," said Russ Kohl, Associate Director for Program Development in Family Life of the YMCA of the United States, "but we realize that we must help provide resources so parents can ensure that their children are cared for." YMCAs across the country are stepping forward. The Y's national office has published a series of manuals to help local YMCAs develop school-age child-care programs.

The Pikes Peak Y of Colorado Springs, Colorado, began its commitment to a latchkey program in January, 1979. An early assessment of the need for such a program indicated that seventy-five percent of elementary children (ages six to twelve) living in northeast Colorado Springs returned to empty houses after school was dismissed each day and that no programs existed to meet the needs of these children.

After a somewhat rocky start, partially due to the program's trying to fly by the seat of its pants without adequate guidance, two comprehensive after-school programs are now functioning, one in an elementary school and one in a local church, as are two activities programs, both located in elementary schools. The Pikes Peak Y, as do most Ys, seems to have great flexibility in negotiating contracts for space with a variety of agencies, schools or churches. And, of course, when convenient, Ys can use their own facilities.

Camp Fire, Incorporated, is another agency that provides a printed manual to help local Camp Fire councils develop programs of care for children during out-of-school hours before and after school. The manual titled *Kids Club: Camp Fire Out-of-School Care Program* was based on the experiences of several councils that offered out-of-school programs for elementary children. The manual describes an ideal program and is especially useful as a detailed guide to councils that have had no experience in operating programs of this type.

SURVIVAL SKILLS TRAINING

As with many other national social service organizations having many somewhat autonomous units, local councils or chapters often develop their own approaches to perceived problems. The Atlanta

Camp Fire Council designed an eight lesson self-reliance program that helps children cope with life situations encountered independent of parental or other adult supervision. The program, called *K.I.D.S.*, which stands for *Kids Independence Development System*, was written for use with groups of children at either the second and third, or fourth and fifth grade levels. The program's objectives include:

1) Developing skills in human relationships and the development of a positive self-image
2) Promoting the well-being of one's mind and body
3) Providing training in how to live safely
4) Helping children to understand themselves in fearful situations, and providing them with skills to cope with fears, real or imagined
5) Developing home management skills
6) Providing information about using money in its various forms: credit, writing checks and consumer education

A second survival/self-reliance course for second to fourth graders has been developed by the Council of Camp Fire, Buffalo, New York. The program, called *I Can Do It*, includes instructions on how to iron, operate washing machines, sew on buttons and doctor minor animal bites in addition to other skills that can improve children's confidence when in self-care.

There are a variety of other survival skills programs available for children. The Boy Scouts of America publishes one called *Prepared for Today*, which teaches children about being home alone, fixing something to eat, home safety, one's neighborhood, caring for younger children, problem solving and feeling good about oneself.

A self-care course for upper elementary-age children and their parents was published in 1982 by the Johnson County Mental Health Center, Olathe, Kansas. The program, called *I'm in Charge*, consists of five sessions. It was developed as part of the Johnson County, Kansas, Latchkey Project.

The course philosophy is that each latchkey situation is the joint responsibility of parent and child, and the *I'm in Charge* manual reflects this philosophy. The first session, delivered only to parents, is designed to help parents structure and monitor their children's self-care situations. The next three sessions instruct children in personal safety skills, emergency responses and care of younger siblings.

The fifth session tries to help parents and children in communicating and negotiating rules and procedures for self-care. "The intent of the course is not to promote or encourage self-care," said Helen Swann, one of the team that prepared the program, "but to help families decide if self-care is appropriate for their child."

The Virginia Cooperative Extension Service and Virginia Polytechnic Institute and State University publish a program called *Survival Skills for Kids.* This six-session program is designed for children between the ages of eight and thirteen and makes liberal use of group activities, especially those associated with food preparation, in order to make the program interesting to attendees. Program instructors are assisted by specially trained small group volunteer leaders who help the children prepare food, but also cover other topics through group discussion. Children are taught how to answer the phone and door, stay safe around the home, handle emergency situations, stay friends with their brothers and sisters, prepare simple snacks and meals, protect themselves from sexual abuse and manage loneliness, boredom and fear.

The Minneapolis Area Chapter of the American Red Cross sponsors training in basic safety and first aid for fourth through sixth graders that includes knowing how to deal with fire, bleeding, poisoning, choking and animal bites, among other things. The program, known as Basic Aid Training, is not intended solely for latchkey children, but certainly provides information that might be useful to unattended children in an emergency.

Little, Brown and Co. published *The Official Kids Survival Kit: How to Do Things on Your Own* in 1981 and Alfred A. Knopf is introducing a small survival skills handbook for children entitled *In Charge* in 1983. Handbooks for young children are really only useful, however, if children get accompanying instructions with them. Parents shouldn't depend on manuals to teach their children how to handle an emergency. There is really no substitute for having an adult show a child what to do and allowing the child to practice proper procedures under adult supervision.

Alfred Higgins Productions, a Los Angeles–based film company, has just completed a short film intended for children who might find themselves alone from time to time. The film, entitled *Alone at Home,* could provide a useful introduction for a survival skills course or as a stimulus for school-age children to discuss feelings associated with the latchkey situation.

## HOTLINES

Other community agencies have approached the needs of latchkey children from a different perspective, recognizing the fact that the children at home alone are usually linked to sources of help by telephone. The Neighborhood Centers Day Care Association of Houston, Texas, began a telephone reassurance service for school-age children, ages eight and older. This service charges enrolled users an annual fee. Children are expected to check in routinely with a telephone counselor and may call periodically if they feel the need to. In the event of an emergency, the counselor is available to come to the child's home. Call-waiting and call-forwarding systems make services like this possible. The Association also provides training in emergency procedures for enrollees. And, in case parents are late or in an emergency situation, the service can coordinate late or overnight care for children.

A similar program operated as a community service project by the State College Branch of the American Association of University Women, State College, Pennsylvania, began operations in January, 1982. This after-school hotline called Phone Friends is a key link in creating a helping network that will provide support and information for children at home without adult supervision. A second goal of the program is to help children help themselves.

Phone Friends, which currently operates on an annual budget of about $4,000, is staffed by trained volunteers. Professionals, largely faculty from Pennsylvania State University, designed the volunteer training program. Contacts and links were established with possible referral and help groups, the police, fire department, school counselors and administrators. Detailed procedures for recording calls, assessing problems and especially understanding medical emergencies were developed. Then the program was announced through the schools and local media. During the first week of operation, 145 calls were received.

The program began operating between 3:00 and 6:00 P.M. "We discovered that the greatest number of calls were received between 3:00 and 4:00 P.M.," said Louise Guerney, consultant to the program, "with about twenty percent of the calls coming in after 6:00 or before 3:00. One of the things we learned was that many of the calls received between 2:30 and 3:00 were from children in a nearby parochial school who arrived home at 2:30. Calls earlier than that were received from children home for the day." The program now operates between 2:30 and 6:00 on school days and from 9:00 A.M. to 6:00 P.M. on weekdays when schools are closed. Full-day coverage can be handled by volunteers in their homes using an automatic call-forwarding arrangement.

During the first months of the operation, the reasons given by children for about thirty percent of the calls to Phone Friends were that they were feeling lonely, scared or bored. These three categories were by far the largest substantive areas mentioned. Children also called for help with homework, help in getting along with siblings, medical problems, reports of a prowler, a rape, and to discuss such issues as fear of being pregnant, feeling hungry or sad. Children called asking volunteers to tell them a story, a joke and for answers to a whole host of information questions.

About ten percent of all calls were referred to another number, most frequently to Tell-a-Tale, a phone company service telling children's stories. In some instances children were requested to call back to let the volunteer know if a situation had worked out. Often, children spontaneously called back, sometimes to tell the volunteer the story they heard on Tell-a-Tale.

The reported ages of callers telephoning Phone Friends has been from four to sixteen; the average age is eight. Children from every elementary school in the area served were reported to have called. And as more children become aware of the service, it is expected that the rate of calls will increase.

While the Phone Friends committee is still learning about the program they have initiated, they no longer consider it a pilot program. "We are convinced that Phone Friends responds to a serious community need," said Marilyn Keat, public relations chairperson, "and we are now trying to resolve such issues as the degree of responsibility we have for the child beyond the phone call."

Questions that need to be resolved by hotlines of this type that do not operate on a subscriber basis include:

a) Should parents be notified when a child reports a serious or repeated problem, or reports that he or she is frightened at home alone?

b) Should schools or other agencies who might have access to the child be contacted for needed follow-up?

Programs like Phone Friends are working. As time goes on they will become more sophisticated. These types of programs are not only offering a service, they are also helping to assess the extent and kinds of needs that exist among the school-age child population when they're not in school. Even programs like Parents in Touch, Indianapolis, Indiana, that were never designed to serve a specifically latchkey population, find that their services like Homework Hotline, a program that allows students to telephone a teacher after school hours for homework help, are also used by unattended children to relieve a variety of other needs.

## SAFE HOME PROGRAM

Sometimes it only takes one parent with purpose to help extend services to unattended children. This is true of Myrna Dorin and Citizen's Crime Watch of Dade County, Florida. Myrna's daughter became a latchkey child at age nine as a result of her mother's divorce and inability to find a reliable babysitter she could afford on a salary of $1.90 an hour. "Sitters, mostly teenagers, were averaging $1.00 per hour then," Myrna said. "I paid and worried about money through several sitters, who stole from me and ate me out of house and home. One day a sitter's mother called and told me to come and get my daughter. I made the decision then for my daughter to stay alone."

Myrna remarried in 1979 and quit working so she could be at home when her daughter, then fifteen, arrived home from school. "My daughter resented my trying to reestablish my control over her activities," Myrna said, "and problems in our home got so bad that she went to live with relatives in Virginia when she turned eighteen."

Myrna attributes many of the problems that developed and subsequently escalated between her daughter and herself to the latchkey situation. "I can tell you that even though I did then what I had to do to raise my daughter alone, I wouldn't do it again. Every child needs an adult to guide them in simple everyday matters, to be there.

"While problems with my daughter grew, I became very depressed and decided I had to get out and do something to help myself. I heard the state's attorney at a meeting talking about helping hand/block home-type programs. I asked if there was one in Miami; I wanted to volunteer. She didn't know of any, but she took my name and number and said she would call me. I figured that was the last of it.

But the next morning she called and said she had been in touch with the Crime Watch group and they were interested in listening to my thoughts about the program.

"I met with the group's president. She liked the idea, except no one knew how to run such a program. I'm still not sure how I got from being a volunteer to running the show. All I knew about it then was that children could go to designated houses in case of an emergency.

"I started to contact other groups for information. I found several groups operating, but there was no written material. Every agency I contacted from Maryland to Florida and west to California sent me information on child abuse, but nothing on block home programs. Finally I wrote my own manual."

Myrna began as a committee of one working within the Citizen's Crime Watch Organization to start a Safe Homes program. Today she has 114 homes with "safe home" signs displayed in their windows that children can go to in case of need. "In a city the size of Miami it seems like so few," said Myrna, "but I feel you have to start somewhere. It's hard to get the program going, there are so many working parents. We're now calling on retired people to participate in our program. This gives them a chance to do something special for the community."

The Safe Homes Program is only a preventative measure. Safe Homes volunteers are told that they are not to serve as community policemen, referees, taxis, babysitters or school crossing guards. They are told that their job is to be there in case a child has an emergency and that the volunteer can assist by calling for help.

Myrna Dorin's manual, which can be obtained from Citizens' Crime Watch of Dade County, Florida, Incorporated, is full of practical advice for parents, including personal safety procedures to help make children streetwise.

Safe home programs work. One, called Helping Hands, has been operating in Seminole County, Florida, for nearly ten years. Another, called Safe Houses, which also maintains good records, is operated by the Office of the Sheriff, Duval County (Jacksonville), Florida. These programs depend on dedicated volunteers and concerned citizens to keep going and to provide a safe haven for children everywhere. "Many people tell me 'ours is a nice neighborhood, nothing like what you're talking about has ever happened here,'" said Dorin. "As usual, it isn't a problem until something happens to you." There are many programs of this type that are also organized by law enforcement agencies.

PROGRAMS INVOLVING THE ELDERLY

Many nursing homes across the country are combining care for the elderly with care for children in an arrangement that seems to benefit everybody. Setting up a child-care arrangement in a nursing home seems like a logical marriage. Many basic principles that apply to care for the elderly also apply to care for the young. Building, fire and health regulations are similar for the two institutions. Codes and regulations concerning adequate indoor and outdoor space, toilet and kitchen facilities and licensing procedures are often handled through the same local authorities who can determine whether major remodeling is necessary. Meals and snacks for children can be prepared in nursing home kitchens. Many nursing homes are surrounded by enough land to allow for outside activities and are conveniently located on bus routes or near populated areas.

More than these physical arrangements, the relationships that develop between children and older people can benefit both the child and the adult. Among younger children such relationships seem to become as warm as those between children and their natural grandparents. School-age children are helped to understand the normal changes in the aging process, and the artificial gap we have produced between the generations in our society is narrowed.

The Generations Day Care Center at the Wright County Retirement Center in Buffalo, Minnesota, was started to help the residents living there get back into the mainstream of life. The program has been more successful than anyone anticipated. The presence of children at a retirement home helps create an atmosphere that is more like a real home. Children visit elderly residents in their day room for wheelchair rides, stories and hugs. Sing-alongs, arts and crafts projects, puppet shows, movies, exercise classes and outings with the residents are regular activities. Young parents often adopt their child's favorite grandparent at the Center, and three generations are spanned.

The Generations Day Care Center is also a community service. Because it uses available resources for two purposes, it can charge less than comparable child care in the area.

Some other child-care centers established at nursing homes provide low-cost child care exclusively for children of nursing home staff. This is the case of the Hill and Dale Day Care Center at the River Hills-West Nursing Home in Pewaukee, Wisconsin. As with many other employer-operated day-care sites, the opening of this center has helped staff recruitment for the nursing home and reduced staff training costs. American Medical Services, the nursing home owner, is able to absorb most of the cost of running the day-care center because staff members stay longer. Nursing care has improved and staff and residents have grown closer through the common bond of "their" children.

Some nursing homes may find full-day child-care programs inappropriate for their situation, but could feel comfortable with operating before- and after-school programs. Before-school programs are needed for about half as many school-age children as are after-school programs and generally are needed for shorter periods of time. Nursing homes could employ staff who would assist with this program and finish a shift working with elderly residents. Serving breakfast, a problem with some before-school programs, should prove less a problem for a residential nursing care facility that is accustomed to serving breakfasts to its residents.

Nursing homes serving as care facilities for school-age children coming from a single school or school district can be designated as acceptable pick-up or drop-off points for children riding school buses. This reduces transportation problems experienced by many parents whose children use care facilities not located on school grounds.

Because nursing homes also ordinarily provide a range of medical services, it is much easier for them to consider arrangements that will accommodate children when they are ill. And nursing care facilities that are constructed to accommodate the handicapped elderly pose no architectural barrier in offering care for handicapped children.

Residential nursing homes actually serve a small minority of the elderly. But even day centers for the elderly could double as care centers for children and thus make use of the talents of those senior citizens who want and would benefit from a relationship with a child. Attitudes might have to change, and special arrangements made, but many sedentary activities engaged in by the elderly are similar to those enjoyed by children, for example: crafts, board games, art, singing. Senior citizens could help with homework. And for most organized active child's play, adults typically serve more as coaches and umpires than as participants, anyway. Since senior citizens who go to senior day centers are generally ambulatory, helping with active outdoor play wouldn't be difficult.

Programs that cross generational lines offer the most promise as a way to relieve child-care burdens. Our older generation is the fastest growing part of our society: it is vigorous, experienced, intelligent, capable. What is needed are many more program models that cross generational lines and can be shown to work. Even children in fifth through ninth grades could profit from such associations. There is no need to assume that these largely misunderstood children are without need for consistent and continuous adult guidance. The fact that this age group (ten to fifteen) congregates in arcades and malls across the country is only testimony that society is not adequately providing for the care of its children.

# Chapter 12
# SUGGESTIONS FOR PARENTS

Parents who decide to try self-care might find the following checklist helpful in evaluating whether or not their children are ready for it:

YES     NO

____  ____   1) Do you consider your child old enough to assume self-care responsibilities?

____  ____   2) Do you believe your child is mature enough to care for him- or herself?

____  ____   3) Has your child indicated that he or she would be willing to try self-care?

____  ____   4) Is your child able to solve problems?

____  ____   5) Is your child able to communicate with adults?

____  ____   6) Is your child able to complete daily tasks?

        7) Is your child generally unafraid to be alone?

        8) Is your child unafraid to enter your house alone?

        9) Can your child unlock and lock the doors to your home unassisted?

        10) Is there an adult living or working nearby that your child knows and can rely on in case of an emergency?

        11) Do you have adequate household security?

        12) Do you consider your neighborhood safe?

If you answered *no* to any of the above questions, it is highly recommended that you delay or abandon plans to leave your child in self-care until positive responses can be given for all of the questions.

YES    NO

        13) Has your child exhibited behaviors in the past that frightened you, such as:

        • playing unsupervised with fire

        • playing unsupervised with dangerous equipment

        • experimenting with dangerous chemicals

        • having unexplained seizures

        • violent or aggressive behavior

        • manifesting

        14) Is your child without a telephone?

        15) While away from home, are you accessible by telephone?

        16) Is your child unable to use a phone?

        17) Is your child afraid of the dark?

        18) Does your child have a handicap that requires special supervision?

        19) Does your child have recurring nightmares or other serious sleep disturbances?

If you answered *yes* to any question between 13 and 19, there is a strong possibility that you shouldn't leave your child in self-care.

21) Is your child

| | | |
|---|---|---|
| 10 or older | _____ | (one point) |
| 9–10 | _____ | (two points) |
| 8–9 | _____ | (three points) |
| 7–8 | _____ | (four points) |
| 7 or younger | _____ | (five points) |

22) How much time each day will your child be in self-care?

| | | |
|---|---|---|
| 1 hour or less | _____ | (one point) |
| 1–2 hours | _____ | (two points) |
| 2–3 hours | _____ | (three points) |
| 3–4 hours | _____ | (four points) |
| 4 or more hours | _____ | (five points) |

23) How much does your child spontaneously tell you about the events occurring in his or her life?

| | | |
|---|---|---|
| everything | _____ | (one point) |
| most things | _____ | (two points) |
| some things | _____ | (three points) |
| few things | _____ | (four points) |
| nothing | _____ | (five points) |

24) How close is the relationship between you and your child?

| | | |
|---|---|---|
| very close | _____ | (one point) |
| close | _____ | (two points) |
| neither close nor distant | _____ | (three points) |

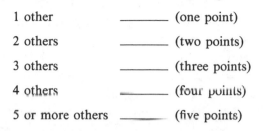

distant _____ (four points)

very distant _____ (five points)

25) Will your child be home with younger siblings?

1 other _____ (one point)

2 others _____ (two points)

3 others _____ (three points)

4 others _____ (four points)

5 or more others _____ (five points)

Add the number of points corresponding to your answers for questions 21 through 25. The lower your score, the better your child's chance, and yours, of managing self-care. The range of possible points accumulated is from five to twenty-five. A score of ten or higher should cause you to be hesitant about starting your child in self-care.

The latchkey experience is not for everyone, and it is not a choice that should be made lightly. Careful planning within one's family is necessary before any action is taken. Caring for oneself and perhaps others demands sophisticated skills of children. So before placing a child in self-care, a parent must carefully assess the child's abilities to carry out the duties and responsibilities demanded.

This chapter contains ideas for parents who have decided their child or children are ready for self-care. Many of the suggestions are based on ideas provided by former latchkey children, parents of latchkey children and latchkey children themselves.

Parents who decide on self-care as a child-care option must prepare their children for the experience: guidelines for behavior must be set and routine and emergency procedures should be taught. Before leaving children alone on a full-time basis, it is helpful to conduct a self-care trial. This can be done by leaving the children alone a few times while shopping or visiting a neighbor to see how they respond. After the trial period, parents should discuss the experience with their children and listen carefully to their reactions before deciding that self-care is a workable option.

## Explaining the Reasons for Self-care

When children are asked to spend some part of each day alone an explanation is in order. The tone of the explanation given by parents will effect how the children feel about staying alone. The explanation should include why both parents are working and why other arrangements are not possible or desirable.

One former latchkey child suggested parents take their children to their workplace for a visit so that they can see where their parents disappear to each day. A visit to the office will not only help children to visualize their parents when they are home alone, it will also help them to understand why their mother doesn't appear at the door for thirty-five minutes, after they've asked her to come right home. This concept of distance is an important one for children to understand, since in an emergency they must learn to act immediately rather than wait for a parent to come home and help.

The absence of an explanation as to why parents are working can lead to needlessly upsetting conclusions: some children felt that their parents went to work to avoid being with them, while others felt they left them alone to be with friends. A clear explanation could have reduced this sense of rejection.

Finally, parents should be careful about the explanations they give. One former latchkey man said, "Don't make your children think they are the reason for a working mother . . . my mother worked to pay for my school tuition. Not only did I miss being cared for, but I also felt guilty about all the hard work my mother did to send me to Catholic school." Finances are certainly a legitimate reason to give a child for working, but should be put in a broader context without specifying tuition or other expenses incurred by one particular child.

### Keys

Many of the children interviewed openly wore their keys on chains or lanyards around their necks. This "housekey necklace" is a certain sign that the child spends some part of the day at home without adult supervision. It is also an open invitation to trouble. Two teachers reported incidents where latchkey children with clearly displayed keys were approached by strangers trying to coax them into automobiles. In order to avoid such approaches, parents should make sure their children wear their "housekey necklaces" inside their shirts, hidden from view.

Parents should also hide an extra key outside or leave an extra key with a neighbor so that children needn't wait if a key is lost. Waiting outside can be traumatic for children. Many are frightened, particularly if it's cold and dark. They also know that their parents will be angry so they often search endlessly for the missing key.

### Survival Kit

Most latchkey children travel to and/or from school alone. They walk, ride school buses and use public transportation. Parents could better prepare children for emergencies between home and school by preparing a survival kit. The survival kit should include an identification card which contains the child's name, address, home phone number and parents' work numbers. This card would prove indispensible to children lost or injured on the way to or from school.

Parents should also include enough change in the survival kit so that an emergency phone call could be made. Some parents include enough money for bus or cab fare home. The survival kit should be placed where it is always accessible to the child. Some parents tape it to the inside of their child's coat pocket. Wherever it is placed, parents who use the survival kit feel safer knowing it's there in case an emergency arises.

### Before School

Children who are alone before school experience stress trying to get ready on time. The easiest way to reduce this stress is by decreasing the amount of responsibility children have in the morning. If possible, parents should make sure their children wake up in time for school, prepare breakfast and lunch for them, and help them pick out their clothes. When parents take responsibility for the morning tasks it increases the stress on parents who are rushing to get ready for work, but it decreases the stress on children who are rushing to get to school on time.

Many children don't eat breakfast before going to school in the morning, either because they don't have time, nothing available appeals to them, they don't want to eat alone, or they're too lazy to prepare something to eat. Those who do eat don't always eat the most nutritious breakfast. Parents should teach children the importance of a good breakfast and help them plan their morning meal. If possible, it is helpful for parents to eat with their children to be sure of what they're eating, and the time spent together can also be seen as an expression of concern and affection. Parents who must leave for work before their children wake up can demonstrate their concern and encourage their children to eat breakfast by partially preparing their child's morning meal. It should only take a few minutes to set the table, put cereal in the bowl so that only the milk needs to be added and put out a glass for juice. Lovingly setting the table with an encouraging note and partially preparing breakfast will encourage children to eat breakfast, though of course there are no guarantees. Parents who find that their children don't eat breakfast should try to find out why in an effort to remedy the situation.

A good time to prepare for school is the night before. Evenings are less rushed than mornings and parents and children can work together as a team to make sure the children get to school on time and well prepared. The night before clothes can be selected, book bags packed and lunches made.

One mother explained how she and her seven-year-old son made a "clothes sculpture" each night of what he is going to wear the next day. "We lay out all the clothes on the floor of his room as if he were wearing them: shirt, pants, socks and shoes. Seth looks forward to it. I can teach him a lot about getting dressed in the process. I show him what things match and what things don't, explain which clothes are appropriate for school and which should be used only for play, and how to pick the right clothes according to the time of year. Eventually, he'll be able to figure it out for himself."

In addition to getting them dressed correctly, some parents have trouble making sure their children are properly groomed for school. If parents suspect that their children are going to school without washing their faces, brushing their teeth or combing their hair, a friendly note or cartoon on the bathroom mirror might serve to remind them to take the time to prepare for school. If this doesn't work, parents might consider pasting a grooming checklist on the bathroom door for their child to check off before leaving for school.

The night before is also a time when parent and child can prepare a lunch for school if one is needed. This can also give a parent an opportunity to teach the child about the importance of good nutrition and the essential components of a balanced lunch. Eventually, children could prepare their lunch alone the night before and have it checked by one of their parents for nutritional content.

Packing for school is also a problem area for most children. Too often children are found running around in the morning looking for their books, homework or other supplies necessary for the school day. If all of this is done the night before, all the child has to do in the morning is take the lunch out of the refrigerator and place it in his backpack and get to school on time. Pick a place by the door, a special chair or an out-of-the-way place on the floor to put all the books and other items necessary for school the next day. Go through your child's schedule with him to make sure he has everything he needs. This is also a good time to make sure that all homework assignments are completed and ready to be turned in. Find out the next day's forecast and place the correct coat, if any is needed, by the door with the rest of the things. If there's been a sudden change of weather overnight, parents can place an umbrella or a different coat by the door before leaving for work in the morning. Planning ahead will reduce the stress the child experiences in the morning and will especially help avoid frustrating situations where that critical item is missing. A list of Do's and Don'ts posted on the refrigerator door can also help remind any child what he or she must do in the morning. This list, made by the mother of a fifth grade girl, might prove helpful to any parent:

### GOOD MORNING

1. Eat your breakfast, it's on the table.
2. Don't forget to brush your teeth, comb your hair and wash your face.
3. Get your lunch from the refrigerator.
4. Take money out of the jar for milk.
5. Let the cat out.
6. Leave for school by 8:15.
7. Lock the door when you leave.
8. Have a great day. See you at 5:15. XXX

Knowing when to leave for school is also a problem for many young children. Many parents who must leave before their children do call home to wake them in the morning, but few call to tell them it's time to leave for school. Parents should signal their children to help them catch the bus or leave for school on time. The telephone can be used to call the child, letting the phone ring once or twice as a signal that it's time to leave. Parents who don't work where a telephone is available can try setting an alarm to remind the child that it is time to leave for school. If everything else fails, children who frequently miss school or are late should have a friend stop by to pick them up on the way. Going with a friend provides personal encouragement to the reluctant child.

### Welcome Home

It is helpful if children who arrive home after school to an empty house are made to feel welcome even though their parents aren't there to greet them. Leaving a light on in the kitchen or hall, or having a radio playing, can make a house feel less empty. Some parents leave a note on the kitchen table with daily instructions or a surprise. A simple "I love you," or "See you at 6:00," can make all the difference to a child who is staying home alone. One mother who draws a cartoon character on a chalkboard every morning before she leaves for work delights her son in finding a "new friend" every afternoon when he returns home from school. Any warm or personal touch such as a snack prepared or a note can put the parent home in spirit and ease the child's loneliness.

### Rules

Parents of latchkey children along with their children should make a list of rules to be followed when no adult is present. Each rule should be explained and discussed so that children understand not only *how* they are expected to behave but *why* they are expected to behave a certain way. All rules should be printed on a large sheet of paper and posted in a conspicuous place, perhaps the kitchen. Once the rules are decided upon and posted they should be reviewed regularly. New rules should be added as situations demand.

The rules decided upon by parent and child will vary from family to family. However, there are some rules that most parents of latch-key children find necessary to ensure the safety of their children. For children who stay alone they are:

1. Come straight home after school (or football practice, piano lesson, or whatever). Wandering around the neighborhood is an invitation to trouble.
2. Keep the door locked at all times. Speak with callers through the door.
3. Don't let *anyone* in the house, not even friends or neighbors.
4. Don't tell people who call on the telephone that you're home alone. Instead tell them that your mother is busy. Take a message and tell them your mother will call them back.
5. In case of a problem or important message, call: _____.

Parents with more than one child at home might want to add the following rules to the list:

6. Don't fight. If there is a problem, write it down and we will discuss it when everyone is home.
7. Everyone does the chores they were assigned. No trading.
8. Limit telephone calls to ten minutes. Give your sisters/brothers a chance to use the phone, too.
9. Don't leave your younger brothers/sisters alone. Stay with them at all times.
10. Do not punish your younger brothers/sisters. Remind them how to behave and wait until everyone is home to discuss problems.

Most parents will find, however, that posting rules is not enough. Children must be made to understand the necessity of following these rules since they are intended to ensure their safety. This isn't easy. Discussions with school personnel indicate that many latchkey children prefer to use their own judgment rather than follow parental guidelines. Principals frequently complain that latchkey children "hang out after school" rather than go straight home. Hanging out after school often leads to other problems, such as missed buses or fights. Proper telephone behavior is usually not followed by latchkey children either. School personnel who call to check on absences frequently find children openly admitting that they are home alone. Even those children who don't volunteer much information answer honestly if asked directly, "Are you home alone?" or "Is your mother home?" A study by the Department of Pensions and Security (DPS) in Madison County, Alabama, provided even more frightening results. DPS workers personally called on children who were home alone. Many children let the workers in the house even though they didn't know who they were and their parents had instructed them not to let strangers in the house.

Parents of latchkey children should check to see if their children are following their established rules. One way parents can do this is to have co-workers call home and ask to talk to an adult. How their children respond to this staged call should give parents an idea of how their children are responding to other callers. Whether parents are pleased or disappointed with their child's response, they can discuss the experience and either praise their children or reteach telephone rules.

Similarly, parents should have a friend whom their children don't know pay a visit to their home. The friend should attempt to enter the home using an excuse like, "My car broke down and I need to use the telephone." Parents who find that their child will admit the stranger should stress the dangers of opening the door for anyone. Parents whose children resist the pressure to open the door should be sure to praise them for it.

### Telephone

The telephone is the lifeline between parent and child. Many parents require that their children telephone as soon as they arrive home. This is a good practice for reducing anxiety, especially the parent's anxiety. Parents should also telephone their children once or twice a day to check on them. Most children regard phone calls as a sign of parental concern.

The telephone not only provides latchkey children with a link to the outside world, it could save their lives in case of an emergency. Parents of latchkey children should post a list of emergency numbers near the telephone, including parents' work numbers, phone numbers of neighbors who are willing to help, the local police and fire departments, ambulance service and the family doctor. Parents should also teach their children how to call these numbers and give the necessary information quickly.

## Time

It is helpful for parents to try to keep the amount of time their children spend alone each day to a minimum. Three hours daily pushes the upper limit of what most children can tolerate. Parents who can adjust work schedules to school schedules should do so when possible. It is also recommended that parents come home immediately after work, saving routine errands to do with their children. A fifteen-minute stop at the grocery store on the way home from work seems short to parents but it can be an eternity to a waiting child.

Parents should also tell their children what time they expect to be home each day, as this tends to reduce anxiety and loneliness for many children. Whenever possible parents should stick to the arrival time they establish since most children become frightened and expect the worst when their parents are late.

## Safety

Both parents and children feel better about the latchkey experience if they feel their neighborhood and home are safe. To ensure safety, parents can have a free safety check of their home conducted by the local police. If children are present during the safety check, it will help to make them feel safer when they're home alone. It is, of course, important to carry out whatever recommendations are made by the police department. The small amount of money invested to install double locks, a smoke detector or other safety features will reduce a child's fear and parental guilt.

## Emergency Procedures

The three most frequent emergency situations experienced by the children and adults interviewed were fires, accidents and robberies. Children should be taught what to do in each of these situations. Many parents avoid preparing their children for emergencies since they don't want to unnecessarily frighten them. But fires, robberies and accidents occur often enough to pose a real threat to latchkey children and should be prepared for. If handled in the right manner, a child's knowledge of what to do in these emergencies can be a source of security instead of fright.

Simply telling children what to do is not enough to impress important procedures on their minds, so it is recommended that correct fire procedures be practiced with children. This can be done by having a parent pretend there is a fire in the kitchen, bedroom or hall and then determine the best routes for getting outside with their children. Parents should also simulate calls to the fire department with their children. A smoke detector, required by law in apartment dwellings of some states, is also recommended for private homes, and the whole family needs to be familiar with its sound. Parents should also impress on their children not to try to put out fires themselves. Many children feel responsible for the fires that start at home when they're alone even if it's not their fault, and try to put them out to avoid being yelled at. Parents should stress to their children that they are more important than any material possession and should follow emergency procedures previously discussed.

Accidents are the main cause of death to children under age twelve. Children home without adult supervision are especially vulnerable. In order to prepare children for emergencies, they should be taught basic first aid for injuries requiring immediate emergency care. Once instructed how to call for an ambulance, children should be encouraged to do so. Many children with serious injuries often wait for their parents to arrive instead of calling for help.

Break-ins or robberies were experienced by a number of the children interviewed. Children can be prepared by telling them where to go if they hear someone breaking in and how to call the police. Children should also be taught to be aware of possible signs of a break-in when they return home from school. Children, like anyone else, should know not to enter the house if they see a door ajar, a window broken or anything else unusual. Instead they should go to a neighbor's house or to whoever else is designated to help in an emergency and call the police.

### Activities

Boredom is one of the major problems of latchkey children, since it magnifies both fear and sibling conflicts. A child who is active is less likely to fight with other siblings or hear noises outside. But keeping a child busy for two hours every afternoon is not an easy task. It requires forethought and planning.

It is recommended that parents plan visits or activities outside the home, since this will provide their children with a change of pace. Children who spend Wednesday, for example, at a friend's home or at a club have a totally different week than children who spend five consecutive days alone. This midweek break divides the week into two-day units and makes the time the children spend alone less routine.

Parents might also consider community recreation or volunteer activities as possibilities for their children. The availability of music, dance or sports activities should also not be overlooked, whether in school, the community, or an affordable private source. An event that takes latchkey children out of the house even one afternoon each week will not only broaden their experience but is sure to make their routine more tolerable.

These activities usually require transportation. Parents can utilize the cooperation of other parents, responsible teenagers and senior citizens to help get their children involved in community activities.

Children should also be encouraged to spend one afternoon a week at the local public library where they can do homework or read, if it doesn't pose an extraordinary inconvenience. Parents could then pick up their children on the way home from work. It's a good idea for parents to become acquainted with a specific librarian who can identify their children by sight, in case contact is needed. Children should be encouraged to participate in activities sponsored by the library and plan library visiting days when special events are scheduled.

Parents might also consider planning exchange visits with children who are home under adult supervision, but care must be taken that true exchange occurs. Parents who don't work can become resentful of being constantly saddled with the children of working parents. If parents let their children go home one afternoon a week with a friend they should be sure to invite the friend over on the weekend for an exchange visit or special activity.

The week can be broken up for older children by spending one or two afternoons a week with another latchkey child. The companionship of a friend always makes the time go by more quickly and reduces the anxiety of both children.

On the days when latchkey children stay home alone, in-house activities should be organized for them. Most children find it difficult to organize time for themselves and consequently become bored. Chores and homework assignments can help pass the time, but other activities are also necessary. The night before, parents might set out pictures for their children to color or puzzles for them to solve. Children who have hobbies, such as stamp collecting or model building, might find their afternoons alone a good time to work on them.

## Chores

Chores are another method of structuring time, though they shouldn't be the only method used. One man who had a successful latchkey experience as a child commented that the time he spent after school went by very quickly. He and his siblings were occupied with chores. "We didn't have time to think about the fact that we were home alone. By the time we were done our parents were home."

Parents shouldn't think of chores as work but rather as something their children might enjoy doing. One way to make chores more interesting is to change the routine so that children don't have to do the same chores every day. Instead try leaving a specific note outlining that day's chores. It is clearer to say, "Vacuum the living room rug, wash the dishes and take out the trash," than "Clean the house." Vague directions have to be interpreted and very often will be misinterpreted. Parents who have more than one child should be sure to assign specific tasks to each child. Leaving the oldest sibling in charge of assigning tasks only leads to conflicts and hard feelings. Instead, parents themselves should hold each child responsible for completing his own assigned tasks.

Complimenting children for their efforts goes a long way in making them feel appreciated and encourages them to do an even better job the next time. It's devastating for a child who has washed the dishes to have these efforts ignored. It's even worse if a child says to a returning parent, "Look! I did the dishes," only to have that parent respond, "But you forgot the pots." In fact, many children who were assigned chores were afraid of doing them incorrectly. One eleven-year-old girl complained that her mother yelled at her for cooking the chicken too long. An eight-year-old boy was afraid to do the dishes because if he broke one his mother would get angry. In order to prevent these problems, parents should assign tasks that are easy for the child to do without adult supervision, and should avoid assigning chores that would have strong negative consequences if done incorrectly.

Although chores do help pass the time, parents should be careful not to give their children too much work to do. A few chores will help structure after-school time and make children feel like contributing members of their families. Children who are asked to set the dinner table can feel good about helping busy parents, but children who are given too much responsibility can feel overwhelmed. Several former latchkey children complained about too much responsibility. "I had to cook dinner, clean the house and watch my younger brothers and sisters. There were five of them," one woman noted. "It was more than I could handle. At times I felt like the mother." The contribution this former latchkey child made to the family was substantial, but overwhelming.

### Television

Most of the latchkey children interviewed watched between four and five hours of television daily. They turned the television on as soon as they got home and left it on all afternoon. Some sat and watched intently while others used it for background noise or companionship. Few were selective about program offerings.

Parents should teach their children to make active program selections rather than be passive television viewers. This can be encouraged by sitting down with the children on Sunday evening and reviewing their television schedule for the week. Then a list could be made of the selected programs and placed by the television. The time alloted for television watching should take into account the time needed to complete homework, chores and other afternoon responsibilities.

Planning children's television watching not only helps to control the amount of television they watch, but also teaches them to be selective consumers. Although planning might not reduce the quantity of viewing, it may cut down on the amount of junk television children watch by increasing the likelihood that they'll take advantage of after-school specials and other educational programs that they may not have been aware of.

Planning can also help parents maximize the educational benefits of the shows they choose to watch. If, for example, you know your children are going to watch a special on gorillas on Thursday, they can be prepared for the program. Preparation might take the form of parents sharing what they already know about gorillas, and could include a visit to the library for gorilla research. Once prepared, children will anticipate Thursday's program and watch with greater interest. Later that evening, parents could discuss the special with their children and give them a chance to share what they've learned.

Finally, planned television viewing can help reduce conflicts when more than one child is involved. Younger siblings often complain that they have to watch the programs their older siblings select. By spending Sunday evening deciding upon the week's program schedule, selections can be made and compromises reached with the advantage of adult input. Children involved in this process will not only learn about program selection, but will also grow in their ability to resolve conflicts.

## Summer Vacations

In order to utilize summer vacations effectively, working parents need to start making plans weeks, sometimes months in advance. The problems latchkey children experience in the school year of fear, boredom and isolation are compounded in the summer when they spend day after day, hour after hour alone. Children need some scheduled activity. It is difficult for even the very mature child to cope with the excessive amounts of free time and independence an unplanned summer can provide.

Besides sending children to live with relatives, parents have numerous options available to them since many private and public agencies are aware of the problems of unattended children in the summer. Whatever arrangements are made, a few simple guidelines are suggested. Parents should discuss all summer plans and activities with children in advance rather than decide arbitrarily how their children should spend their summer. The number of places children spend their summers should also be kept to a minimum. It is better for a child to spend eight weeks in a single program, rather than spend two weeks at each of four or five different centers.

Parents frequently use summer-school programs offered by private and public schools to provide day care for their children. Summer school is generally offered at a reasonable cost and can be used to strengthen academic skills. The problem with summer-school programs is that most of them are only scheduled for half a day (usually in the morning) leaving the children to care for themselves for the rest of the afternoon. Another disadvantage of summer school is that, after nine months of regular school, most children don't want to attend. In general summer school should be utilized by those who are academically deficient and could use the extra time to catch up. It's much better that students who are performing satisfactorily be given a different type of experience rather than enroll in summer school, which might quell their enthusiasm for the opening of school in the fall.

Home care, a less popular alternative, can provide the family with several children's being cared for at a reasonable cost. This type of summer care provides children with the security of their own home and neighborhood and continuous adult supervision. The problem is that most babysitters are hired to watch children rather than entertain them, and children are still in the position of providing their own structure to long summer days.

Day-care centers or day-care programs are designed to deal with the needs of working parents. They open early, provide a full day of activity and stay open late so that parents can pick up their children on the way home from work. They don't have the facilities a day camp or summer camp can offer but they do offer convenience.

Day camps are intended to provide children who don't want to spend the summer away from home with a summer camp experience. They generally offer a full range of sports and structured activities. The problem is that they usually don't correspond to the schedule of working parents and transportation is often not provided. Working parents who want their children to attend a day camp must arrange a carpool or other transportation and realize that their children will probably spend part of the afternoon alone since most day camps are dismissed in the late afternoon.

Children who attend summer camp sleep away from home for part or all of the summer. This is possibly the best arrangement for working parents whose children are bored with spending the summer with grandparents. The arrangement not only offers parents relief from the stress of child care for a few weeks a year, it gives children the opportunity to make new friends and gain an added sense of their own independence and maturity. Parents should, however, be careful not to give their children the impression that they are being sent to camp to get rid of them. Instead, children should go away to camp because they want to go and spend only a week or two their first time away. The second year a lengthier trip can be planned if the first year was a positive experience.

## Neighbors

Helpful neighbors can be the key to a successful latchkey experience. They can assist children in emergencies and provide moral support when necessary. Because of their proximity to latchkey children, neighbors tend to provide a safety net that minimizes parental fears. Developing such supportive relationships isn't always easy, however; neighbors must be carefully selected and cultivated.

In selecting a neighbor parents must first be sure that the neighbor is willing to help if needed. It's better to select someone three doors away who doesn't mind children phoning or visiting than a next-door neighbor who resents the time requested.

Second, parents should be sure to select someone who is usually home after school. Neighbors can't be expected to stay home just to help latchkey children, but some are home more than others. Cooperative neighbors who are seldom home are little help in an emergency. Senior citizens or women with children under three usually spend a good deal of their time at home, particularly in the late afternoon.

Parents should have an explicitly understood arrangement with the person who agrees to be a neighborhood resource. Children can't be expected to go to someone who hasn't been previously contacted for help. To become better acquainted, parents could invite the neighbor over for coffee, share their concerns and see if the neighbor is willing to help. Once a willing neighbor is found, the neighbor and child could spend some time meeting and getting acquainted. It is important that the neighbor personally invite the children to come over in case of an emergency to help them feel comfortable in requesting help. Many children reported having a neighbor who they were supposed to call for help yet, when an emergency arose, they

sat at home waiting for distant parents. Neighbors who are supportive and encourage children to come over will help latchkey children
get over their initial feelings of shyness.

Latchkey parents and children can demonstrate their appreciation
for their neighbor's help by sending flowers, remembering them in
other special ways on holidays, baking a cake or mowing their lawn.
It is most important not to take a kind neighbor for granted. Parents
whose children begin to spend too much time at a neighbor's house
should consider paying the neighbor for babysitting or find some-
place else for their children to stay, unless the neighbor expresses
delight at having the child around.

### Siblings

Parents who have more than one child staying at home should try
to minimize the possible areas of conflict. Rules should be clearly
established for telephone and television usage.

Experience indicates that parents with children who are close in
age shouldn't assign one the job of supervising the other. Rather,
each child should be made responsible for his/her own behavior. As
a rule children less than ten years old shouldn't be expected to watch
younger siblings, and children under six shouldn't be left in the care
of their older brothers and sisters. Parents who have children who
are several years apart should teach older children to accept the
responsibility graciously. It's not wise for parents to abdicate their
role as disciplinarian to a twelve- or fourteen-year-old. Instead, the
primary role older children play is to ensure the safety of younger
children. A parent's expectations of each child should be clearly
communicated, holding each accountable for his/her actions. Disci-
plinary problems can then be handled with less turmoil and hard
feelings when the parent returns.

### Quality Time

A problem common to virtually all parents is finding time at the end
of a busy work day to spend with their children. From the time they
arrive home until their children go to bed three or four hours later,
dinner must be cooked and served, dishes washed and homework

checked. Yet probably the most important thing parents can do during that time is also the thing most often overlooked: make their children feel loved. One of the most frequent complaints of former latchkey children is, "My mother was always too busy or too tired to spend time with me." When children think their parents are too busy to spend time with them, it may compound the feelings of rejection they may already be having about being alone. One former latchkey child, whose mother was a teacher, found herself jealous of her mother's students. "She always did things for her students that she was too busy to do for us. I felt hurt and rejected." Children need to be told and reminded in little ways that they are loved.

In addition to cuddle time, which helps to build closeness and open communication between parent and child, parents should also try to spend some time each day doing something with each child. That might be baking cookies, reading a book or building something out of legos. It's not so important what parents do with their children, but that time is being spent with them.

Parents often try to compensate for lost time during the week on weekends. This time can be made even more special by spending part of one day each weekend as "Children's Day." Sunday afternoon makes an excellent Children's Day. The children themselves should decide the afternoon's activities from a list of choices parents find manageable. They will feel more secure if parents try to make the time they spend with their children special and help them to understand that they want to be with them at other times, too.

### Homework

Ideally homework should be used to foster a close relationship between home and school and parent and child, if the parent is able to help the child with homework assignments. If parents are unqualified to help they may only confuse the child with incorrect explanations. If they are unwilling to help the child complete assignments and punish him or her if they're incomplete, homework becomes a source of stress and tension between them. Ideally, every parent should plan to help children with assignments every night, if only to communicate to their children the value they place on education. But this demand is often difficult to meet, even in families with one parent at home. If there are nights when parents are unable to help their children with homework assignments, ask that they complete them when alone after school. Parents should then reward their children for these independent efforts. One method would be to place a calendar on the refrigerator. Every time the child has his/her homework assignment completed by a specified time, the child gets a check on the calendar. After a certain number of checks, for example five, the child receives a reward. This way the child is encouraged to develop independent work habits. If the child cannot or does not complete the assignment, it's better to simply help him or her complete the assignment rather than resort to punishment. In any case, the parent and child should always check completed assignments together.

## When Children Are Sick

If children are sick enough to stay home from school they should be given continuous care. Most latchkey children find spending two or three hours alone a day stressful; asking the same child to spend eight or nine hours alone while sick places the child in a very difficult situation. Sick children need to be nurtured. Recovery is as much psychological as it is physiological. Oftentimes sick children are more vulnerable to their own fears and feelings of isolation and would benefit a great deal from having a caring adult or an older sibling present. Obviously, the child's parent is the person best suited to stay with a sick child. If job constraints prohibit a parent from spending the day at home, then a nearby neighbor or relative might be willing to have the child spend the day with him or her. It is better for a child to be taken to someone else's home where he or she will receive continuous care and companionship than to be left alone in his or her own home.

If it's impossible to find a friend or relative to care for your child, some communities now offer home care for sick children. In cooperation with United Way, the Tucson Association for Child Care has created a network of trained on-call providers to care for sick children in their homes. Parents call the service any time after 6:00 A.M. and an aide is there within an hour. The aides are trained to assess the children upon entering the homes and will determine whether or not to send them to a hospital if they are sufficiently sick. Otherwise, armed with playthings and first aid items they provide companionship for sick children.

Generally, day-care centers are forbidden by law to admit sick children. But one program in Albany, New York, called Wheezles and Sneezles, is specifically designed to accommodate sick children. Housed in a three-bedroom apartment in Albany, Wheezles and Sneezles provides sick children with a nap room and a quiet place to play in a home atmosphere.

If all alternatives fail and parents must leave their children alone when they are sick, they should minimize the time they are continuously alone. One way to do this would be for parents to only work half a day. In two-parent families parents could alternate working in the morning and afternoon, which would allow for continuous care. If a half day is impossible, returning home for lunch is a good alternative, since it would break up a long day at home alone. If distance to and from work prohibits such a visit, parents might be able to enlist a friend or neighbor who would be willing to pay a lunch-time visit to the child to monitor his or her progress and provide needed companionship.

When a sick child must spend a half or a whole day alone because no other arrangements can be made, extensive preparations to assure the child's comfort are necessary. Preferably the child should be placed on a bed or sofa with easy viewing of a television and within reach of a telephone. Lunch and snacks should be prepared in advance and placed near the child, in a cooler if appropriate. A coloring book and crayons, a good book for reading or other favorite quiet activities should also be nearby. Medication should be portioned into individual baggies and clearly marked with the time the child is to take the drug. All of these preparations not only help make the child feel comfortable, but also communicate the parents' concern and affection. Under no circumstances should young children or children with a fever be left home to care for themselves. The danger of a fever rising rapidly or improperly taken medication is too great.

## Communication

When former latchkey children were asked what could have been done to make their experience more positive, most often their responses implied closer communication between parent and child.

Communication is the key and should be nurtured, since it plays a decisive role in how well children adjust to the latchkey experience.

Generally, children are most eager to talk about their day right after school. One tip for working parents is to ask children to write down all the important things that happened that day when they return home from school on a pad or chalkboard, then nothing will be forgotten. Their children's enthusiasm may have waned somewhat in the meantime, but enthusiasm can be restimulated if parents take an active interest in their children when they do get a chance to talk.

In a recent book, entitled *The Private Life of the American Teenager,* authors Jane Norman and Myron Harris surveyed 60,000 teenagers regarding their relationship with their parents. Sixty-one percent of the teenagers surveyed felt as though their parents listened and cared about what they had to say. The other thirty-nine percent felt that their parents didn't listen or didn't care.

Being a good listener and communicating interest is more difficult than it first appears, especially with teenagers, who typically isolate themselves to some degree from parents. Parents should start by selecting a comfortable place to talk. Somewhere that is private and free from distractions will increase the likelihood of an open and honest interaction. The kitchen and television room are generally poor choices, since they are the busiest rooms in most households. Parents with more than one child should talk to each of them individually, since children are less likely to discuss their concerns in front of other family members.

Parents demonstrate to their children that they have time to listen to their concerns by sitting down and maintaining eye contact. They shouldn't try to listen while folding the laundry or cooking dinner, even if they're alone. Sitting down and maintaining eye contact communicates "I have time to listen to you now. I'm not going anywhere."

In trying to open up a conversation with a teenager, remember to use questions that give him or her a great deal of freedom in answering and avoid questions that only require a yes or a no answer. Yes or no questions provide parents with little information about how their children are really coping. Questions like, "What did you do in math today?" or "Tell me how you feel about being alone" demonstrate interest and concern rather than a sense of giving a child the third degree. A general rule to follow is to ask questions that allow the child to do the talking while the parent listens.

Parents who feel their children are having difficulty coping with staying alone should try to find out why. Questions like, "What do you do when you feel lonely?" or "How do you and your sister get along when I'm not here?" can open the door to discuss problems. It's important to note that listening doesn't mean that solutions will be found right away. But parents who allow their children to express their concerns and demonstrate understanding will help them to feel better just by airing their grievances.

Parents can also encourage communication by accepting whatever their children have to say. While many children's concerns seem irrational to parents, they are very real to the children who experience them and shouldn't be deprecated. If a child doesn't like to be alone during an electrical storm, parents shouldn't respond by saying, "There's nothing to be afraid of." This discounts the child's feelings. Instead parents should listen to their child's whole story, trying to put themselves in his or her place. To comfort him or her and demonstrate their understanding parents should then try to express what they think the child is feeling, such as "It frightens you to be home alone during a storm."

Nonverbal communication is just as significant as verbal communication. Children's behavior will often communicate how they feel about being alone, even if they won't talk about it. Parents who notice their children acting sullen or depressed, angry or quiet, should share these observations with their children. A quiet discussion might help parents learn why their children are acting differently.

Nagging, judging and criticizing are obviously communication turn-offs, though parents may understandably be low on patience at times. Because of the limited amount of contact parents have with their latchkey children, however, it's important to try not to waste the time together in anger or with hard feelings.

The latchkey experience can be a challenging one for any family. Parents who communicate frequently and openly with their children have taken the first step to solve many of the problems that do occur. But if communication is sparse or shallow, the problems which will inevitably follow will be magnified. Communication is the key. Parents should use it to develop a team approach to solving problems.

## Evaluating the Experience

Placing a child in self-care doesn't have to be a permanent arrangement. It is recommended that parents who for any reason suspect that the arrangement is less than positive seek alternative child-care arrangements. The following is a checklist to help parents evaluate whether or not their child is having difficulty staying alone.

YES   NO

_____ _____    1. Have you come to believe that your neighborhood is no longer safe for your child?

           2. Has your child begun to suddenly exhibit behavior that frightens you, such as:

_____ _____       • playing unsupervised with fire, dangerous household tools or chemicals

_____ _____       • experimenting with alcohol or other drugs

_____ _____       • having seizures

_____ _____       • demonstrating violent or aggressive behavior

_____ _____    3) Has your child lost access to any adult living or working nearby that he or she knows and upon whom he or she can rely on in an emergency?

_____ _____    4) Are you no longer accessible to your child by telephone?

_____ _____    5) Do any of your children refuse to stay alone with other siblings?

If you answer yes to any of these questions, you should reevaluate your decision to leave your child in self-care or in the care of a sibling. The latchkey arrangement has probably become an unacceptable one for your family.

6) Does your child say he or she would prefer *not* to stay alone?

      _____ almost never    (one point)

      _____ sometimes     (two points)

      _____ almost always  (three points)

7) Does your child say he or she is afraid while alone?

_____ almost never    (one point)

_____ sometimes       (two points)

_____ almost always   (three points)

8) Has your child begun complaining about being afraid of the dark?

_____ almost never    (one point)

_____ sometimes       (two points)

_____ almost always   (three points)

9) Has your child begun to have nightmares or other sleep disturbances?

_____ almost never    (one point)

_____ sometimes       (two points)

_____ almost always   (three points)

10) Has your child begun to have difficulty gaining access to your house?

_____ almost never    (one point)

_____ sometimes       (two points)

_____ almost always   (three points)

11) Has your child begun to complain about having difficulties with siblings?

_____ almost never    (one point)

_____ sometimes       (two points)

_____ almost always   (three points)

12) Do you think that your relationship with your child is becoming distant?

_____ almost never    (one point)

_____ sometimes       (two points)

_____ almost always   (three points)

Add the number of points corresponding to your answers for questions 6 through 12. The higher the score, the less likely it is that you should continue your child in self-care. A score of 15 or higher should cause you to be hesitant about continuing your child in self-care.

13) Is your child on time for school?

_____ almost always   (one point)

_____ sometimes        (two points)

_____ almost never     (three points)

14) Does your child arrive home from school (or call you) on time?

_____ almost always   (one point)

_____ sometimes        (two points)

_____ almost never     (three points)

15) Does your child tell you where he or she is going before leaving home?

_____ almost always   (one point)

_____ sometimes        (two points)

_____ almost never     (three points)

16) Does your child discuss his or her feelings and problems about self-care?

_____ almost always   (one point)

_____ sometimes        (two points)

_____ almost never     (three points)

17) Do you believe your child is truthful with you when he or she is asked what happened during the day?

_____ almost always   (one point)

_____ sometimes        (two points)

_____ almost never     (three points)

18) Does your child complete the tasks he or she has been assigned?

_____ almost always  (one point)

_____ sometimes     (two points)

_____ almost never   (three points)

19) Does your child seem to solve problems that arise in self-care?

_____ almost always  (one point)

_____ sometimes     (two points)

_____ almost never   (three points)

20) Does your child appropriately ask for help in making decisions about problems in self-care?

_____ almost always  (one point)

_____ sometimes     (two points)

_____ almost never   (three points)

Add the number of points corresponding to your answers for questions 13 through 20. The higher your score, the more likely it is that your child is beginning to have trouble with self-care. The range is from 8 to 24 points. A score of 13 or higher should alert you to a general problem developing.

Parents who find that their children are having trouble entering or maintaining the latchkey arrangement would be wise not to force the situation. Being a latchkey child can be dangerous and shouldn't be attempted if parents or children feel distressed by the arrangement. There are usually alternatives that can be found.

Parents would benefit a great deal by talking about their needs and the needs of their children with friends and neighbors. Bringing the problem out into the open might present solutions that are novel. Oftentimes parents fail to mention their problems concerning child care because they don't want their friends, relatives or neighbors to feel imposed upon. The real consequence is that where another alternative to self-care may exist, the family's support group doesn't know there's been a problem.

Parents across the nation are having problems providing adequate care and supervision for their children—it's no longer a matter touching the lives of only a few families. The partnership we need to care for our nation's children grows out of the family into our neighborhoods and communities, our cities and states and the nation as a whole. But the best solution to the latchkey problem will be found closest to the family.

# Chapter 13
# THOUGHTS OF
# THE FUTURE

In addition to the many programs and policies facilitating the care of children that were mentioned in Chapter Eleven, there are three areas of change that can help parents become the direct providers of out-of-school care for their children. One is to increase the interplay between school and work policies. A second is the move toward the household as the workplace; the third is the development of a renewed sense of community.

## Changes in School and Work Calendars

While there is a growing reluctance nowadays simply to hand over our children to schools, parents still look to schools to provide the major portion of the care and training of children outside the family. Parents and employers would find it to their advantage to alter the current disjunction of school and work calendars.

The school year was developed on an agricultural calendar when America was largely a nation of farmers. As America became less and less an agrarian society, cautious minor adjustments were made to adapt the school to the new industrial calendar. In general, families have been expected to span the gap between needs in the workplace and schooling.

In an industrial society that blessedly came to protect children from being used as cheap labor, there was less reason for children to have time to do farm chores and so less reason for a tightly limited school day. But the length of the school day or year was not changed accordingly. Families filled in with free play and mothers were at home to supervise while fathers worked. We convinced ourselves that this was the best arrangement. And the arrangement worked, as long as mothers were willing to stay out of the labor force in large numbers.

We kept our eyes closed to differences in the educational calendars in Europe and the more serious business of education in many nations abroad. We told ourselves that America's grand experiment in universal education was unlike anything else on earth and that educational practices followed by other, far distant countries did not, could not apply to us. It worked, as long as we were an industrial economy that could train our brightest and most talented offspring for more years to fill our needs for highly skilled workers, while we absorbed the bulk of our citizenry in industrial tasks that demanded less training and more physical than intellectual ability. Today, however, the world economy is coming to be dominated by technicians and information processors rather than clerks and laborers, and there is a need for a better educated citizenry all around. With an increased need for the education of our young, and the fact that the majority of mothers are in the labor force full-time, we find that the old arrangement no longer works; mothers aren't available to supervise children during many out-of-school hours. Hence, the need to bring the school year and day and the work year and day into greater conformity is stronger than ever.

The signs that doing this could work in America are already evident. Nations such as France and Sweden already provide their workers five weeks of paid vacations plus holidays; West German workers average more than four weeks of vacation. Among the member countries of the European Economic Community, the standard minimum annual vacation is four weeks. The American worker averages two weeks of vacation plus holidays with about twenty percent of all workers deprived of paid vacations. Add to this the fact that a significant number of American workers indicate that they are willing to trade some income for more leisure time, there is reason for believing that we could, even now, make it possible for parents to spend more time with their children and less at work.

When people view the current American economy, with one eye on the past and the other on competition from abroad, shortening the work year seems unthinkable. Yet, other countries compete favorably while their employees spend fewer days on the job. If we look only at what employers are doing, progress is slow. In general, work schedules have remained unchanged since before the Second World War. But labor schedules, employee benefits and company-provided services do not materialize simply as the result of market forces. These things are also influenced by social change, government intervention and employee demand. We expect that as labor becomes less plentiful and our concern about producing better-educated children increases, changes favoring worker preference will take place.

In reality, changes in the work week are already under way. Predictions are that in less than ten years the standard work week in America will be reduced from forty to thirty-six hours and will often be achieved by working nine hours a day for four days, a plan that would fit nicely with school calendars that operate on a four-day week with extended school hours each day. Such four-day school weeks have operated in several western states since 1974 and are currently under consideration in school districts in states such as Minnesota and Florida. Polk County, Florida, for example, is considering experimenting with such a plan next year for the 60,000 students it services.

Besides sorely needed efforts in revising educational approaches to guarantee a better-educated future generation of adults, educators should also consider the extension of the school day and year to allow for more time to meet the increased demands for a literate society. A parallel decrease of work-time demands from employees would mean a greater correspondence between the schedules of children in school and those of their working parents, thus allowing greater opportunity for parents to maintain full employment while allowing more time for them to be with their children.

## Work at Home

A second strong future force that may close the child-care gap is the possibility that large numbers of workers will be allowed to carry out their work at home. Reconceptualizing the workplace, combined with a close correspondence between school and work calendars, could almost eliminate the need for extra familial child care for school-age children.

The wheels that would allow for family life that included one or both parents working at home are already in gear. Even in the current manufacturing sector the number of workers who actually have to manipulate goods is declining. As industries change and technology advances, people will be able to carry out more of their work wherever they are, including in their homes, in increasingly less time.

What would happen to the education and care of children if the majority of parents were able to conduct their work at home? What, indeed, would happen to families? There is a clear indication that the most rapidly expanding work classifications are also those that offer the best possibilities for work in one's home, so the possibility of a mass transfer of work from the office to the home is very much a reality, despite evident difficulties in effecting such a transfer.

There are powerful forces at work to cause a change in the places work is done. These include: the escalating costs of transportation; the increase in the time workers spend commuting as a proportion of the time they spend at work; the increased costs of maintaining offices; the possible increase in the labor pool as more women would be able to hold a job and supervise children; the decrease in pollution and the cost for controlling it; and the possible increases in family interactions, stable community relationships and community participation.

One trend that supports the possibility of increased work-at-home options is self-employment. Since the beginning of the twentieth century, the number of self-employed people in the United States has declined from nearly fifty percent of the work force in 1900 to only seven and a half percent of the work force in 1970.

However, during the early 1970s the number of self-employed began to rise from 7 million people in 1970 to 8.5 million in 1980.

Most of these new business people are information entrepreneurs who work out of their homes.

Work-at-home options should be especially popular with the members of the baby boom generation that peaked in 1958. Many of these young adults will be forming new families and rearing children during the 1980s. Given the appeal of flexplace work arrangements for working parents, plus the energy and time savings of working at home, it seems that approximately twenty-five percent of all white-collar work will be done at home within ten years.

Transfer of work to the home could have other benefits for society as we look at more husbands and wives, even children, working together. Even today, many fathers and mothers involved in the computer industry find that children as young as eight become excellent computer operators and programmers. One example of such cooperation is a family business called Earthware Services, Inc., producer of a simulation called *Volcanoes* and other company software. This Eugene, Oregon, company is owned and operated by the Goles family. The father, Gordon, is the code designer of Earthware's simulations. Donna, along with son Edward, thirteen, designs program graphics. She also handles marketing and bookkeeping for the company. Fifteen-year-old Mark Goles is the company's chief programmer.

If any sizable proportion of a community shifted to working at home, greater community stability would result. Employees who performed their work at home wouldn't have to move every time they obtained a promotion or changed jobs. As forced mobility declined, fewer transient relationships would occur, people would become more willing to enter into close neighbor relationships and greater zeal for participating in community life would result, to say nothing of the economic gains families would realize by elimination of commuting costs.

The difficulties that would be encountered in implementing the above suggestions should not be underestimated, however. Problems of motivation, management and corporate structure would have to be resolved. Some jobs would have to continue to be carried out in person, in an office setting. Yet, the possibilities offered by work-at-home options are enormous, with a variety of experiments in work-at-home arrangements already under way.

## A New Sense of Community

Community has many meanings, and many different things facilitate our coming together. The mood of society is to search for greater community. The more we are surrounded by high technology, the greater is our need for it. The emergence of community is also part of the decentralization movement in the country. Because we have grown weary of waiting for effective top-down solutions that never seem to come, we next look for solutions in our neighboring areas. Because of a long tradition of local control, education is a natural focal point for community, and is the main reason why people will probably continue to look to community schools to help balance their work-family conflicts.

As forced job relocation subsides, stronger attachments to the region in which one lives should increase. There has been a surge of movement back to small towns and rural areas, facilitated by the fact that people are not as tied to access to a center city in order to hold a job. Smaller towns and rural areas are known for their sense of community. They also feel safer to people, a significant change in reducing some of the negative impact on latchkey children.

In a collaborating society the importance of the family grows as the most natural setting for small group cooperation and as the principal building block of local communities. Some have proposed the establishment of family corporations, profit-making institutions that extend over and draw together generations within family groups. These groupings would be able to enjoy the benefits of a corporation while they collaborate in producing one or more products or provide one or more services. In such a family corporation social services would be provided to all the members of the corporation, using rather than replacing family ties.

The family as a cooperative economic unit is not novel in western society. Incorporating a family is simply a way of pooling intergenerational and extended family resources, thereby returning to the family a utility it had in an agrarian society. But it would also be a way for acknowledging mother/homemaker contributions to the gross national product. Within this model the family could provide continuous care of children as a corporate family business expense delivered by one or more employees of the corporation, who also are shareholders.

These are exciting possibilities. Unfortunately, as with most collaborative plans, upper- and middle-income households, especially intact families, will be the major beneficiaries. Their relative wealth already provides them with a degree of insulation from most of the negative impacts of a shrinking social net. At the same time, these families are best able to purchase, because of greater financial resources, and profit, because of better education, from the new technologies and the trend toward collaborative enterprise, self-employment and computerized networking. Without financial and educational resources, America's poor will be ill-equipped to adapt to their changing environment. Some of the changes suggested would remove from upper- and middle-income families the need to leave children unattended, but not from disadvantaged families; this could create an even larger gap between rich and poor.

A national child-care policy would still be needed to provide for those who cannot be self-sufficient. The federal government has never responded to the needs of children with a comprehensive plan. In fact, until recent years, the government more or less ignored the existence of the family.

If public policy is effective in encouraging many families to respond to the needs of their own members independent of social support programs, then perhaps there will be sufficient resources and impetus to provide the comprehensive social supports needed for those who have not been able to provide for themselves.

# EPILOGUE

The basis for much of the information in this book was obtained from families living in the metropolitan Washington, D.C. area. Families in this area tend to lead the nation in new life-style trends such as fewer children per family, increased numbers of working women, greater diversity in types of households and rising household incomes. In this area employees who have children are more likely to have a working spouse or be living with other working adults than employees who have no children. In this area, too, having children look after themselves is the most frequently used child-care arrangement of employed parents.

Despite concern expressed throughout this book with the cost and availability of child care, the kind of child care employed parents use is largely determined by the number of children in each household and their ages, and the presence or absence of persons in the household who can serve as child-care providers. Parents are likely to use first the resources they happen to have in their homes for child care no matter what the family income level. This factor seems to indicate that the best way for increasing continuous adult supervision for children is to increase the availability of adult members of the household. Households with the least resources for child care at home are those headed by a single parent.

It is evident from our findings that while children *can* be stressed by self-care arrangements, there is no clear indication of how many children are ultimately harmed by such arrangements. Except for child care by a spouse or other adult resident in the household, all other child-care arrangements carry with them some form of liability. These liabilities include the unrealiability of the care-giver, the cost of care, and the extra time and distance demanded to transport children to child-care sites.

The nation, government, communities and employers should be concerned about the care arrangements parents make for children, among which self-care is rapidly becoming paramount. Not only are children put at greater or less risk depending on the child-care arrangement selected for them, but the national economy is affected by the drain on employees caused by parental responsibilities. Working parents using self-care as a child-care arrangement suffer nearly double the absenteeism rates as do those working parents with a spouse or other adult available at home for child care.

Many suggestions for employer and community involvement to help parents carry out family responsibilities were offered. And many more approaches are needed, especially to assist single parents who tend to have their children look after themselves disproportionately more than two-parent families and to be less able to afford other types of paid child care.

Changes in society, technological advances, changes in the hours and place of work, and the hours and days of the school calendar may all create changes in opportunities for managing the care of children. Until these changes appear, the greatest help will come from increasing emphasis on the responsibilities of parenting, helping to improve parent-child relationships, putting parents in touch with existing child-care providers and training children to survive in their environment. The short-term outlook is going to be much improved as awareness grows that children need more, not less adult attention if they are to become well-adjusted adults and generous parents themselves in due course.

# RESOURCES

Many groups have become interested in promoting policies and programs that will benefit latchkey children, either directly by fostering programs that provide day care for children, or indirectly by facilitating changes in social and work policies and procedures that allow parents more options for safeguarding their children. The following list is representative of groups across the nation that in one way or another are working to improve children's environments. This list is intended to help you become familiar with and involved in the work now in progress.

SOCIAL WELFARE ORGANIZATIONS

The following groups are active in a great variety of child-related projects. These range from operating survival skills programs to advocating federal policy changes beneficial to all children. Some simply provide data on a specific aspect of child welfare. Many of the organizations listed are only partially involved with children in self-care or school-age day-care projects. But all have some commitment to children and/or their working parents and therefore may be of help to you.

American Red Cross
17th and D Streets, N.W.
Washington, D.C. 20006
202-737-8300

Association for Volunteer Administration
P.O. Box 4584
Boulder, CO 80302
303-497-0238

Association of Junior Leagues
825 Third Avenue
New York, NY 10022
212-355-4380

Big Brothers/Big Sisters of America
117 South 17th Street
Suite 1200
Philadelphia, PA 19103
215-567-2748

Boy Scouts of America, Inc.
P.O. Box 61030
Dallas/Ft. Worth Airport, TX 75261
214-659-2000

Boys Clubs of America
771 First Avenue
New York, NY 10017
212-557-7755

CampFire, Inc.
4601 Madison Avenue
Kansas City, MO 64112
816-756-1950

Child Welfare League of America
67 Irving Place
New York, NY 10003
215-254-7410

Children's Defense Fund
122 C Street, N.W.
Washington, D.C. 20001
202-628-8787

Children's Legal Rights Information and Training
2008 Hillyer Place, N.W.
Washington, D.C. 20009
202-332-6575

Children's Rights Group
693 Mission Street
San Francisco, CA 20009
202-332-6575

Day Care Council of America
1602 17th Street, N.W.
Washington, D.C. 20036
202-745-0220

Girl Scouts of the U.S.A.
830 Third Avenue
New York, NY 10022
212-940-7500

Girls Clubs of America
205 Lexington Avenue
New York, NY 10016
212-689-3700

National Assembly of National Voluntary Health and Social Welfare
Organizations
291 Broadway
New York, NY 10007
212-267-1700

National Association for Child Care Management
1800 M Street, N.W.
Suite 1030N
Washington, D.C. 20036
202-452-8100

National Association of County Human Services Administrators
c/o National Association of Counties
1735 New York Avenue, N.W.
Washington, D.C. 20006
202-783-5113

National Association of Girls Clubs
5808 16th Street, N.W.
Washington, D.C. 20011
202-726-2044

National Association of Neighborhoods
1651 Fuller Street, N.W.
Washington, D.C. 20009
202-332-7766

National Committee for Prevention of Child Abuse
332 South Michigan Avenue
Suite 1250
Chicago, IL 60601
312-565-1100

National Fire Protection Association
Batterymarch Park
Quincy, MA 02269
617-328-9290

National Safety Council
444 North Michigan Avenue
Chicago, IL 60611
312-527-4800

National Self-help Clearinghouse
Graduate School and University Center
City University of New York
33 West 42nd Street
New York, NY 10036
212-840-7606

Parents without Partners
7910 Woodmont Avenue
Suite 1000
Washington, D.C. 20014
202-654-8850

Save the Children Federation
54 Wilton Road
Westport, CT 06880
203-226-7271

Volunteer: The National Center for Citizen Involvement
P.O. Box 4179
Boulder, CO 80306
303-447-0492

Young Men's Christian Associations of the United States
101 North Wacker Drive
Chicago, IL 60606
312-977-0031

Young Women's Christian Associations of the United States of America
ica
600 Lexington Avenue
New York, NY 10022
212-753-4700

## EDUCATIONAL ORGANIZATIONS

Schools play a vital role in child care in America. There is increased demand that this role be expanded. The organizations listed below may provide technical assistance for developing a school-based child-care program or may bring together chief state school officers who can have wide-ranging impact on whether schools change to accommodate changing life-styles. No matter what these organizations' general focus, some part of their educational endeavor is directed toward the continuous care of children while their parents work.

American Association of School Administrators
1801 North Moore Street
Arlington, VA 22209
703-528-0700

Association for Childhood Education International
3615 Wisconsin Avenue, N.W.
Washington, D.C. 20016
202-363-6963

Bank Street College of Education
610 West 112th Street
New York, NY 10025
212-663-7200

Council for Exceptional Children
1920 Association Drive
Reston, VA 22091
703-620-3660

Council of Chief State School Officers
379 Hall of States
400 North Capitol Street, N.W.
Washington, D.C. 20036
202-833-1925

Home and School Institute, Inc.
Special Projects Office
1201 16th Street, N.W.
Suite 228
Washington, D.C. 20036
202-466-3633

National Association for the Education of Young Children
1834 Connecticut Avenue, N.W.
Washington, D.C. 20009
202-232-8777

National Association of Elementary School Principals
1801 North Moore Street
Arlington, VA 22209
703-528-6000

National Association of State Boards of Education
444 North Capitol Street, N.W.
Suite 526
Washington, D.C. 20001
202-624-5844

National Commission on Resources for Youth
36 West 44th Street
New York, NY 10036
212-840-2844

National Council on Year-round Education
c/o Dr. Charles Ballinger
6401 Linda Vista Boulevard
San Diego, CA 92111
714-292-3679

National Education Association
1201 16th Street, N.W.
Washington, D.C. 20036
202-833-4000

National Head Start Association
635 South Main Street
South Bend, IN 46601
219-234-2150

National PTA
700 North Rush Street
Chicago, IL 60611
312-787-0977

Parents Rights, Inc.
12571 Northwinds Drive
St. Louis, MO 63141
314-434-4171

School-age Child Care Technical Assistance Project
School of Education
Tennessee State University—Downtown
10th and Charlotte Avenues
Nashville, TN 37203
615-251-1540

Wellesley College Center for Research on Women
School-age Child Care Project
Wellesley College
828 Washington Street
Wellesley, MA 02181
617-235-6360

## PUBLIC AFFAIRS ORGANIZATIONS

Changes affecting children often come about because the community is changing. Organizations such as those that follow focus their attention on ways to strengthen and make communities better.

American Association of University Women
2401 Virginia Avenue, N.W.
Washington, D.C. 20037
800-424-9717
202-758-7798

Community Design Center Directors Association
981 16th Street, N.W.
Suite 603
Washington, D.C. 20006
202-659-4982

League of Women Voters of the United States
1730 M Street, N.W.
Washington, D.C. 20036
202-296-1770

National Association for Better Broadcasting
7918 Naylor Avenue
Los Angeles, CA 90045
213-641-4903

National Association for Community Development
161 West Wisconsin Avenue
Suite 7156
Milwaukee, WI 53203
414-272-5600

National Association for the Advancement of Colored People
1790 Broadway
New York, NY 10019
212-245-2100

National Community Development Association
1620 Eye Street, N.W.
Suite 503
Washington, D.C. 20006
202-293-7587

National Congress for Men
P.O. Box 147
Mendham, NJ 07945
201-543-6060

National Council for Alternative Work Patterns
1925 K Street, N.W.
Suite 308
Washington, D.C. 20006
202-466-4467

National Organization for Women
425 13th Street, N.W.
Washington, D.C. 20004
202-347-2279

National Pro-family Coalition
721 Second Street, N.E.
Washington, D.C. 20002
202-546-3000

National Self-help Resource Center
1722 Connecticut Avenue, N.W.
Washington, D.C. 20009
202-387-1080

National Urban League
500 East 62nd Street
New York, NY 10021
212-310-9000

New Ways to Work
149 Ninth Street
San Francisco, CA 94103
415-552-1000

### INFORMATION AND REFERRAL SOURCES

Some states have county offices that deal with child-care information, such as the Department of Pensions and Security in Alabama, the Division of Human Services in Oklahoma, or the South Carolina Department of Social Services. Some states have established regional offices such as Wisconsin's Department of Health and Social Services. Most states have some type of licensing division or information and referral service that can help when child-care information is needed. The following list of referral agencies might prove helpful.

*Alabama*

Department of Pensions and Security
64 North Union Street
Montgomery, Alabama 36130-1801
205-832-6175

*Alaska*

Division of Family and Youth Services
Department of Health and Social Services
Pouch H-05
Juneau, AK 99811
907-465-3206

*Arizona*

Department of Health Services
Bureau of Day Care Licensing
1740 West Adams
Phoenix, AZ 85007
602-225-1112

*Arkansas*

Arkansas Social Service Day Care Licensing Division
Central Office
P.O. Box 1437
Blue Cross/Blue Shield Building

Seventh and Gaines
Little Rock, AR 72203
501-371-7512

## California

Community Care Licensing Division
Department of Social Services
1232 Q Street
Sacramento, CA 95814
916-920-6855

## Colorado

Colorado Department of Social Services
1575 Sherman Street
Denver, CO 80203
303-866-3362

## Connecticut

Office of Child Day Care
1179 Main Street
Hartford, CT 06101
203-566-2893

## Delaware

United Way Information and Referral Service
Porter State Service Center
511 West 8th Street
Wilmington, DE 19801
302-575-1052

## Florida

Telephone Counseling and Referral Service
P.O. Box 20169
Tallahassee, FL 32304
904-224-6333

## Georgia

State Department of Human Resources
Child Care Licensing Section
618 Ponce de Leon Avenue, N.E.
Atlanta, GA 30308
404-894-4142

*Hawaii*

Child Care Switchboard
1352 Liliha Street
Honolulu, HI 96817
808-935-1077

*Idaho*

Department of Health and Welfare Services
450 West State Street
Boise, Idaho 83720
208-334-4085

*Illinois*

Department of Children and Family Services
Office of Child Development
1 North Old Stage Capital Plaza
Springfield, IL 62706
217-785-2459

*Indiana*

Department of Public Welfare
141 South Meridian
Indianapolis, IN 46225
317-633-3876

*Iowa*

Children's Bureau
Iowa Department of Social Services
Hoover State Office Building, fifth floor
Des Moines, IA 50319
515-281-5657

*Kansas*

Wichita Child Care Association
155 South Hydraulic
Wichita, KS 67211
316-265-0871

*Kentucky*

Department of Human Resources
Office of the Inspector General

Division of Licensing
142 Chenoweth Lane
Louisville, KY 40207
502-893-3678

## Louisiana

Licensing and Certification
333 Laurel Street, sixth floor
Baton Rouge, LA 70821
504-342-5773

## Maine

Bureau of Resource Development
Licensing Division
Department of Human Services
221 State Street
Augusta, ME 04333
207-289-3456

## Maryland

Maryland State Department of Health and Mental Hygiene
Division of Child Day Care
201 West Preston
Baltimore, MD 21201
301-383-4009

## Massachusetts

The Office for Children
120 Boylston Street
Boston, MA 02111
617-727-8900

## Michigan

Office for Young Children
701 North Logan, Suite 435
Lansing, MI 48914
517-371-3430

## Minnesota

Minnesota State Department of Public Welfare
Centennial Building

St. Paul, MN 55155
612-296-3971

## Mississippi

Mississippi State Board of Health
P.O. Box 1700
Jackson, MS 39205
601-982-6505

## Missouri

Day Care Licensing Unit
Division of Family Services
P.O. Box 88
Jefferson City, MO 65103
314-571-2450

## Montana

Social Rehabilitation Services
Licensing Division
1211 Grand Avenue
Billings, MT 95102
406-252-5601

## Nebraska

Nebraska State Department of Public Welfare
301 Centennial Mall South, fifth floor
Box 95026
Lincoln, NE 68509
402-471-3121

## Nevada

Nevada Child Care Service Bureau
505 East King Street, Room 603
Carson City, NV 89710
702-885-5911

## New Hampshire

New Hampshire Division of Welfare
Bureau of Child and Family Services
Hazen Drive
Concord, NH 03301
603-271-4395

## New Jersey

Bureau of Licensing
Division of Youth and Family Services
1 South Montgomery Street
Trenton, NJ 08625
609-292-1878

## New Mexico

Division of Human Services
P.O. Box 2348
Sante Fe, New Mexico 87503
505-827-4065

## New York

New York State Department of Social Services
40 North Pearl Street
Albany, NY 12207
800-342-3715

New York City Agency for Child Development Information Service
240 Church Street, Room 113
New York, NY 10007
212-553-6423

## North Carolina

Statewide Care-line
800-662-7030

## North Dakota

Social and Rehabilitation Services Center
Randal Building
Rural Route 1, Highway 83
Bismarck, ND 58505
701-224-2304

## Ohio

Day Care Licensing Unit
Ohio Department of Welfare
30 East Broad Street, thirtieth floor
Columbus, OH 43215
615-466-3822

## Oklahoma

Division of Human Services in Oklahoma
P.O. Box 25352
Oklahoma City, Oklahoma 73125
405-424-5818

## Oregon

Children's Services Division
198 Commercial Street, S.E.
Salem, OR 97310
503-378-3178

## Pennsylvania

Day Care Division
State Office Building, Room 502
1400 Spring Garden Street
Philadelphia, PA 19122
215-351-5603

## Rhode Island

Department of Children and Their Families
Day Care Licensing
610 Mount Pleasant Avenue
Providence, RI 02908
401-227-2804

## South Carolina

South Carolina Department of Social Services
P.O. Box 1520
Columbia, South Carolina 29202-9988
803-758-8460

## South Dakota

Office of Children, Youth and Family Services
Department of Social Services
Kneip Building
Illinois Street
Pierre, SD 57501
605-773-3227

*Tennessee*

Tennessee Department of Human Services
111 Seventh Avenue North
Nashville, TN 37203
615-741-3284

*Texas*

Neighborhood Centers Day Care Association
5005 Fannin
Houston, TX 77004
713-529-3931

*Utah*

Department of Social Services
Field Services Division of Family Services
Children, Youth and Families
150 West North Temple, Room 370
Salt Lake City, UT 84103
801-533-7123

*Vermont*

Vermont Department of Social and Rehabilitative Services
Licensing and Regulation Unit
103 South Main Street
Waterbury, VT 05676
802-241-2158

*Virginia*

Commonwealth of Virginia
Department of Welfare
Licensing Division
Blair Building
88007 Discovery Drive
Richmond, VA 23288
804-281-9204

*Washington*

Department of Social and Health Services
Bureau of Children's Services
State Licensor

Olympia, WA 98504
206-753-7002

## Washington, D.C.

Family Services Administration
122 C Street, N.W.
Washington, D.C. 20010
202-737-9342

## West Virginia

West Virginia Department of Welfare
1900 Washington Street, E.
Charleston, WV 25305
304-348-7980

## Wisconsin

Wisconsin Department of Health and Social Services
P.O. Box 7850
West Wilson Street
Madison, Wisconsin 53707
608-266-3681

## Wyoming

Wyoming Information and Referral Service
1780 Westland Road
Cheyenne, WY 82001
800-442-2744

### EMPLOYER-SUPPORTED INFORMATION AND REFERRAL SERVICES

The following is part of a growing list of employer-supported information and referral services.

## California

Expanded Child Care Referral
1838 El Camino Real
Suite 214
Burlingame, CA 94010

Family Day Care Network
Children's Home Society
3200 Telegraph Avenue
Oakland, CA 94609

Hemet Valley Hospital Child Care Center
1116 East Latham Avenue
Hemet, CA 92343

Huntington Memorial Hospital Child Care Center
100 Congress Street
Pasadena, CA 91105

National Semiconductor Employee Assistance Program
MIS 16257
2900 Semiconductor Drive
Santa Clara, CA 95051

## Florida

Community Coordinated Child Care for Central Florida, Inc.
816 Broadway
Orlando, FL 32803

## Massachusetts

Child Care Resource Center
187 Hampshire Street
Cambridge, MA 02139

Rodgers and Rudman, Inc.
93 Abbottsford Road
Brookline, MA 02146

## Michigan

Steelcase Child Care Resource and Referral Service
P.O. Box 1967
Grand Rapids, MI 49501

## Minnesota

Child Care Information Network
111 East Franklin
Minneapolis, MN 55404

Honeywell, Inc.
Corporate and Community Responsibility Department
Honeywell Plaza
Minneapolis, MN 55408

Northern States Power Company
414 Nicollet Mall
Minneapolis, MN 55401

## Missouri

Child Day Care Association of St. Louis
915 Olive Street
St. Louis, MO 63101

## New Jersey

Roche Child Care
500 Kingsland Street
Nutley, NJ 07110

## New Mexico

Digital Equipment Corporation
Personnel Office
5600 Kircher Boulevard, N.E.
P.O. Box 82
Albuquerque, NM 87103

## New York

Citibank, N.A.
111 Wall Street
New York, NY 10043

Corning Children's Center
Box 11
Corning, NY 14830

## North Carolina

Duke Medical Center
Child Care Referral Service
Box 3017
Durham, NC 27710

## Ohio

Center for Human Resources
3030 Euclid Avenue
Cleveland, OH 44115

## Oklahoma

Community Connection
1001 Southwest 44th
Oklahoma City, OK 73109

## Pennsylvania

Children's Circle
1000 Wood Circle
Philadelphia, PA 19151

# INDEX